Eat Me: The Food and Philosophy of Kenny Shopsin

Kenny Shopsin and Carolynn Carreño

Alfred A. Knopf, New York, 2008

THIS IS A BORZOI BOOK
PUBLISHED BY ALFRED A. KNOPF

Library of Congress Cataloging-in-Publication Data

Shopsin, Kenny.
Eat me : the food and philosophy of Kenny Shopsin /
by Kenny Shopsin and Carolynn Carreño.—1st ed.
    p. cm.
"A Borzoi book."
ISBN 978-0-307-26493-0
1. Shopsin's (Restaurant)   2. Shopsin, Kenny.   I. Carreño,
Carolynn.   II. Title.
TX945.5.S52S56 2008
647.95068—dc22
2008017642

Book design and uncredited photographs
by Tamara Shopsin and Jason Fulford

Manufactured in China
First Edition

OCT 2008

This book is dedicated to

EVE

Contents

ABAGIAL   SARA

1977

Don't Mention It:
The Hidden Life and Times of a
Greenwich Village Restaurant

Calvin Trillin

I published this article in the spring of 2002, when Shopsin's was coming to the end of its tenancy in the original location—Bedford and Morton, a couple of blocks from where I live. I remained a regular customer when it moved to Bedford and Carmine. I've been to the latest Shopsin's, in the Essex Market, even though it's now too far to be considered an extension of my kitchen. Kenny's disposition has not improved.

I suppose Kenny Shopsin, who runs a small restaurant a couple of blocks from where I live in Greenwich Village, could qualify as eccentric in a number of ways, but one of his views seems particularly strange to journalists who have had prolonged contact with proprietors of retail businesses in New York: he hates publicity. I've tried not to take this personally. I have been a regular customer, mainly at lunch, since 1982, when Kenny and his wife, Eve, turned a corner grocery store they had been running on the same premises into a thirty-four-seat café. Before that, I was a regular customer of the grocery store. When the transformation was made, my daughters were around junior-high-school age, and even now, grown and

living out of the city, they consider Shopsin's General Store—or Ken and Eve's or Kenny's, as they usually call it—an extension of their kitchen. Normally, they take only a brief glance at the menu—a menu that must include about nine hundred items, some of them as unusual as Cotton Picker Gumbo Melt Soup or Hanoi Hoppin John with Shrimp or Bombay Turkey Cloud Sandwich—and then order dishes that are not listed, such as "tomato soup the way Sarah likes it" or "Abigail's chow fun."

When Kenny gets a phone call from a restaurant guidebook that wants to include Shopsin's, he sometimes says that the place is no longer in operation, identifying himself as someone who just happens to be there moving out the fixtures. Some years ago, a persistent English guidebook carried a generally complimentary review of Shopsin's that started with a phrase like "Although it has no décor." Eve expressed outrage, not simply at the existence of the review but also at its content. "Do you call this 'no décor'?" she demanded of me one evening when I was there having an early supper—the only kind of supper you can have at

Shopsin's, which has not strayed far from grocery-store hours. (Aside from a Sunday brunch that began as a sort of family project several months ago, the restaurant has never been open on weekends.) She waved her arm to take in the entire establishment.

I looked around. Shopsin's still looks a lot like a corner store. It has an old pressed-tin ceiling. There are shelves, left over from the grocery store, that are always piled high and not terribly neatly with ingredients and supplies. There are always newspapers and magazines around for the customer who might need reading material while eating alone. A table setup might include a constantly varying assortment of toys and puzzles—a custom that started when the Shopsins' children were young and continues for the more or less grown-up customers. The counter, which no longer has stools, is taken up mainly by buckets of complimentary penny candy. One wall has, in addition to a three-dimensional advertisement for Oscar Mayer beef franks, some paintings of the place and its denizens. The portrait of Kenny shows him as a bushy-haired man with a baby face that makes him look younger than he is, which is nearly sixty, and a girth that may reflect years of tasting his more remarkable creations; he's wearing a Shopsin's General Store T-shirt, folded over in the way the cognoscenti know how to fold it in order to form the words "Eat Me." A large sign behind the tiny kitchen that Kenny shares with his longtime assistant, José, says "All Our Cooks Wear Condoms." When I had taken in all of that, or whatever part of it was there at the time, I said, "I absolutely agree, Eve. A

reviewer might comment on whether or not the décor is to his taste. Conceivably, he could prefer another type of décor. But you can't say that this place has no décor."

Normally, mentions of Shopsin's in print are complimentary, in a sort of left-handed way—as in *Time Out, New York*'s most recent guide to the city's restaurants, which raved about the soups and described Kenny ("the foul-mouthed middle-aged chef and owner") as "a culinary genius, if for no other reason than he figured out how to fit all his ingredients into such a tiny restaurant." To Kenny's way of thinking, a complimentary mention is worse than a knock. It brings review-trotters—the sort of people who go to a restaurant because somebody told them to. Kenny finds that review-trotters are often "petulant and demanding." Failing to understand that they are not in a completely conventional restaurant, they may be taken aback at having the person next to them contribute a sentence or two to their conversation or at hearing Kenny make a general remark in language not customarily heard in company unless the company is in a locker room or at being faced with deciding among nine hundred items and then, if they have selected certain dishes, having to indicate the degree of spiciness on a scale of one to ten. (Before Shopsin's began restricting its serving staff to Eve, it employed a waitress who narrowed at least that choice by refusing to take an order higher than a six, on humanitarian grounds.)

Ken and Eve have found that review-trotters often don't know their own minds. If a customer at Shopsin's seems completely incapable of deciding what to order, Eve will, in the interest of saving time, reveal her own favorites, which these days happen to be three dishes with chicken in them—Chicken Tortilla Avocado Soup, Pecan Chicken Wild Rice Enchiladas, and Taco-fried Chicken. But she doesn't do it with a song in her heart. Kenny is less flexible. "If somebody comes in here and is flabbergasted by the number of things on the menu and tells me, 'How can I choose?' " he has said, "I realize that they're essentially in the wrong restaurant."

The place can handle just so many people, and Kenny was never interested in an expansion that would transform him into a supervisor. "The economic rhythm of this place is that I run fifteen meals a week," he used to say before Shopsin's offered Sunday brunch. "If I do any five of them big, I break even; if I do ten of them big, I'll make money. I'll make a lot of money. But if I do fifteen, I have to close, because it's too much work." Kenny requires slow periods for recouping energy and ingredients. The techniques that enable him to offer as many dishes as he does are based on the number of people he has to serve rather than on what they order. That's why he won't do takeout, and that's one of the reasons parties of five are told firmly that the restaurant does not serve groups larger than four. Pretending to be a party of three that happened to have come in with a party of two is a very bad idea.

Not all the rules at Shopsin's are based on the number of meals that the kitchen has to put out. For years, a rule against copying your neighbor's order was observed fairly strictly. Customers who had just arrived might ask someone at the next table the name of the scrumptious-looking dish he was eating. Having learned that it was Burmese Hummus—one of my favorites, as it happens, even though it is not hummus and would not cause pangs of nostalgia in the most homesick Burmese—they might order Burmese Hummus, only to have Eve shake her head wearily. No copying. That rule eventually got downgraded into what Ken called "a strong tradition," and has now pretty much gone by the wayside. "I realized that the problem was not that they were trying to imitate the other person but that they weren't capable of ordering anything themselves, and it was just unnecessary cruelty to point that out to them," Kenny told me not long ago. He said he was getting more and more people of that sort.

"Why is that?" I asked.

"The country's going that way," he said glumly.

Because Shopsin's has a number of rules and because Kenny is, by his own admission, "not a patient person," it's common to run into people who are afraid to enter the place. I've escorted a number of them to their first Shopsin's meal, in the way a longtime businessman in a Midwestern town might escort a newcomer to Kiwanis at noon on Wednesday. Since the *Seinfeld* Soup Nazi episode became part of the culture, people sometimes compare Kenny to the brilliant but rule-obsessed soup purveyor who terrified Jerry Seinfeld and his friends. Kenny would say that one difference between him and the Soup Nazi is that the Soup Nazi is shown ladling out his soup from a steam table; at Shopsin's, most soups are made from scratch when they're ordered.

Some people think of Shopsin's as forbiddingly clubby, chilly to outsiders. Actually, Shopsin's does not have a crowd, in the sense of a group of people who go in assuming they'll run into someone they know—the way the old Lion's Head, a few blocks uptown, had a crowd, built around *Village Voice* writers. At a play reading once, I was surprised to run into a Shopsin's regular I hadn't realized was an actor; all I'd known about him was that he doted on a dish called Turkey Spinach Cashew Brown Rice Burrito. Still, there are a lot of regulars, and they seem more at home than they might at a conventional restaurant. "You're really not allowed to be anonymous here," Kenny has said. "You have to be willing to be who you really are. And that scares a lot of people." One evening, when the place was nearly full, I saw a party of four come in the door; a couple of them may have been wearing neckties, which wouldn't have been a plus in a restaurant whose waitress used to wear a T-shirt that said "Die Yuppie Scum." Kenny took a quick glance from the kitchen and said, "No, we're closed." After a brief try at appealing the decision, the party left, and the waitress pulled the security gate partway down to discourage other latecomers.

"It's only eight o'clock," I said to Kenny.

"They were nothing but strangers," he said.

"I think those are usually called customers," I said. "They come here, you give them food, they give you money. It's known as the restaurant business."

Kenny shrugged. "Fuck 'em," he said.

Anytime there seemed to be a threat of my becoming entangled in a piece of unauthorized publicity about Shopsin's, I have resorted to rank cowardice, spooked by the fear of a lifetime banishment that might not even carry the possibility of parole. Once, I asked Kenny if an acquaintance of mine who'd been eighty-sixed some years before but greatly missed the place and its proprietors could come in for lunch with me sometime. "Sure, she can come in for lunch," Kenny said. "And I'll tell her she's a scumbag bitch." I told him I might hold off on that lunch for a while.

In the mid-nineties, I got a phone call from a reporter named D. T. Max, who was doing a piece for the *New York Observer* on Shopsin's, without the cooperation of the proprietor. After assuring him of my belief that reporters have an obligation to talk to other reporters on the record and informing him that I had been quoted by name insulting most of the people I've ever worked for, I told him that in this instance I intended to be exceedingly circumspect and to keep Kenny informed of everything I said. Max was most understanding.

When I did report back to Kenny, I was asked what information I had surrendered. "Well, the subject of Egyptian Burritos came up," I said. Egyptian Burrito was then listed on the breakfast menu, although I'd never eaten one. On the rare occasions that I had been to Shopsin's for what people in some other trades might call a breakfast meeting, I'd always allocated my calories to Shred Potatoes, a fabulous dish that Kenny claims to have stolen from a short-order cook in the Carolinas through intense observation that required only ten minutes.

"And?" Kenny asked.

"Well, he seemed interested in what an Egyptian Burrito was," I said.

"So what did you say?"

"I said, 'An Egyptian Burrito is a burrito, and inside is sort of what Kenny thinks Egyptians might eat.' "

Kenny considered that for a moment. "Well, that's accurate," he finally said. He sounded relieved. By chance, though, the *Observer* piece ended with an anecdote, accurately gathered from someone else, that involved me: One morning, a Sanitation Department officer had come in to ticket Kenny for some minor infraction like wrapping his garbage incorrectly or putting it in the wrong place. Kenny, who was at the stove, lost his temper and threw a handful of flour he happened to be holding at the sanitation officer, who thereupon summoned a police officer to write a citation. When I was told about the incident at lunch that day, I asked Kenny, "What was the citation for—assault with intent to bake?" A couple of months after Max's piece appeared, Kenny said he had finally concluded that I, frustrated at not having been able to work the assault-with-intent-to-bake line in anywhere, might have instigated an article in the *Observer* just to get it into print. I had a defense for that: within days of my exchange with Kenny about flour-throwing, I had, without mentioning any names, eased the anecdote into a newspaper column that was on a completely different subject.

Yes, I've managed to write about Shop-sin's from time to time, always observing the prohibition against mentioning its name or location. That is one reason I've never been offended by Kenny's refusal to recognize a reporter's God-given right to turn absolutely everything into copy. In a piece about Greenwich Village a few years ago, for instance, I asked a restaurant proprietor "who tends not to be cordial to people wearing suits" what the difference was between the Village and uptown, and he said, "I don't know. I've never been uptown." Kenny has never objected to any of the mentions. He has always thought of us as being in similar fields, and, as someone who has to be prepared every day to turn out any one of nine hundred dishes a customer might ask for, he has a deep understanding of waste not, want not.

In the mid-seventies, in fact, when my daughters were little girls, I wrote an entire article for this magazine about a corner store in the West Village which was run with rare imagination and a warm feeling for community—a store with a rocking chair and bean-counting contests and free circulating paperback books. At that time, the store struck me as being about as close as Greenwich Village got to the Village conjured up by reading, say, "My Sister Eileen"—even to the point of having a proprietor, described in the piece as a young man from a prosperous background who'd always had what he called "a little trouble with authority," capable of making occasional allusions to Camus or Sartre as he sliced the roast beef. At the time, Kenny owned some dazzling old gumball machines, and I simply referred to Shopsin's by the name my girls always used—the Bubble Gum Store.

So why am I calling it Shopsin's now? Because not long ago Kenny told me that it was no longer necessary to abide by the rule against mentioning the place in print. The building that Shopsin's is in, an undistinguished five-story brick structure that consists of the restaurant and eight apartments, changed hands several months ago. Kenny, who was faced with having to renegotiate his lease, at first treated the situation philosophically. When I asked him what the new owner, Robert A. Cohen, of R. A. Cohen & Associates, was like, he shrugged and said, "He's a real-estate guy," in the tone that New Yorkers customarily use to mean that asking for further details would be naïve. Then Kenny and Cohen had a meeting at Cohen's office. ("I went uptown!" Kenny told me, as a way of emphasizing a willingness to put himself out.) According to Kenny, Cohen offered the Shopsins a one-year lease at more or less market rent. He also offered a three-year lease, contingent on one of their daughters vacating a rent-stabilized apartment she occupies in the building. A one-year lease is obviously not practical for a restaurant, and the attempt to include Kenny's daughter in the transaction did not please him. All in all, I would say that Robert A. Cohen was fortunate that the offers were made when Kenny wasn't holding a handful of flour.

Kenny decided that he would leave at the end of May rather than sign a new lease. He hopes to reopen nearby. He is aware, though, that the tone of his business has a lot to do with the physical space it has occupied for more than thirty years, including what I suppose you'd have to call the décor—the old-fashioned booths that Kenny ran across and cut down to fit his space, the music from tapes he puts together himself from songs of the twenties and thirties (supplanted, occasionally, by a modern Finnish group that concentrates on the tango). Kenny says that what really distinguishes his place from other restaurants is the level of human involvement in every detail. As he has put it, "I've been peeing on every hydrant around here for thirty years." In other words, the Shopsin's my daughters have known—Kenny's, Ken and Eve's, the Bubble Gum Store—can no longer be affected by publicity because it will no longer exist.

The God of New York real estate is an ironic god, and he works in ironic ways. What propelled Ken and Eve into the restaurant business in the first place, twenty years ago, was a bump in their rent. They figured that their choices were to start opening on weekends or transform the store into a restaurant. By that time, Kenny was doing a good business in takeout sandwiches like chicken salad and egg salad. "Zito would bring me over bread and I would just have a line out the door every lunchtime," he recalled not long ago. "Essentially, if anyone asked me what I did for a living, I said I sold mayonnaise—mayonnaise with chicken, mayonnaise with shrimp, mayonnaise with eggs, mayonnaise with potatoes. The key was that essentially you sold mayonnaise for eight dollars a pound and everything else you threw in for free." He had also been making what he calls "restaurant-style food to take out of a non-restaurant"—turkey dinner every Wednesday, for instance, and chicken pot pie. When Ken and Eve closed the store for the summer—because they had young children, Shopsin's was the rare Village business that often observed the *fermeture annuelle*—Ken, a reasonably adept handyman who had worked as a building superintendent before he went into the grocery business, turned Shopsin's General Store into a restaurant. When it opened, the menu listed a conventional number of more or less conventional dishes, although there was some hint of the future in items like Yiddishe Melt (grilled American cheese on rye over grilled Jewish salami) and Linda's Frito Pie, a Texas specialty whose recipe has to begin, "Take a bag of Fritos..."

Kenny had Frito Pie on the menu because one of his customers, who's from Texas, was comforted by the knowledge that less than a block from her house in Greenwich Village she could order a dish that most Texans identify with the snack bar at Friday-night high-school football games. The menu grew because of what customers wanted or what Kenny was struck by in reading cookbooks or what new ingredient he happened across or what he figured out how to do as he taught himself to cook. "I don't make too many decisions," Kenny once told me. "I react." Lately, for instance, a lot of dishes have been inspired by the tchotchkes he's bought on eBay. Because of some tortilla bowls he snapped up for a bargain price, he is now offering Mexican moo shu pork, which can also be ordered with chicken or turkey and has

something in common with a former dish called Thai Turkey Torpedo. Some large plastic bowls split in two by a curving divider led to what he calls Yin/Yang Soups—a couple of dozen soups and a couple of dozen kinds of rice that can be ordered in any combination, like Sweet Potato Cream Curry Soup with Piña Colada Rice or Toasted Pumpkin Seed Soup with Ricotta Pignoli Rice.

There is almost no danger of a customer's ordering Plantain Pulled Turkey Soup with Strawberry BBQ Rice only to find out that there isn't any more Plantain Pulled Turkey Soup and he might have to settle for, say, Mashed Potato Radish Soup. In the twenty years my family has been eating at Shopsin's, putting our meals on the tab we established when Ken and Eve were selling milk and paper towels and cat food, nobody at our table has ever ordered anything the restaurant was out of. When I asked Eve recently if that held true with other customers, she said that she thinks she remembers running out of chicken cutlets sometime within the past year.

"I think I have everything all the time," Kenny says. "That's part of the system." What does happen occasionally is that Kenny gets an idea for a dish and writes on the specials board—yes, there is a specials board—something like Indomalekian Sunrise Stew. (Kenny and his oldest son, Charlie, invented the country of Indomalekia along with its culinary traditions.) A couple of weeks later, someone finally orders Indomalekian Sunrise Stew and Kenny can't remember what he had in mind when he thought it up. Fortunately, the customer doesn't know, either, so Kenny just invents it again on the spot.

As the menu at Shopsin's grew, I half expected to come in for lunch one day and find Kenny being peered at intently by a team of researchers from the institution that foodies are referring to when they mention the CIA—the Culinary Institute of America—or maybe even a team from the other CIA. The researchers would have their work cut out for them. It's true that if you listen to Kenny talk about cooking for a while, you can see the outline of some general strategies. For instance, he freezes pre-portioned packages of some ingredients that take a long time to cook and then pops them into the microwave—"nuking 'em" for a couple of minutes—while he's doing the dish. He fiddles with his equipment, so that he's drilled out the holes on one burner of his stove and rigged up a sort of grid on another. He runs a new idea or a new ingredient through a large part of his menu. ("I love permutations.") On the other hand, Kenny has said, "There's no unifying philosophy. I do a lot of things special, and not only do I do a lot of things special but I commingle them."

To get an idea of Kenny's methods, I once asked him how he made one of Eve's favorites, Chicken Tortilla Avocado Soup, which he describes as a simple soup. "When someone orders that, I put a pan up with oil in it," he said. "Not olive oil; I use, like, a Wesson oil. And I leave it. I've drilled out the holes in the burner so . . . it's really fucking hot. . . . On the back burner, behind where that pan is, I have that grid. I just take a piece of chicken breast and throw it on.

The grid is red hot, flames shooting up, and the chicken sears with black marks immediately and starts to cook. If there were grits or barley or something, I would nuke 'em. . . . At that point in the cook, that's what would happen if this were Chicken Tortilla Avocado with barley in it. For this dish—this is a fast dish—I shred cabbage with my knife. Green cabbage. . . . I cut off a chunk and I chop it really finely into long, thin shreds. I do the same with a piece of onion. Same with fresh cilantro. At this point, José has turned the chicken while my back is still to the pan. I throw the shit into the oil, and if you rhythm it properly, by the time you have the onions and everything cut, the oil is just below smoke. Smoke for that oil is about three-eighty-five. After three-eighty-five, you might as well throw it out. It won't fry anymore; it's dead. But I turn around just before smoke and I throw this shit in. And what happens is the cabbage hits it and almost deep-fries—it browns—and now we get a really nice cabbage, Russian-type flavor. The onions soften immediately, and I now turn back and I take one of any number of ingredients, depending on what they've ordered, and in this particular instance, for someone like you, I would add crushed-up marinated jalapeño peppers to about a five, which is about a half a tablespoon. They're in a little cup in front of me. . . . In front of me, in, like, a desk in-out basket, I have two levels of vegetables that don't need to be refrigerated and I have plastic cups full of garlic or whatever. So now the soup is cooking. So then I reach under the refrigerator. On the refrigerator floor there's another thirty or forty ingredients, and I'll take for this particular soup hominy—canned yellow hominy—and throw in a handful of that. Then I go to the steam table and take from the vegetarian black-bean soup—it has a slotted spoon in it—a half spoon of vegetarian cooked black beans. And then I switch to the right, because the spice rack is there, and I put in a little cumin. Then I take the whole thing and I pour chicken stock in it from the steam table. And at this point José has already taken the chicken off the flame. The chicken now is marked on the outside and the outside is white, but it's not cooked. It's pink in the center. He cuts it into strips, we throw it into the soup, a cover goes on the soup, it gets moved over to the left side of the stove on a lower light and in about three minutes José takes a bowl, puts some tortilla chips that I've fried the day before in the bowl with some sliced avocado and then pours the soup over it. And that's Chicken Tortilla Avocado Soup." There are about two hundred other soups.

Presumably, Kenny can arrange his ingredients around a customized stove in some other storefront. Presumably, it will be convenient to our house. The last time I discussed the move with him, he mentioned a couple of possibilities. One is convenient, but it's somewhat larger than the present restaurant and it seems less vulnerable to being shaped by Kenny's personality. Another has the appropriate funkiness but also has what everyone, Kenny included, believes is "the world's worst location." That tempts Kenny, of course. He is someone whose contrariness is so ingrained that he can begin a description of one cooking experiment like this: "At the time I was interested in baba ghanouj, I was reading a James Beard article about eggplants and he said never put eggplants in a microwave. So I went and put an eggplant in a microwave...."

When Kenny mentioned that the second place was on such an awful block that my daughters and I would probably come only once, I assured him of their loyalty, assuming he continued to turn out "tomato soup the way Sarah likes it" and "Abigail's chow fun." They confirmed this when I phoned them to bring them up to date on the latest Shopsin's developments. They also expressed some concern about the possibility that writing about Shopsin's even now carried the risk of causing overcrowding or inadvertently saying something that could lead to the banishment of the author—and, presumably, his progeny.

"Don't worry," I told one of them. "Kenny says it's OK."

"Just be careful," she said.

—The New Yorker, *April 15, 2002*

Prologue

One of the things that's happening to me as I'm getting older is I'm seeing my beliefs, the tenets of my existence, coming back to me through my children. I cast my bread upon the waters, and it's flying back in my face, fully baked. My kids—I have three boys and twin girls—have taken everything I've given them and developed it to the point where they're superior to me when it comes to discussing and acting on a lot of my own ideas. My girls especially are more unyielding in my beliefs than I am.

All their lives my kids have known me to have a leave-me-alone attitude toward the media and the public eye. In running my restaurant, Shopsin's General Store, I've done everything I could to avoid articles and accolades of any kind. I have talked about how the media was evil, about the dangers of celebrity, and about the pitfalls of losing your self-doubt. And they took me at my word. What they didn't know, because how *could* they know—I certainly never vocalized it—was that behind absolute statements, like those that I made on a regular basis, is a complex set of emotions. Inherent in those absolutes were compromises. It's like there was a tug-of-war inside of me that, in an attempt to resolve itself, took sides.

For me, writing this book was one of those compromises. On the one hand, it was tremendously satisfying to my ego to have someone ask me to write a book. On the other hand, I knew that in writing this book I would be allowing strangers a look into our private lives—something I have vehemently avoided since I started my business in 1973. Even worse, I knew that a book would encourage these strangers to come into my restaurant.

A few years back, Melinda posted a sign in front of the restaurant that read, "Restaurant for Customers Only." That pretty much explains our attitude at Shopsin's. It's pretty straightforward, but it also says more than it might seem to.

My approach toward the customer is something a lot of people don't understand, and I guess I shouldn't expect them to. Customers in this country have been raised to believe that they are "always right." Their neuroses are coddled and their misbehaviors are tolerated for their patronage and their money by every restaurateur in America. But not by *me*. My approach at Shopsin's is the exact *opposite* of "the customer is always right." Until I know the people, until they show me that they are worth cultivating as customers, I'm not even sure I *want* their patronage.

For me, customers are not just people who give me money, and my restaurant is not for just anyone who wants to come in. It's not for a film crew doing a movie on the block to get a cup of coffee to go. It's not a place for you to bring your out-of-town friends to look at us as if we are exhibits in a zoo. And it is also not—if we have anything to do with it—someplace to come because you read about us in a magazine. By writing a book, I was putting myself at risk of attracting *wrong* people who want to come here for *wrong* reasons.

The brilliance of my restaurant is my ability to control my clientele. The thing that makes my restaurant special is my relationships and interactions with my customers—and the way they relate and interact with one another. With the wrong people in here, those interactions don't happen, so to keep the wrong people out, in addition to avoiding publicity, I have rules that people have to abide by in order to be here. (You'll hear more about those later.) And I kick people out when I don't like them. I probably ax at least one party every day—and usually more than that.

As for why I decided to write the book anyway, a question I'm asked often by people who are familiar with my feelings about publicity, my typical response is that I did it for the money. This is partly true, but, of course, there's also a deeper reason. In a nutshell, I decided to write this book because I was asked. Peter Gethers, who is now my editor, and Janis Donnaud, who is a literary agent, had been regular customers for many, many years, and for the last several of those years they've been telling me I should write a book. Despite my resistance, it was clear to me that unlike people in the media who write articles in order to exploit me for their own purposes, Peter and Janis weren't trying to get anything out of me or to do anything *to* me. They were just expressing their honest feelings of interest and thought I had something to say that would be of value to the audiences that they're used to working with.

Although I wasn't sure that what I had to say—about food or my restaurant or anything else—was of value or interest to anyone, much less somebody buying a cookbook, the fact that they believed this meant a lot to me. I was really touched by their appreciation. And because I appreciate them and consider them to be people of quality—they are well read, well fed, well traveled, and, more important, really know the book business—I believed them. I put my trust in them, and I decided to do the book based on that trust.

Once I started writing, my biggest fear was that, by its very nature, a book is a stagnant thing. Once it's printed and bound and out there, there's no changing it. It's done. My restaurant, on the other hand, is *never* done. It is constantly changing. I change the menu just about every day, and the feeling and personality of the restaurant are different as different customers come in from day to day. I am different, my thoughts are different, my personality is different, and the conversations I have are different from one day or from one minute to the next.

My cooking is the same way. I don't even have recipes. My regular customers know that if they order the same thing they got last week, there is a good chance I will make it so differently that they won't even recognize it. I don't do it differently on purpose. It's just that everything I cook, every time I cook, is an event in and of itself. It's like when you have sex: you approach it each time to do the best you possibly can, as if it were the only time. You don't have to think about what you're doing because you are 100 percent in the moment—and each time it turns out just a little bit different. That's how I cook. And I think that in order to enjoy cooking, that's how you *have* to cook.

As I got into writing the book, I was surprised to find out that I actually had something to say that might be of value to the home cook. I often compare my ideas about cooking to the children's book *Goodnight Moon,* by Margaret Wise Brown, where the little boy discovers that everything he needs in life is in his life already, right in his own room. In a *Goodnight Moon* world, it's pretty easy to be a good home cook. It's really not about having some terrific skills or exotic ingredients or expensive high-tech equipment. It's not even about having the right secret recipe. To be a good cook, to turn out good, honest food that satisfies your individual tastes, it is all about having the kind of confidence and self-awareness that comes from *Goodnight Moon* living, in which you are happy with what is already in your life.

It's about using ingredients that you know and that you like. As an eater, the advantages to cooking with ingredients that you know and like are obvious, but there are also advantages as a cook. When using ingredients you're familiar with, you are a lot less likely to mess up what you're cooking. If you like melted cheese, for instance, you probably know that if you put cheese under the broiler, it's going to melt, and if you leave it there long enough, it will get brown and bubbly on top. So you not only know why you're putting the cheese under the broiler, you also know what to expect when you put it there. On the other hand, if someone tells you to add peach juice to a beurre blanc, you not only have no idea why you're adding it, you more critically don't know how the juice is going to react to the beurre blanc—you may not even know what the fuck beurre blanc is. As a consequence, your chances of screwing it up are pretty high.

I learned this lesson the same way I learned most of my cooking lessons: by screwing up. When we were a grocery store, we used to get a lot of cabbies coming in for coffee and tea. One time one of them told me I should try tea with milk and lemon in it. I'd never heard of putting milk and lemon in tea, but I did it anyway because this guy told me to. I made the tea, squeezed lemon in it, and then added milk. The first time I did it, the milk curdled; it was bad. So I threw out the milk, threw out the tea, and started over. I did this four more times, each time throwing away another carton of milk before I figured out that the milk wasn't bad. *None* of the milk had been bad. The acidity from the lemon had caused it to curdle in the tea, but I didn't know that because I wasn't familiar with the combination of milk and lemon. I was just doing what someone told me to do, which is exactly what following a recipe is and exactly why you're in trouble if you use recipes that are out of your field of knowledge. I was such an idiot that it took me five times to figure out the lemon was causing the curdling. But guess what? I've never put lemon and milk together again. And not because I'm thinking about it, but because I now *know,* from somewhere deeper than my brain, *not* to do it. Call it what you want—instinct, experience, familiarity—but I've learned to trust that internal guide.

In my *Goodnight Moon* kitchen I don't use any exotic ingredients. I don't subscribe to some intellectual school of thinking where I care about the provenance of every ingredient I'm cooking with and where every single component of a dish has to be homemade with the utmost integrity. I don't use fancy cooking techniques or expensive equipment. The base of my cooking philosophy is to get the job done with as few ingredients, as little effort, and in as short a time as possible. And if I were to take a wild guess, I'd say that this is how most people cook at home— or how they want to cook, anyway.

I hope you like the book. I guess I'm not that different from everyone else in that I, too, would like to be loved by the masses for the right or the wrong reasons.

•

If anything in this book is wrong or untrue, it wasn't intentional. I didn't mean to lie. I don't live in the past. My wife, Eve, who died in 2002, was the one who was good at remembering details and dates. My life is right here, right now. Even though I'm not sure I remember everything correctly, I still thought it was important to start with the beginning, because the beginning is what brought me to where I am today. It has all been one slow evolution, like the line in the poem by Carl Sandburg that goes: "The fog comes on little cat feet." Everything in my life is like that. My life moves inexorably forward. It might be flowing at the speed of molasses, but it is definitely flowing.

Introduction

Shopsin's started as a small neighborhood grocery on Bedford and Morton Streets in Greenwich Village. In those days, stores like mine were on practically every corner and were an essential part of the pulse and rhythm of New York life. We became a restaurant in 1983 after the landlord raised the rent to a price we could no longer pay by selling groceries. We ran the restaurant in the same space until the landlord raised the rent again in 2002, which forced us to move to a different location down the block, and in 2007, we moved to Essex Street, where we are now.

Eve and I raised our family in the original store. We had our first child, Charlie, a few years after we opened, in 1976. Our daughters, Melinda (Minda) and Tamara (Mara), were born a few years after that. Then Danny and then Zack.

When our children were first born, we had them in the store with us all the time. The building had a window on either side of

The first store

the front door, and we had a crib in one window and a playpen in the other. We usually just held the kids, and if we got too busy, we handed them off to a customer. When we became a restaurant, we opened only on weekdays so we could spend Saturdays and Sundays together as a family. But even when the restaurant was open, the kids were there with us every day. We didn't even have to watch them. They had toys and games, and they had one another to keep themselves occupied—plus we knew our customers had their eyes on them.

When the kids got to be school age, they would come into the store in the mornings and order whatever they wanted to take to school for lunch. And they'd come back after school to do their homework. Eventually, when it became economically impossible to stay closed on weekends, we opened up for Sunday brunch, with the kids all working with me in various capacities—and Eve

Eve at work

kept the day off. It was like playing in the sandbox next to my kids, playing real hard all day long. It was a wonderful physical experience, and it is one that continues to this day.

●

Today, three out of my five kids work with me. Since Eve died, Minda has taken her place in terms of running the restaurant. She serves customers every day, and she also keeps track of all the money stuff. Melinda, not me, is basically in charge of Shopsin's. Along with other jobs Zack is in charge of at the restaurant, he is becoming a really great cook; he's especially good with scrambled eggs, which is not an easy thing to be good with. On Mondays when we're closed, I do all the shopping, and Zack helps unload all the stuff into the store. Mara cooks with me on weekends. She doesn't need the work; she's a graphic artist. She works with me because she likes it; she likes being elbow to elbow with her dad all day long, talking and cooking and just being together.

It was great growing up in a restaurant. We lived in a very small apartment, so my sister and brothers and I spent all our time in the store. I've basically worked at the store all my life. I helped out the way kids help their parents out. When Mom needs help, you help. When I was really young, I bussed tables. Later, if my mom had to do something like go to a parent-teacher conference for Zack, I'd waitress for her. And even when I had a full-time job, if she was sick or had an appointment, I would just tell my boss, "I have to work at the restaurant today." The restaurant was always more important.

It actually wasn't my dad's decision to open on Saturdays. It was something my sister and brothers and I came up with as a plan to help alleviate the financial difficulties we knew he was having. On weekends it was just us—no outside employees—because we could save more money that way. We all had other jobs at the time, and we were living all over the place. I was living in Brooklyn; Danny had his own apartment; and Mara was living in an apartment above the store. So this was also a day when we came together to work and be a family.

I don't have a favorite dish. There are lots of things on the menu I like. For breakfast, I like the Cathy: raspberry and mac n cheese pancakes, which is basically Mac n Cheese Pancakes (page 90) with some raspberries thrown on top while they're cooking. There is a sandwich named after me—chicken salad and turkey bacon on garlic rye bread—but it has nothing to do with me. It was originally named after someone else. Either my dad got mad at that person, or that person stopped coming in, I don't remember which, but my dad wanted to change the name so it became Melinda. Customers love it, but it's not really my thing because I am not a big mayo fan.

My current favorite thing to eat at the store is Shrimp Lefses (page 6). Lefses are very thin Norwegian potato crepes. My dad heard of them on the foodie Web site Chowhound, so he ordered some from North Dakota. I guess there's a big Norwegian population out there. He didn't know what he wanted to do with them, and he experimented a lot without much success. I don't remember exactly how Shrimp Lefses came about, only that I was instrumental in their development because I was the one my dad knew he could count on to eat the experiments. The final version is shrimp, jalapeño peppers, Jack cheese, and salsa all melted on the grill, piled on top of this crepe thing, and then folded over. It's really yummy.

—Melinda Shopsin

The store as a restaurant

Kenny and Minda

Shrimp Lefses
Makes 2 lefses

This is pretty much just an assembling of ingredients—very quick for the cook. I buy the lefses from a place called Freddy's Lefse in North Dakota (phone number: 701-235-2056). Making lefses from scratch would be more work than it's worth. That's not what my cooking is about. I came up with this recipe because I found this premade product that I thought was very good and I wanted to use it. If you go to the trouble to order the lefses, you might want to use them for more than just these roll-ups. You can also use them like I do with the tortillas to make other types of crepes (see Crepes, page 81). Or just fill them with scrambled eggs and top with lemon zest, pine nuts, ricotta, and a dollop of lingonberry preserves. It makes a nice sweet-and-savory breakfast item. If you don't want to order the lefses, you could probably make these using flour tortillas, but be sure to get thin ones.

Ingredients

½ pound small shrimp (see Shopsin's Prep: Shrimp, facing page), thawed if frozen
1 heaping tablespoon minced fresh garlic
6 tablespoons butter
½ to 1 fresh jalapeño pepper, sliced (see How Spicy Do You Want It? on page 128)
1 heaping tablespoon finely chopped fresh parsley
2 teaspoons good olive oil
¼ cup Salsa Roja (page 63) or any fresh chunky salsa
¼ cup shredded Monterey Jack cheese
¼ cup grated Parmesan cheese
1 ripe Hass avocado, chopped
2 lefses (or flour tortillas)
2 big handfuls of prewashed arugula or spinach (about 2 heaping cups)

Instructions

Put the shrimp in a 5-inch stainless-steel bowl. Stir in the garlic, butter, jalapeño pepper, parsley, olive oil, Salsa Roja, Jack cheese, Parmesan cheese, and avocado. Heat a large skillet over high heat. Invert the bowl onto the skillet and cook the mixture, with the bowl covering it, for 1 to 2 minutes, until the cheese melts and the shrimp are pink and cooked through.

Meanwhile, put the lefses in a separate large skillet and heat over high heat until warm. Do not turn. Place a handful of arugula or spinach on the side of 2 plates and put one lefse on each plate. Dump half of the shrimp mixture on half of each lefse. Fold each lefse over to make a semicircle. The dark brown dots on the lefses make them pretty, so any other decoration is unnecessary.

Shopsin's Prep: Shrimp

When we get a shrimp delivery, we divide the shrimp into 4- or 5-ounce portions and freeze them for later use. We put them in plastic sandwich bags and lay them flat so the shrimp thaw evenly; it's not necessary to seal them because when frozen, the shape of the bag will become rigid and seal itself through that rigidity. When anything calling for shrimp is ordered, I put one of the small bags of shrimp in the microwave for 2½ to 3 minutes, until thawed. This cooks the shrimp a little bit. They end up somewhere between just thawed and a bit steamed. Both are okay. If you don't have a microwave, thaw them overnight in the fridge.

"Keep cool, Charlie."

I live in San Diego, so I miss the restaurant a lot. My dad is very up-front about trying to get me to move back. He says, "Honestly, I'd prefer you were here. It might be better for *you* out there, but it would be better for *me* if you were *here*."

My favorite dish has changed over the years. When I was younger, I really had a thing for Patsy's Cashew Chicken (page 119). I used to love that dish. In high school, during my first year at Bronx Science, my dad used to cook a sausage; then he'd take a baguette, hollow it out, and stick the sausage in the hollowed-out area so it was like a really good pig in a blanket. But now my favorite dish is definitely Huevos Rancheros (page 210). It's the only thing I make sure to have every time I go back. I don't think I've ever had Huevos Rancheros as good as my dad's. I am perpetually disappointed if I order them somewhere else. He serves the tortillas on the side so I can use them to dip into the egg—like when you're eating Middle Eastern food—instead of having a sloppy tortilla underneath everything. Plus, the quality of the ranchero sauce is good and the eggs are always cooked perfectly.

The last time I was there, Zack made my huevos. They were really good. I was impressed. I mean, Zack is my baby brother. He's so much younger than I am that I brought him to school for show-and-tell when I was in second grade. I think he was about a week old. I asked my parents, "Can I borrow Zack for show-and-tell?" And they said, "Okay." I carried him to school and showed him to my class: "This is my baby brother." And then I carried him back.

—Charlie Shopsin

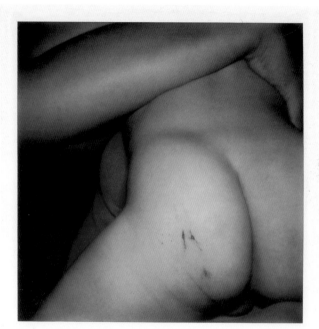

7/10/77
SINK ACCIDENT

Shopsin's is a family business, but I consider anyone who is a significant part of my life in any meaningful way part of my family. There is no "us" and "them" at Shopsin's. That's what a lot of people don't understand. Anyone can come here. *Anyone.* You don't have to be beautiful. You don't have to be successful or smart, rich or famous, clever or sophisticated. You don't have to be perfect. And you don't have to know us. You just have to be willing to talk to us and to other customers while you're here. Everyone who comes here (or *almost* everyone, anyway) is given a glass of water and a menu. From there it is up to them what happens.

We can usually tell if someone is going to work out the minute he or she walks through the door—or even sooner. Most people who are coming to Shopsin's know they're coming to Shopsin's, and they walk right in. But some people walk by the restaurant and slow down to contemplate whether they want to come in. Sometimes when I see someone doing this, I think, "Keep going, buddy." I can just tell by their demeanor or the way they look that it's not going to work out between us.

I hang a menu out in front of the restaurant, which a lot of places do in the hope of enticing customers to come inside by showing them what they have to offer. I do it for the opposite reason. I put the menu there to *dissuade* people from coming in. My menu is six pages long, and there is a *lot* of stuff crammed on those pages. I've never counted, but I've been told that at its largest, it has been up to something like nine hundred items. (Now it's less than half of that.) People who aren't familiar with a restaurant look at a menu in order to conceptualize the place, and when they look at my menu, the only conception they have is that it's out of their conception. If that's the case, hopefully they will keep walking.

Sometimes we get these people who are on the border, and we just *know.* Melinda and I look at each other, and I say to her, "This isn't going to work." They're easy to spot. They come in with blinders. They're totally insensitive to their surroundings or the people around them. They have no desire to interact. Depending on our mood and how offensive we find them, we

Titty Man

may ask them to leave or we may give them a chance. But the minute they give a "tell," something that makes us *sure* they're not right, we get rid of them.

What people don't understand—and what makes those people who have gotten kicked out of Shopsin's feel obligated to think I'm an asshole and hate me for life—is that the acceptance process goes both ways. This even applies to how we look.

I know that the way my restaurant looks isn't appealing to everyone. Shopsin's is very quirky, and we don't do anything to try to camouflage our oddness. If I had to describe the way the restaurant looks, I would say it's not design and it's not décor. It's an assemblage. I don't pay attention to the overall picture. I care about the dots that make up the picture. Each individual object has meaning either for me or for somebody I really care about: my kids or my customers.

When you walk in, there's one of those black bulletin boards with the pressed-on plastic letters that go in the crevices. The words—often put on by customers sending messages to one another—might look like they're stuck there in an arbitrary way, but there are definitely feelings expressed all over that thing. There is the "grocery" sign from the old store that the girls put up, and a rotating crystal that Mara likes. There are some snapshots of people in the store over the years, and there's a little postcard that Espo, a graffiti artist and a regular, sent me from someplace. There is some artwork that I gave to my mother as a gift; she didn't like it so I took it back. And there is the Bi-Polar Bear poster that Danny put up because he's bipolar. There is a whole wall of boxes filled with candy that I give away. And there are toys in all the windows that are, in spirit, a remnant of the days when my kids used to play in the store—although most of the toys are things I have found recently on the Internet.

We don't try to hide the more mundane elements of running a restaurant. There might be a pile of linens that just got delivered sitting on a chair, and boxes that also got delivered that morning could be stacked right near the entrance area. There's a bowl of very speckled bananas up on the counter next to the ice-cream maker, and there are boxes and big cans of all sorts of crap piled way up on the high shelves—strapped back with a bungee cord that I cleverly strung so the cans can't fall on anyone's head. Basically, there's shit all over the place. I feel really comfortable here, and if you don't, that's fine.

A lot of people get out of here *real* fast. They can feel that it's not right for them. Maybe they don't like the way the place looks, or maybe they don't like the way *I* look. Either way, they've made a good decision. But some people aren't as intuitive or as bright as that. Even though my place is not right for them on every level, they think they should like it, so they stay. By kicking them out, what I'm doing is respecting the fact that they don't belong here. And, in fact, I've helped them out. Because if it didn't start out right, it's never going to be right. It's like going out with a guy you don't find attractive; no matter how nice he is, you're never gonna want to fuck him.

Crocodile Dentist

Most of the reasons people get kicked out have to do with ignorance, and it's not really their *fault* at all. They're just being themselves, which works for them everywhere else, but not at Shopsin's. When people come in and ask for coffee to go, we tell them, "You can get the 'to go' part." We've learned from experience that if we give them the coffee, they'll want something else. Next, they'll want to use the bathroom. Or maybe they'll change their mind and decide they want to sit down and have their coffee in a warm, comfortable room. But you can't have just coffee here; you have to eat a meal. (That's one of the rules.) I am not the government providing shelter, and I am not Barnes & Noble that lets you use the bathroom even though you've never bought a book in your life.

I don't blame people for trying. I'm guilty of going to Barnes & Noble to use the bathroom, but if the person running the place told me that it wasn't okay, I would respect that and I would leave. When I get angry is when I tell people that what they're asking of me doesn't work for me, and they refuse to believe it. They keep pushing. They're so used to getting whatever they want wherever they go, they have no way of understanding that someone is telling them they *can't* have what they want. There was one guy I refused to serve. I don't remember why. I just remember that Melinda told him I didn't want to cook for him, and he got so furious that he walked into the bathroom and ripped the toilet out of the floor.

The rules have changed over the years as both the restaurant and I have evolved. A lot of the rules that people talk about either are myths or are rules that I no longer enforce. Twenty-five years ago I used to have a "no copycat ordering" rule. Because the menu is so large, first-timers are often daunted by the selection, and their way of getting around the problem is to point to what someone else in the restaurant is eating and say, "I want that." My refusal has nothing to do with them. It just doesn't work for *me*.

I cook every single meal that is served in my restaurant, and when I'm done, I don't want to have to start all over and cook the same thing again. There's a *lot* of stuff on the menu. Order something else! The other reason for this rule is that I don't like people who can't think for themselves. Ultimately, that is not who I want as a customer. So what I'm really trying to do is help them along in their own development. I could have just told them to get out, but instead I gave them a chance to explore something pretty basic within themselves—what they feel like eating. I've gotten soft on that rule. I still don't like to do it, but if people order the same thing, I don't refuse. I usually just change the ingredients or some step in the method to keep myself interested.

The "no Cobb salad without bacon" rule, which is also no longer enforced, is part of a general philosophy that I still believe in, which is not to send food out of my kitchen that I don't like or that I'm not proud of. I started this rule after a semi-famous actress came in and ordered lentil soup. She didn't want it my way; she wanted all these strange things in it. I don't remember what she was asking me to put in the soup; I just remember that I didn't agree with the changes, but I did it anyway because deep down I'm a star-fucker. Well, the soup turned out terrible (she didn't eat it, so she must have thought so, too), and I *felt* terrible even though I'd only done what she'd asked me to do. I've learned a lot of things at the nadirs in my life, and that was one of them. After that, I said to myself: If someone orders something in such a way that I'm not going to like the finished product or I even think that I *might* not like the finished product, then fuck 'em! I'm not going to do it.

A Cobb salad has many tasty ingredients in addition to bacon, like blue cheese and avocado, but it is a simple fact: a

Cobb salad isn't as good without bacon as it is *with* bacon. I've gotten soft on that rule, too. Today, I will make Cobb salad without bacon even though I think it's a stupid idea—and if you're doing it because bacon is fattening, then it's a *really* stupid idea because blue cheese and avocado are even fattier than bacon. I also do corn chowder without bacon even though I don't agree with that, either. But I won't do a Cheesy Steak (my name for a Philadelphia cheese steak) without onions. It's just wrong. A Cheesy *is* onions. Without the onions, it's just a meat sandwich with some cheese melted on top. It's nothing special. If you don't want onions, order something else.

Kate Peterson and Kenny, Halloween

Corn Chowder
Serves 2 to 4

Kate Peterson was a great waitress at Shopsin's, and stories about her total autonomy, which I encouraged, are legend. One time in the old place a woman ordered Corn Chowder, and soon after she tasted it, she complained that it had bacon in it and tried to send it back. Kate responded by asking if someone else at the table would like the soup. She then explained to the woman that all our Corn Chowder is made with bacon and that therefore she would be charged for the soup because all soups were made to order and what were we to do with it? The lady said, "Don't be a hard-ass with me." At this point Kate picked the woman's soda up off the table and poured it over the woman's head. We have since made a policy of asking customers whether or not they want bacon in their Corn Chowder.

Ingredients
6 slices bacon
1 baked potato, cut into ⅜-inch cubes
¼ cup Clarified Butter (page 44), regular butter, or ghee
2 cups frozen corn
1 big yellow Spanish onion, finely chopped
2 carrots, finely chopped
3 tablespoons masarepa (Hispanic cooked cornmeal) or cornmeal
A pinch of Mara Spice (page 95) or pumpkin pie spice
3 cups Chicken Stock (page 123) or any stock or broth
½ cup feather-shredded cheddar cheese
¾ cup heavy cream
2 tablespoons grated Parmesan cheese, or more to taste
Salt and pepper

Instructions
Cook the bacon until crisp in a heavy sauté pan over very high heat. Remove the bacon from the pan. Add the potato cubes to the rendered fat and cook, shaking the pan occasionally, until they are very crisp and brown on all sides.

Heat the butter in a large sauté pan over high heat. Add the corn, onion, carrots, and any other good chowder vegetables you have around, like arugula, spinach, or green beans. Cook on high heat for about 1 minute, but don't let anything burn. Add the masarepa and Mara Spice, and stir with a whisk to mix in the masarepa. Add the stock, cheddar cheese, and cream, and bring the soup to a simmer. Reduce the heat to low and simmer until the carrots are tender, about 5 minutes. Just before serving, stir in the Parmesan, potato, and bacon. Don't stir too much or wait too long to serve the soup because you want the potato to retain some crispness and the bacon to retain some crunch. Season with salt and pepper if desired.

Cheesy Steak
Serves 2

The authentic way to make a Cheesy is with rib-eye meat, which is the same thing as prime rib, but a little lower down on the cow. It's very expensive, but that's what I use. The meat is semifrozen so I can slice it paper-thin on a slicing machine. When cooked, it disintegrates into something that is not chopped and not sliced. It is its own thing, and it melts in your mouth. The problem you'll encounter when making these at home is how to get the meat as thin as I do. Probably the best way is to have your butcher do it on a slicing machine. It won't get *as* thin because he won't have frozen it first, but it'll be thinner than anything you could do at home, assuming you don't have a meat slicer.

The second component of a Cheesy is the onions, and I use a lot of onions—a whole big yellow Spanish onion for every sandwich. Classically, the onions are cooked on the griddle, but I cook mine in the deep fryer. You can also use this cheesy steak filling, as I do, as a filling for other things, like tacos and quesadillas. A lot of people think the traditional Cheesy bread is important to the sandwich. I use ciabatta rolls instead, but trust me: the Cheesies are even better this way.

Ingredients
2 big yellow Spanish onions, thinly sliced
Good olive oil
½ pound rib-eye meat or roast beef, very thinly sliced
Beef or Chicken Stock (pages 123–24), or any stock or broth or olive oil
Butter for buttering the rolls
2 ciabatta rolls, sliced in half
2 slices American cheese, or any cheese you like

Instructions
Fry the onions in a deep fryer or a pot of oil until browned and crispy (see Fried Onions, page 171).

Pour enough oil to coat the griddle or a large sauté pan and heat it over high heat until it is very hot. Add the beef and cook until the meat is brown, about 2 minutes. Drizzle with a splash of stock to give the meat a nice mushy texture. Butter the rolls and place them, open, over the sliced cheese. When the cheese has melted, scoop up the meat under each roll and flip them onto a plate to serve.

In most cases the reason I don't do special requests has to do with the customer's reason for making it. Most of the time when a customer makes a special request, it's not about the food but about his own desire to be in control and to establish his own specialness. Making people feel special through this kind of ass kissing is one of the services that a restaurant can provide to people who need it, but it's not a service that *I* want to provide.

I have been cooking for thirty years and I've got a thousand things on the menu, and you're going to take one thing and make it different? Uh-uh. Try it my way for once. The way I often get rid of these customers is to negative them. They say, "Can I get X?" And I tell them no. Then they say, "Can I get Y?" And I say no to that, too. Depending on the person, they might need to ask for three or five things before they figure out that they can't get anything except *out.*

Not too long ago, Melinda gave me a check for a burrito that normally came with cheese, only with no cheese. The customer said she was lactose intolerant. But that same customer got a side order of pancakes, and pancake batter is *all milk.* Her need to make her burrito special was not about not wanting to or not being able to drink milk. It was about her need for control. I didn't just tell her I wouldn't do it. I gave Minda back the check and told her to get rid of the whole table.

Some people tell me that they're deathly allergic to something and that I have to make sure it's not in their food. I kick them out, too. I don't want to be responsible for anyone's life-or-death situation. I tell them they should go eat at a hospital. Often after I do that, they'll back down and tell me, well, they're not *that* allergic. And then I *really* want them to leave because now I know they're assholes.

Anybody who makes special requests is putting himself at risk, but if it's a regular customer who wants something a little different, I usually accommodate his or her desires. I am, after all, in the service business. I love cooking, and I love feeding people. Probably half the items on my menu started as special requests and eventually made their way onto the menu. And for a lot of customers, I cook to their requests regularly. For Barry Sheck I make a chorizo omelet with no toast and no-carbohydrate ingredients in the omelet. Jon Korkes, a regular customer, is on a low-salt diet, so I cook a specific way for him. And for my best friend, Steven Casko, who recently became diabetic, I make an egg white omelet that is cooked according to what he can and cannot eat.

●

I enjoy cooking and giving what I can to my customers, and, in turn, my customers don't just enjoy giving me money, they enjoy receiving what I have given them. Once we've established a rapport, we're absolute equals in my restaurant. But I guess I shouldn't expect newcomers to understand this. In all fairness, they're right and I'm the asshole, because my way is hardly the traditional you-give-me-money-I-give-you-a-bagel. I want more from them. I want a relationship.

●

The rules are printed on the menu in clear type, so there is no reason anyone needs to break them or be surprised by them. Today, there are only three official rules left:
1. Limit of four people per group
2. No cell phone use
3. One entrée per person minimum

The party-of-four rule is something that developed in the original space. Implementing the rule was my way of controlling my wife, Eve. When we would start to get too busy, I used to tell her to quit letting people in. But Eve had an obsession with making people happy, and when customers came in, no matter how slammed she could see I was, she just kept letting them in. She would pack the place, and it didn't matter how many times I told her not to, I'd still find myself back there like an automaton on an assembly line trying to get the food out. I simply couldn't accommodate large parties on a production level. The kitchen was tiny, and I had so few burners that I couldn't cook that many dishes and get them all to the table at the same time or even *around* the same time. I finally got tired of having to rely on Eve to control the pace of the restaurant, so I just made it a rule. When we kick out a large party, the people will almost always >

Steven Casko's Egg White Omelet *Serves 2*

This thing is so healthy, except maybe for the ham, that it must be as close as you can get to not eating and still getting to chew. I've never tried it. It's not my thing. But Steven likes it. Honestly, I'd cook it for Steven Casko even if it didn't taste good because I would do anything for Steven. He has saved my life more times than I care to admit or that I can count. He is a contractor but is so much more than that to me. He is good with carpentry and electrical stuff but is also just *so* smart and *so* clever and *so* good at following through and finishing what he started. I can't tell you how much he does for me—whether it's a technical thing in the kitchen or some kind of problem solving in terms of food. My son Daniel asked me recently, talking about Steven Casko, "What do you do when someone is so important in your life and so selflessly generous? How do you repay him?" I said I would presume that someone who is that generous gets some kind of pleasure from being generous, so what you do is appreciate what he does for you and show your appreciation for him as best you can. And if he ever asks you to do something, no matter what it is, you do it. The problem is, I can rarely figure out what to do for Casko besides cook for him.

This isn't really an omelet because it's not folded; it's more like a white frittata. If you want to make more than one, you need to make them one at a time.

Ingredients

Good olive oil
1 slice of ham, chopped
½ red bell pepper, cored, seeded, and
    chopped (see Cutting Peppers, page 55)
2 slices tomato, chopped
6 extra-large egg whites, whisked

Instructions

Pour a thin coating of oil in a large egg pan over medium heat and heat until the oil is warm. Add the ham, pepper, and tomato. Put the lid on the pan and let the ham and vegetables cook for about 3 minutes, until the peppers soften. Pour the egg whites over the vegetables and cook (see Cooking Eggs, page 46) until the bottom side is pretty solid. Flip the whole thing with a flick of your wrist and cook the omelet on the other side for another 2 to 3 minutes, until the egg whites are cooked through.

Casko

PARTY OF FIVE

You could put a chair at the end
or push the tables together
but don't bother
This banged-up little restaurant
where you would expect no rules at all
has a firm policy against seating
parties of five

And you know you are
a party of five

It doesn't matter if one of you
offers to leave or if
you say you could split into
a party of three and a party of two
or if the five of you come back tomorrow
in Richard Nixon masks and try to pretend
that you don't know each other
It won't work: you're a party of five

Even if you're a beloved regular
Even if the place is empty
Even if you bring logic to bear
Even if you're a tackle for the Chicago Bears
it won't work
You're a party of five
You will always be a party of five
a hundred blocks from here
a hundred years from now
you will still be a party of five
and you will never savor the soup
or compare the coffee or
hear the wisdom of the cook
and the wit of the waitress or
get to hum the old-time tunes
among which you will find
no quintets

—*Robert Hershon*

> ask if they can split up into two tables. But it's still the same thing, and our answer is still no. They're all still going to order at the same time, and they're all going to want their food at the same time. It's hard on me. I don't want to do it.

Besides, the *real* reason for the rule is that large parties are no fun. They come into the restaurant, and they're an entity unto themselves. When there are more than four people to a party— whether they are seated at one table or divided between two— they don't interact with other customers. They're not a part of what is going on in the restaurant. Let them have their powwow somewhere else. I don't want them here.

We do occasionally bend the party-of-four rule. (In fact, we bend all the rules whenever we happen to want to.) We reserve the right to count kids or not count them depending on whether we like the people and if we feel like letting them in. And once in a while, for no particular reason, we just seat a party of five (or even six) adults. When that happens, it's usually because Zack did it. Zack's best and worst quality is that he has a big heart, and sometimes in a bighearted moment he lets the people in. Then he comes and tells me, "Look, Dad. There was nobody in here. Plus they're really nice."

I started working here full-time out of necessity. This other kid who was working here got fired, and at the same time I needed a job. Also, with my mom passing, I knew my dad needed the help.

I'm happy here. I've worked here full-time for a few years now, but really we've all worked here our whole lives. We got paid most of the time. It wasn't always good pay, but it was fun work. I liked growing up in the restaurant. Everyone in the neighborhood knew us. There was never a day when I walked down the street and somebody didn't point and say, "You're a Shopsin!" I think we always felt more special than the other kids because of the restaurant. At least I did.

People always ask me if I'm like my dad. I think they ask all of us that. But out of the five of us, I'm probably the most like both our parents. Maybe all of us combined are like my dad, like the Transformer, Voltron.

Chicken Chow Fun is my favorite thing to eat at the restaurant. When we were kids, Chicken Chow Fun (facing page) was everyone's favorite. We always had it with extra broccoli. It has all the good things of the chow fun you get in Chinatown except it doesn't have dried-out crappy chicken. The chicken has a nice flour coating that gets glazed when it's cooked.

—Zack Shopsin

Chicken Chow Fun
Serves 2 to 4

Chow fun noodles are made of white rice that has been boiled down and run through a press. I buy them at a vegetarian Chinese restaurant at Grand and Bowery Streets. No one who works there speaks English. I say, "Ten dollars forty cents," and they give me my noodles. The noodles have a very short life. I portion them and freeze them in plastic bags.

Ingredients
Two 5- to 6-ounce boneless, skinless
   chicken breasts
All-purpose flour for dredging
¼ cup good olive oil
2 cups Asian-type vegetables (whatever is
   available to you, such as bok choy,
   jicama, snow peas, scallions, shiitake,
   broccoli, long beans, and peas), chopped
   if applicable
2 cups fresh chow fun noodles (or 8 ounces
   dry pad Thai noodles that have been
   soaked in hot water according to
   package instructions to soften)
1 lemon
2 tablespoons soy sauce
¼ cup Chicken Stock (page 123), or any
   stock or broth

Instructions
Cut the chicken into strips the size of a baby's index finger. Pour the flour on a plate or in a small bowl. Dredge the chicken in the flour and shake off the excess flour.

Heat the olive oil in a large, heavy sauté pan over high heat until it is hot but not smoking. Gently drop the chicken in the pan, evenly distributing it around the pan. (Be careful; this can be dangerous because the oil is very hot. If you carelessly drop the chicken in, it'll splatter on your arms and face.) Let the chicken cook, sitting in one spot. Check the underside of one piece. When it becomes medium brown, use the handle of the fry pan to toss the pan and flip the chicken pieces in the pan. It is really hard to flip every piece; just toss the pan a few times to get most of the chicken turned and then use tongs to turn the few remaining pieces so that all the brown faces up.

Add the vegetables. Cut the noodles with scissors so they drop in the pan, and toss. Squeeze the juice of the lemon over everything, drizzle with soy sauce, and then add the chicken stock. Agitate the pan to coat the chicken and noodles with a sticky brown-black glaze and finish cooking for 1 to 2 minutes. Serve in a stainless-steel Chinese dome set if you have one.

anywhere else. Owning a store on that block felt like a womb to me, like something I wanted to go back to.

Neither of the stores was for sale, but the way it worked in New York at that time was that if you wanted to buy any small business, you just went into the store every day for a few days or weeks, whatever it took, and told the owner you wanted to buy it. You'd ask him what it would take for him to sell, and eventually you would make a deal. I went into both stores, and both owners wanted the same amount of money even though one store was three times as large. I decided to buy the smaller store because it seemed more manageable. I paid—or, rather, my father paid—$25,000 (this was 1973, remember), which included the stock and goodwill.

Back then, goodwill counted for a lot. In fact, it was all you had. Regular customers never paid for what they purchased at the time they purchased it because every store gave them credit. We had a book in which people would write down what they bought. The majority of our customers lived from week to week, and the delay in paying was comforting to them. You floated them, and in return you owned them. Your customer had credit in your store, so that was the only place he or she would—and for the most part *could*—shop.

Besides, there was no reason for anyone to leave a certain radius to go to a different store, because none of the stores did anything distinguishable from one another. The food and grocery business was very different then, and competition for business didn't exist like it does today. There were very few supermarkets. There was only one in the Village, and it was not popular, especially with older people who liked the personal attention they got from stores like mine. And there were no specialty markets like you have now. Soho Charcuterie, a prepared-food store that was the first of its kind, had not yet opened in Chelsea. Giorgio DeLuca had not yet started Dean & DeLuca.

The majority of people in the city did all their shopping at small, independently owned grocery stores like mine, and we all sold the same stuff, which was a little bit of everything: fresh meat and vegetables, frozen vegetables (still a novelty), beer (lots), drink mixers (lots), soda, dairy, eggs, cat food, toilet paper, dish soap. In the delicatessen you could expect to see cold cuts and premade sandwiches as well as potato salad, coleslaw, and fresh bread. That was it. The only thing I did differently from everyone else was that I made roast beef for sandwiches. The previous owner's wife had made roast beef, and I simply continued that tradition. But even that wasn't so unusual. The nitrate system for preserving meats hadn't yet been perfected, so there was no commercial roast beef—none that was any good anyway—so a lot of people made their own.

•

After I bought the store, the guy I bought it from, an Armenian immigrant, stayed with me for a few days, maybe a week, to show me how it was done. The way it worked, not just at my store but at many stores in New York City, is that customers didn't just wander around the store and pick stuff off the shelves. They told you what they wanted, and the proprietor would get it off the shelf for them. A workingman buying groceries was serviced as though he was in Cartier buying diamonds.

When I bought the store, the Armenian said to me, "The one thing you're going to know in this business is your customer. You may not know anything else, but you'll know your customers by what they order." And it was true. The very first time this was made clear to me, I was standing in the store behind the counter, wearing my gray coat. I think it was my first day. The Armenian said to me, "Oh, it's Thursday. Here comes Mrs. Constable." He began pulling things off the shelves: a six-pack of seven-ounce seltzers, a jar of Smucker's strawberry jam, and a few other things. When Mrs. Constable walked in the store, she placed her order, which included everything the Armenian had already picked out for her.

When he left after that week, I was terrified. I felt the way you do the first time you leave the hospital with a baby, like you're responsible for this really important thing and you're totally incapable of handling it. But I got the hang of it pretty quickly. I wore a gray clerk coat because that's what he wore, and I always had a pencil stuck behind my ear. And I felt really good running the place. I worked really hard, and I loved it.

From the time I opened at seven in the morning until I

Painting by Dorthy Eisner

closed at eight o'clock at night, I was moving: helping customers, taking things off shelves, adding things up. I didn't have an adding machine, so I would take the bag I was packing the groceries in and the pencil stuck behind my ear and I'd write the order up on the bag. When customers left, the bag was their receipt.

We had a steady stream of customers coming in the morning for coffee, a line of customers between eleven and two o'clock in the afternoon waiting to get lunch, offices calling up waiting to get large orders to pick up, and customers coming all day long to buy groceries. Half the time I had to slip in a quarter pound of sliced this or half a pound of sliced that, which meant I had to go over to the meat slicer and get that together. We had orders going out, and we had grocery deliveries coming in that had to be unloaded and put on the shelves. Then one of the gumball machines would break—I always had gumball machines because kids like them, and I like kids—and I would have to stop everything to fix it. It would go on and on all day long like this. It never stopped. It was like I was sitting on a chair with a really good ball bearing in it, and every once in a while someone would take a bat and spin me around. And then, just when I'd start to slow down, they'd spin me again. They were long, long days, but they flew by like a blink. I did it five days a week, sometimes six or seven, for thirteen or fourteen years.

We had two employees working for us at that time: Danny Midler, Bette Midler's brother, whom I had hired as a favor, and a guy named Jimmy, a skinny, dynamic, diabetic black guy with a Sammy Davis Jr. face. Jimmy had a girlfriend named Elaine who was really fat. When the Health Department came out with new regulations, I sent her down to take the inspections course for me. I hated the Health Department even back then. I think I'd rather go out of business than take that fucking course. People said, "How can you have *her* take the test for you? She can't pass for you." But she was perfect. Who the hell is going to ask a three-hundred-pound black lady if she's really Kenny Shopsin? Of course, nobody did. Anyway, Jimmy had worked at a lot of different places before he worked at our store, so he always had ideas. One day he suggested that I make egg salad in addition to roast beef, so I said, "All right," and I did.

Egg Salad

Makes enough for 2 sandwiches

Egg salad is like guacamole: The contrast of smooth and chunky makes its texture exciting enough that it would be good even if it had no flavor. But almost as a bonus, egg salad made with fresh eggs explodes with flavor. Little seasoning is needed. In fact, it's best when there is no seasoning at all, so the eater can season it as he goes along, sprinkling a little salt and pepper on immediately before taking each bite. It tastes better if it gets its creamy texture from being more yolky, not by adding more mayo, which is why it's important to separate the yolks and whites when you make it.

Ingredients

6 extra-large eggs
Mayonnaise (I like Hellmann's; use what
    you like)
Salt and pepper

Instructions

Place the eggs in one layer in a large pot and add enough water to cover by ¾ inch. Put the pot over high heat and stir the water occasionally, until there are lots of small bubbles on the bottom and sides of the pot but the water is not yet boiling. At that point, cover the pot, remove it from the heat, and let the eggs sit in the water for 9 minutes (less for smaller eggs). Drain the eggs and run them under cold running water to cool to room temperature. Peel. (This should be easy if you have done everything right and the eggs are fresh.)

Break the eggs apart with your hands and separate the yolks from the whites. The yolks should be bright yellow, flaky-dry, not dense and powdery looking, and definitely not with a gray ring around them, which means they are severely overcooked. Pat the whites dry with paper towels. Crumble the yolks into a bowl to a fine, slightly spongy texture. Add mayonnaise gradually until the mixture is just creamy but not wet. Be careful not to add too much. Hand-crumble the egg whites into the bowl with the yolks and mayonnaise mixture. Don't crumble them too much because you want the texture of the bigger pieces. Stir the whites and yolks together and season with salt and pepper if desired.

I had no conscious intention of going into cooking, and I certainly never tried to set myself apart. But because I was different, because I was coming from such a different existential place than the Armenian immigrant I bought the store from or the other store owners in the neighborhood, my intentions and my approach to the craft were different, too. So even though my business appeared to be the same as the others, even though I seemed to be engaged in the same occupation, and even though it seemed to be the same shit I was selling, my business was *not* the same—or at least not for long. My store became a new creation, a new *type* of store, in terms of both the world we created there through our daily banter with the customer and the food we sold.

Vase by Kenny, 1966

In the natural course of events, I began cooking more and more items. I started out in life as a sculptor because I liked working with my hands, and now I just took whatever was in front of me, which happened to be food, and did whatever I felt like in that moment. After the Egg Salad, I started making other mayonnaise-based salads, like Chicken Salad (page 36) and shrimp salad. I took pork tenderloin, shaped like a big round bologna, and cooked it with onions and duck sauce and then sliced it for sandwiches. I made one soup—Chicken, Mushroom, and Barley Soup (page 37)—which I was really proud of. And I started making takeout dinners—turkey dinners, meatloaf dinners, potpies, stuff like that. We had a different dinner special for every night of the week, and people went crazy over all of them. Pretty soon we had a line out the door.

Radically Chic...

MR. AND MRS. KEN SHOPSIN, proprietors of Shopsin's corner grocery store, enjoying the party at Jimmy's.

Chicken Salad
Makes enough for 2 sandwiches

Chicken salad has a long history at Shopsin's. It's been made in a number of different ways, none of which I totally remember—though I do remember that originally I made chicken salad with turkey. Don't ask me why I didn't use chicken for the chicken salad because I really don't know. Probably it's because I was a grocery store, so I didn't have cooked chickens, but I did have the cooked turkey breasts that we used for making sandwiches.

People immediately got stuck on my chicken salad. I served it on bread sharp enough to cut your gums, from Zito's, a place that used to be around the corner on Bleecker Street. My regular customers would come in and start to order something different, and then they would change their mind and say, "No. I think I'll have the chicken salad." Bob Dylan, who lived in the neighborhood, was hooked on it for years.

Ingredients
5 ounces cooked turkey or chicken, cut into
    1-inch chunks
Mayonnaise
Salt and pepper

Instructions
Put the turkey or chicken chunks in a bowl and massage the chunks between your thumb and first three fingers until they are frayed on the edges and semisoft in the center. Once you have the proper texture, start adding mayonnaise. Because breast meat has a dry texture, it will absorb the oil from the mayonnaise, so what's left on the outside will be the white, creamy, tasty part of the mayonnaise. As for how much mayonnaise you add, it's a feel thing. It's like making risotto where you add broth a little at a time until the rice is cooked. Add the mayonnaise a little at a time, and as soon as the molecules of the meat have been filled and the mayonnaise has nowhere else to go, stop. You can then season the salad with salt and pepper if you like. I don't.

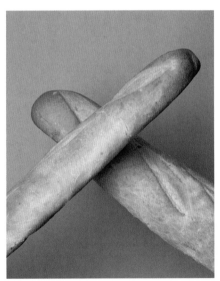
En garde

Chicken, Mushroom, and Barley Soup *Serves 4 to 6*

A long time ago, when we were still a grocery store, Bud (Calvin) and Alice Trillin invited us to a function at their house. Bud is a well-known writer for *The New Yorker*, and he and his wife, Alice, who died a few years ago, were longtime customers and friends (Bud still is). One of their guests, whom I was talking to, was a real big shot of some kind, and somehow the subject of chicken soup came up. Alice had an effect on people where they really wanted to be in her social circle. This big shot was trying to challenge me in front of Alice to establish his superiority over me and to gain her approval. This was going to be hard for him to do in terms of chicken soup, because I'd been making my Chicken, Mushroom, and Barley Soup four days a week for years. In fact, for many years it was the only soup I made, and it was my pride and joy. I stayed really quiet, probably because I was stoned. Besides, I've only gotten real noisy in the last five or ten years, although there are some people who might not agree.

Anyway, the guy persisted, and at one point he asked me if I used chicken feet in my soup. I didn't. I made my soup using old chickens, or fowls. And I cooked the barley long enough that it gave up some of its starch into the broth, so the broth had a special viscous, slimy, barley kind of thickness. When I told the guy that, no, I didn't use chicken feet, he said, "Well, you really don't know how to make chicken soup then, do you?" Sometime later, Alice told me the guy

had removed himself from her circle with that comment. He was out of line, and she told him so. I was unsure about Alice until then, but after that, I realized that she was really sweet, that she cared about people.

Old chickens, which they now call hens, make the best soup. As chickens get older, they also get more savory, just like there's something more savory about a woman who has a few years on her than a young, shallow girl. You don't see hens in stores much anymore because they have to be fed for a longer period than young chickens, so they are not cost-effective to raise, but if you can get them, use them for this soup.

Ingredients

1 whole chicken
A small handful of fresh dill (about ½ cup)
2 carrots, chopped
2 celery ribs, chopped
1 big yellow Spanish onion, chopped
2 big handfuls of white mushrooms (about 2 cups), thinly sliced
2 cups barley
Salt and pepper

Instructions

Put the chicken in a large pot of water over high heat. Add the dill, carrots, celery, onion, and mushrooms. Bring the soup to a boil, reduce the heat, and simmer until the chicken is done, 45 minutes to 1 hour, depending on the size of the chicken.

Turn off the heat, take the chicken out

of the pot, and rip the meat off the bones. Discard the skin and bones, and toss the ripped chicken back into the pot. Add the barley and cook the soup for another half hour or so, until the barley is just barely tender. Season with salt and pepper if desired and serve. If you are making this for later, refrigerate and then heat up just as much soup as you want to serve to avoid overcooking the barley.

Life in Eggville

I believe that one of the secrets to happiness is to work within the parameters of the reality of your life. As a restaurant owner I have learned that if I'm going to be happy doing what I do, I have to go with the zeitgeist. When Shopsin's first became a restaurant, it was a soup joint. I got to be known for having all these different kinds of soups, so that's what people typically came here for. Then the Soup Nazi came along, half a dozen places opened in the neighborhood that sold soup, and people just stopped ordering soup so much, at least from me. Also, at that time dinners were my biggest meal, but then due to changes in the neighborhood, my customer base shifted and dinners got slow. Eventually they got so slow that I closed the place at dinnertime.

Back in the dinner days we had a separate breakfast menu that ended at 11:00 a.m. Customers who came during the afternoon or evening would often ask, "Can I get breakfast?"

We'd respond with "Sorry. We're done with breakfast."

And they'd say, "Oh, shit. I really wanted eggs. Can you *please* do me some eggs?"

We'd tell them, "No, it's after eleven." It just didn't make sense. After a while I got tired of being an asshole. I thought I wanted to make soup and dinner, but what I wanted more was to make what my customers wanted, and what my customers wanted were eggs. I started offering eggs all day long, and now I'm in Eggville. The irony is that until I landed in Eggville I didn't even *like* eggs—eating them or making them. Now I've found that it really doesn't matter what I make because, for me, cooking is all about the process.

I cook about ninety dozen eggs every Saturday and every Sunday, and I enjoy cooking them each time I do it. I like cracking the eggs into a bowl. I like breaking the yolks and whisking them with cream for scrambled eggs. I like watching the ripples form as they cook, and I like the process of gently running my fork through cooked eggs to create space for the raw egg to hit the pan. When I'm making fried eggs and sunnies, I like heating the butter in the pan; I like sliding the eggs into the butter; and I like sliding the finished eggs from the pan onto a plate. I like everything there is about making eggs, and no matter how many times I do it, I *still* like doing it. There's nothing else I'd rather be doing. I don't come to the task from a place of drudgery or boredom. I come to it from a place of curiosity and love. To be a good cook you have to.

Clarified Butter

I use only clarified butter for cooking eggs—and for any sauté cooking where I want the flavor of butter instead of olive oil. Clarified butter is butter that has been melted and then the milk solids and water removed, so all that you're left with is the golden buttery-flavored butter. Because it has no milk in it, it doesn't burn, which means you can cook at a higher temperature than when using regular butter without fear of the butter's browning or burning.

Clarified butter

To make clarified butter, melt butter over low heat. Skim the white foam off the top, then let the butter sit until the milk solids drop to the bottom. Pour the butter into another container so you now have just the golden liquid. You could also buy clarified butter, called ghee, which is used in Indian cooking. I think you can get it at most grocery stores—and definitely at Indian-type or at health food stores. In my recipes you can use regular butter instead of clarified butter where I call for it. You'd just have to be careful not to let the butter brown.

Buying Eggs

There are two basic types of eggs in the world: fresh eggs and storage eggs. Storage eggs, which are kept in a special room with special conditions, can be as much as a year old when you get them in the supermarket. I use only fresh eggs. They have better flavor. The only real way to discern whether or not you're getting good eggs is to buy one some-place and then go home and cook it. A good fresh egg will have a bright yellow yolk and a flavor with lots of subtlety and nuance. An old egg will have a lighter-colored yolk. It will *look* like an egg, but that's about as far as it goes. I don't have a preference for cage-free or free-range eggs. It sounds nice, the hens running free and all that, but frankly I don't notice a difference in the taste.

If you have a good Teflon pan, one that costs a little more than the minimum, you shouldn't have a problem cooking sunnies or over-easies. It's about the weight: A heavy pan is a good pan because it stays hot even when you put something cold in it.

Cooking Eggs

There are certain foods that are not malleable but dictatorial in how they are cooked. That's definitely true of eggs, which is why a lot of places, probably most places, turn out eggs that really suck. When you're cooking eggs, you have to give up your macho stance and do what they say. The secret to cooking eggs—no matter what style—is not to rush them. Eggs are really finicky. There is a proper speed to cooking them, and if you mess with that, you're going to get *wrong* eggs. When you're cooking eggs, you can pretty much count on a formula: If they look right, they will taste right. I don't salt eggs. I like to let my customers season them as they desire, but if you like salted eggs, by all means add salt to any of my egg recipes.

To make SCRAMBLED EGGS it's important to be gentle with them. Cook them slowly over a low fire and try to control yourself in terms of playing with them. If you cook them correctly, you'll end up with nice big curdles, and the low-heat cooking preserves the bright yellow color. If you cook them too fast, over heat that is too high, or mess with them too much, they get tough and may even brown. (For more detailed instructions, see Scrambled Eggs and Toast, page 48.)

Cook SCRAMBLED EGG WHITES like regular scrambled eggs, only over hotter heat (medium-low) and for a longer time. You have to make sure there are no translucent bits left in the eggs, or they'll have a slimy albumen texture—and you'll be amazed at how long this takes. If you really want to be low-fat, you can even poach egg whites. Just slip them in the water and cook them the way you'd poach any egg. I don't know if this is true of the stuff that comes in cartons because I don't use that shit. If you like it, use it, but even without trying it, I think it sucks. I guess it's like eating at McDonald's. There's nothing wrong with their hamburgers if you like them, but you shouldn't delude yourself into thinking you're eating an *actual* hamburger.

The first thing you should learn in making SUNNIES is to break the eggs into a small bowl, not directly into the pan. It makes it a lot easier to remove any shell bits or deal with a broken yolk. You have to look carefully at the yolks to make sure they haven't broken and are not going to leak when you drop them into the pan. Preheat the clarified butter in an egg pan at somewhere between low and medium. Gently slide the eggs into the pan and cook until the whites are perfectly opaque. If the eggs sizzle when they hit the pan, turn down the heat; otherwise you'll end up with a crispy browned crust on the edges and bottom of the whites.

For OVER-EASIES, the purpose of flipping them is not to cook them on the second side but just to hide the yolks. So cook sunnies until they are done, then flip them and leave them on the second side for 20 seconds. For over-medium eggs, leave them on the second side for an additional 30 seconds.

There's a whole mystique about making POACHED EGGS that I've never understood. It's just like making sunnies: You crack the eggs in a bowl, heat the pan, slide them in—only there's water in the pan instead of butter. The way I make them, they're simple—no swirling shit around. No vinegar. No little cups to break the eggs in. You do have to pay attention to the heat, though. You don't want the water to boil rapidly, but you don't want the water to stop boiling, either, so you have to make adjustments to the heat while the eggs are cooking. And you *do* need a slotted spoon to get them out. That's the only special tool. They are so easy and really delicious. Poached eggs have all the runny, eggy goodness of a sunny without the distraction of the butter flavor. As I get older, I'm less and less prone toward gilding something that is already perfect. There's nothing better than a poached egg on a piece of crunchy buttered toast or English muffin. *Nothing.*

Scrambled Eggs and Toast *Serves 2 to 4*

I read someplace years ago, and I still believe it's true, that if you go to a restaurant and want to know whether or not the kitchen knows what they're doing, order scrambled eggs. If the eggs are good, you can almost be sure that anything you eat there will be good. If the kitchen doesn't know how to cook scrambled eggs, chances are they can't cook anything. Scrambled eggs and toast is a really good deal at my place. It's only $4.95 for three perfectly cooked eggs and two thick slices of really good toast. And if I do say so myself, my scrambled eggs are perfect.

Ingredients

1 teaspoon Clarified Butter (page 44), regular butter, or ghee
6 extra-large eggs
½ teaspoon heavy cream
Buttered toast

Instructions

Heat the butter in a nonstick egg pan over medium heat. Whisk the eggs and cream together in a bowl and pour into the pan. Let the eggs sit for a bit until you sense that somewhere around the edge they're setting, but they don't yet look like they're setting. Pull a fork gently through the eggs as though you're drawing a line down the center of the pan. The line you drew through the center will fill up with raw egg, and now all of a sudden there will be ridges in the eggs, a discernment between the raw and the cooked eggs. When the flat raw egg looks like it is setting, pull the fork through it again slowly. When you do this the third time, pull the fork across in a few places and lift up the center of the eggs so that some of the raw egg gets under them and they don't overcook. At this point the eggs are cooked enough for me, but I like my eggs soft, with different levels of cookedness within them. If you like your eggs more cooked, cook them more. Serve with the toast.

Variations on Scrambled Eggs

Eggs are wonderful by themselves, but they are also good as a vehicle for other flavors. I have God knows how many scrambles on my menu. I can't tell you how to make every single one, but I can give you the ingredients and let you figure it out for yourself. Refer to the method for Scrambled Eggs (facing page) for detailed instructions on how to cook any of these. My menu is so huge that half the time I get an order for something and don't even remember what it is. I look at the menu to see what ingredients are in it, and I use that list like a road map to take me to the end of the dish. You should try doing the same. To be a good cook you have to be willing to take risks.

Eating Eggs

In my years of cooking and watching people eat, I have noticed that of all the foods I sell, eggs are eaten the most habitually. Everyone who eats eggs has a special way of eating them. If you were to watch ten or twenty people eating eggs, you would find that no two people eat them the same way. And if you were to track those people eating eggs over a period of time, you would find that they eat them the same way each time.

Eating eggs is a very personal thing and something that people find enormously satisfying. Just the way I am when I cook them, for that moment in time when a person is eating eggs he or she is totally consumed. Maybe it's some ontological recapitulation of childhood, of eating a mother's product. Most people get a peaceful look on their face and go someplace else. I don't know where the hell they go, but they are taken away.

Cutting Avocados

To cut an avocado cut it in half with a big chef's knife. If you are using only half of it, set the half with the pit aside and proceed with the other half. Separate the flesh from the skin with a big spoon but leave it in the shell. Score the avocado into chunks in the shell, then turn it over and squeeze the chunks into whatever you are adding it to.

Favorite tools

Auntie Scrambled Eggs, Blue Cheese, Avocado, and Spinach *Serves 2 to 4*

This dish is mainly a lot of avocado. It's an expensive dish to make, but it's right in terms of the flavor of the dish. I add the blue cheese after the eggs are cooked. Otherwise, it melts into the eggs, and you hardly notice it's there. Ideally, when you take a bite of these eggs, you will feel your teeth going through the spinach, the avocado, the egg, and the chunks of cheese.

Ingredients
1 teaspoon Clarified Butter (page 44), regular butter, or ghee
2 big handfuls of prewashed spinach (about 2 heaping cups)
6 extra-large eggs
½ teaspoon heavy cream
2 to 4 tablespoons crumbled blue cheese (depending on your taste)
1 ripe Hass avocado, cut into chunks

Avocado at the ready

Instructions
Heat the butter in a nonstick egg pan over medium heat. Add the spinach and cook until it heats up and wilts a bit, but not until it gets dark and spinachy. Whisk the eggs and cream together in a bowl; pour into the pan with the spinach and cook as for Scrambled Eggs (page 48) until the eggs are almost done (I mean *really* almost done), then fold in the cheese and avocado and serve.

Bayou Scrambled Eggs, Okra, Salsa, and Cheddar Cheese *Serves 2 to 4*

Sometimes an ingredient will come into my mind, and I'll think, "I should use more of that," and I proceed to build a dish from there. These eggs started with the okra.

Ingredients

1 teaspoon Clarified Butter (page 44), regular butter, or ghee
6 extra-large eggs
½ teaspoon heavy cream
2 handfuls of frozen cut okra (about 2 cups), heated to room temperature in whatever way you like
2 big spoonfuls of Salsa Roja (page 63) or any fresh chunky salsa
A big handful of feather-shredded cheddar cheese (about 1 cup)

Instructions

Heat the butter in a nonstick egg pan over medium heat. Whisk the eggs and cream together in a bowl and pour into the pan. Cook as for Scrambled Eggs (page 48). When they're almost done, fold in the okra, salsa, and cheese. Gently fold all the ingredients together while you finish cooking the eggs.

Bayou with whole-wheat toast

Frozen okra

Marblehead Soft Scrambled, Corn, and Cheddar Cheese *Serves 2 to 4*

I named this for Lloyd Kramer, a regular customer and a onetime pretty famous reporter, now director, who's from a suburb outside Boston called Marblehead. Lloyd is on a healthy diet now, but before that, when he ordered what he wanted, this is what he ate. It has a ton of cheese in it. The frozen corn cools down the eggs, allowing me to cook them over a higher fire than I normally cook scrambled eggs and still have really creamy eggs.

Ingredients
1 teaspoon Clarified Butter (page 44), regular butter, or ghee
6 extra-large eggs
⅓ cup feather-shredded cheddar cheese
½ teaspoon heavy cream
A big handful of frozen corn kernels (about 1 cup)

Instructions
Heat the butter in a nonstick egg pan over medium heat. Whisk the eggs, cheese, and cream together in a bowl. Pour into the pan and cook the eggs as for Scrambled Eggs (page 48). When the eggs are almost done, add the corn and continue to cook until the eggs are done and the corn is warmed through.

Squaw Eggs Bacon, Peppers, and Hominy *Serves 2 to 4*

To my mind, this is the scrambled American Indian version of a western omelet. At the time I came up with it, the feminist Andrea Dworkin was making a huge racket about things that were offensive to women, and I thought Squaw Eggs would be offensive without being *too* offensive—so I put it on the menu to piss her off even though I don't know her and she's probably never heard of this dish. I put hominy (dried corn kernels) in them, which has a squaw feeling for me because American Indians used to grind hominy to make all kinds of breads and shit like that. You can buy it canned, frozen, or dried. And I added tricolored peppers because they remind me of the colors in an Indian girl's dress. This is the kind of egg dish that has more non-egg ingredients than egg, so the egg just binds those ingredients together. If you want it eggier, add more eggs.

Ingredients
1 teaspoon Clarified Butter (page 44), regular butter, or ghee
6 extra-large eggs
½ teaspoon heavy cream
8 slices bacon, cooked and crumbled
½ cup chopped bell peppers (red, green, and yellow)
⅓ cup chopped onion
1 tablespoon Salsa Roja (page 63) or any fresh chunky salsa
2 tablespoons canned or frozen hominy (about 15 pieces)

Minced fresh or pickled jalapeño pepper to taste (see How Spicy Do You Want It? on page 128)

Instructions
Heat the butter in a nonstick egg pan over medium heat. Whisk the eggs and cream together in a bowl, pour into the pan, and cook the eggs as for Scrambled Eggs (page 48). Just before they're done, fold in the bacon, bell peppers, onion, salsa, hominy, and jalapeño pepper.

Fellini Tomato, Garlic Bread, Ricotta, and Egg Casserole *Serves 2 to 4*

This is a dish that Mara makes. I got the idea from an Italian deli in Red Hook, Brooklyn, that is known for a sandwich in which they take a potato, fry it, put it on a piece of bread, and then put a big clonk of super-cold, super-fresh ricotta cheese on top. I like ricotta in general, but when it's fresh like theirs (they make it on the premises), it's particularly sweet and delicate—and just wonderful. If you want, you can melt the cheese under the broiler. If you are going to do this, remember to preheat the broiler and use an ovenproof skillet.

Ingredients

1 teaspoon Clarified Butter (page 44), regular butter, or ghee
6 extra-large eggs
½ teaspoon heavy cream
2 pieces Garlic Bread (page 150), cut into roughly 1-inch chunks
2 whole canned peeled tomatoes (preferably San Marzano)
½ cup fresh whole-milk ricotta cheese

Instructions

Heat the butter in a nonstick egg pan over medium heat. Whisk the eggs and cream together in a bowl, pour into the pan, and begin to cook as for Scrambled Eggs (page 48). Fold in the garlic bread chunks and tomatoes. Continue to cook until the eggs are done, and then spoon the ricotta on top of the eggs. At this point you can either serve the eggs or put them under a broiler to melt the cheese a bit.

Cutting Peppers

The way I cut peppers is nothing special unless you don't know how to do it, and then you'll be glad you learned. Hold the pepper upright and pretend it has four distinct sides. Hold on to the core and cut down on one side of the pepper so you just get the slab of pepper and none of the seeds and bad stuff connected to the core. Do this on the remaining three sides so you have four clean slabs of pepper. Discard the core, which, if you've done what I have told you, still has all the seeds attached. I cut apples in the very same way.

The inherent reward for my sincere efforts to cook eggs is that every once in a while, I think of something new to do with them. I probably have close to a hundred different egg dishes on my menu. In addition to the basics like scrambled eggs, poached eggs, and fried eggs, I make traditional fluffy French-type omelets. I cook egg white omelets. I scramble eggs with bread cubes in the Fellini (page 55) and with tortillas to make Migas (page 214). In fact, I've got a whole lineup of Mexican dishes I make with eggs, including egg enchiladas (see Carmine Street Enchiladas, page 208, and fill the tortillas with scrambled eggs instead of chili), egg quesadillas (make a quesadilla and add scrambled or fried eggs), Egg Nachos (page 62), and Egg Guacamole (page 66). And I make another whole line of dishes using flat browned Jersey omelet–style eggs.

Lake Glen Wild

Jersey Omelet Eggs

Serves 1 or 2

These eggs are flat and browned in the style you get if you order an omelet in a diner in Jersey. I learned to make them from a woman who worked the griddle at a little restaurant in the town where we had a lake house. When the girls were about six or seven, they started taking gymnastics classes. The class was close by, but our house was about a mile down a crummy road. It was a two-way road wide enough for only one car, so you had to stop every time a car was coming in the other direction to let it go by. It was a chore every time you needed to go to the outside world. I didn't want to go down that shitty road back to the house, but I also didn't want to sit there and watch the girls jump over the side horse a hundred times. I don't have the patience. But more important, a major part of my child-rearing philosophy was that if they hit someone in class or they fell and hurt themselves, or even if they did something really good, I wanted the experience to be *their* thing. I didn't want them to have to look to me or to Eve to validate what they were going through. I thought they should harvest their own crop from life. The third reason, which might in fact be the real reason, is that I didn't want to sit behind a wall with all the other parents for an hour. They had nothing to say, and I knew I would just get in trouble for what I *did* say. So, instead, while the girls were in class, I would drive to the restaurant in town and have breakfast.

The restaurant was an old house in which the wall between the kitchen and the living room had been knocked down. A counter had been installed, with a view of the griddle, where the living room had been. By this time in my life I was running a restaurant, and I had begun cooking with some degree of creativity and consciousness about what I was doing. So while I sat there watching the lady at the griddle, it wasn't just idle entertainment for me. I was in the frame of mind to notice things. What I noticed in watching her was that everything she did was wrong.

I am no expert, but when I order an omelet, I think of omelets cooked in the style of Mont-Saint-Michel, an island off the coast of France where omelets were supposedly invented. Saint-Michel omelets are light and fluffy. The cooked eggs puff up like a head of cauliflower. My understanding is that to make one, you have to stop cooking the eggs when they are still slightly wet-looking, but this lady in Jersey, she just cooked the shit out of the eggs over really high heat, so her omelets were dried out and brown and lay totally flat. If you had a cheese omelet, she would cook the eggs, drop the cheese in the center, and then take all four corners up like she was closing an envelope. That is how flat they were.

I have to admit that her food tasted good even though it misrepresented the title she gave it. In fact, some people *like* their eggs cooked the way she cooked them. Today, I use her omelet method to make some of my egg dishes—notably those that I want flat, such as the Egg Pizza (page 64) and Egg Nachos (page 62). What I don't do, though, is call them omelets. To make them I use regular (nonclarified) butter because unlike with my other egg dishes, I want these eggs to brown. If you want to make more than one, double the ingredients, but you have to cook them one at a time—unless you use more than one pan.

Ingredients

2 tablespoons butter
3 extra-large eggs, beaten

Instructions

To make Jersey Omelet Eggs, heat the butter in a large nonstick egg pan over medium-high heat. Pour the eggs into the pan, spread them out so they form a large semicircle, and cook the hell out of them until the undersides are brown and only a thin layer of wet remains on the top. That's it. You don't even flip it. If you want to fill this omelet, put whatever you want in the middle and fold the sides toward the middle like an envelope. You now have a New Jersey–style "omelet."

Pastrami and Eggs *Serves 2 to 4*

This is a classic Jewish egg dish. When I was growing up, my mom used to make salami and eggs using kosher salami. Kosher salami is not like Italian hard salami. It's made of beef, not pork, and it's soft, like a lunch meat. It's also really salty, really garlicky, and *loaded* with fat. I love it. My mom would cook the salami over high heat to render the fat. Cooking eggs in that rendered fat is the common denominator of all Jewish egg dishes, which, like Jersey Omelet Eggs (page 57), are cooked until they are brown. The thing that's really nice about Jewish eggs is that they're almost impossible to mess up. It's like watering a cactus. You don't have to water it often, and if you don't water it at all, even better. This recipe works with kosher salami, pastrami, or corned beef, but not brisket, because brisket is too dry. I find that most people put catsup on Jewish eggs. Who doesn't like catsup and eggs?

both sides until it is just this side of burnt. Reduce the heat to medium, add the eggs, and cook, using a fork to jiggle the pastrami and the eggs so the uncooked eggs touch the surface of the pan, until the eggs are done to your liking.

"Pick up"

Ingredients

6 extra-large eggs
1 teaspoon butter
6 to 8 ounces thinly sliced pastrami

Instructions

Whisk the eggs in a small bowl with no cream or milk. Heat the butter in a large nonstick egg pan over high heat. Add the pastrami (either whole or torn) and cook on

Egg Nachos
Serves 2 to 4

There's not a person alive who doesn't like a pile of chips with all that nacho gooey stuff on top. The important thing with nachos is that when you take a chip, you get a little bit of each of the topping ingredients with it. Still, with 99 percent of the nachos you order, you eat the stuff on the top with the first few chips, and then you're left with nothing but plain dry chips. It's a rip-off and really disappointing. What I do to avoid that common pitfall is after I nuke the cheese, I pour the molten stuff over the chips, making sure each and every chip gets cheese on it. The eggs I lay on top of the chips are Jersey Omelet Eggs (page 57), but you should scramble yours however you like. If I were serving multiple people, I would either make it family style, cooking the eggs in two batches and laying them side by side on the nacho platter, or cook the Jersey eggs for each person separately so that each pile of chips is topped with a neat little circle of cooked eggs. To make regular cheese nachos, follow this recipe, but leave out the eggs.

Ingredients
2 handfuls of shredded Monterey Jack cheese (about 2 cups)
6 extra-large eggs
¼ cup butter
Corn tortilla chips
1 cup canned black beans, drained
1 cup feather-shredded cheddar cheese (or more if you like things really cheesy)

Salsa Roja (facing page) or any fresh chunky salsa

Instructions
Preheat the broiler or oven until it's as hot as it goes.

Melt the Jack cheese until molten in the microwave or in the oven; if you do it in the oven, make sure to use an ovenproof bowl and be careful not to let the cheese burn.

If you are making two omelets, melt half of the butter and cook them like Jersey Omelet Eggs (page 57). Repeat with the remaining butter and eggs. While the eggs are cooking, pile the chips onto as many ovenproof plates as you are using. Pour the molten cheese over the chips, making sure it touches each and every chip, and spoon the black beans over the chips and cheese. Pick up the big round egg circle (or circles) and flop, cooked side up, over the chips. Sprinkle the eggs with the cheddar cheese and put the nachos under the broiler (or in the microwave) just long enough to melt the cheese a bit more. Serve with a big dish of salsa on the side.

Salsa Roja

Makes about 1½ cups

We make this fresh chunky salsa every morning and use it as a subset ingredient for a lot of different rice and scrambled egg dishes, and we serve a little cup of it on the side of any dish that is remotely Mexican.

Ingredients

1 14-ounce can of chopped peeled tomatoes (preferably San Marzano)
3 tablespoons fresh or frozen corn kernels, thawed if frozen
1 teaspoon torn or chopped fresh cilantro leaves
1 teaspoon or more to taste minced pickled jalapeño peppers (see How Spicy Do You Want It? on page 128)
½ teaspoon minced fresh garlic
Salt

Instructions

Combine the tomatoes, corn, cilantro, jalapeño peppers, garlic, and salt to taste. This will keep up to three days in the refrigerator.

Egg Nachos

Salsa Roja

Egg Pizza
Serves 2 as an entrée or 4 as a starter

This is just like pizza except that a normal crust is replaced by a very thin sheet of well-cooked egg. I can't tell you how I came up with it except to say that when I'm doing the reps, something like egg pizza just pops up.

I cut it into four wedges like pizza. You can eat it all by yourself, or you can share it like pizza. It's really hard to pick up an egg pizza, so I suggest you eat it in the 1940s way. Back then, when people first started eating a lot of pizza in this country, almost every pizza place in America, or at least in the New York area, had a sign that showed you how to eat pizza. Without the instructions, because people were just really stupid, I guess, they would pick up a slice in such a way that everything—all the cheese and sauce and topping—would slide off, and they'd be left holding a wedge of crust. The way the signs told you to eat pizza and the way I recommend you eat this egg pizza is to take the wedge, fold it up into a V, and then fold the tip of the V back toward the wide part of the crust. The last part where you fold the tip back is key, and that's the part that has really been forgotten.

If you don't have an ovenproof pan, cook the egg "crust" in whatever pan you do have and then transfer it to a baking sheet before dressing it with the sauce and cheese to finish it off in the oven. With toast or a salad, this pizza makes a nice light meal.

Ingredients
1 tablespoon Clarified Butter (page 44), regular butter, or ghee (or enough to cover the bottom of a 12-inch pan)
4 extra-large eggs, beaten
1 cup grated mozzarella cheese (or more if you like really cheesy pizza; about 3 ounces)
¼ cup Marinara Sauce (page 236) or any marinara sauce
A big pinch of dried oregano
1 tablespoon chopped fresh parsley
Salt and pepper
¼ cup grated Parmesan cheese
Good olive oil for drizzling
Pizza Topping (see below)

Instructions
Heat the butter in a large ovenproof skillet over high heat. Pour the eggs in and twirl the pan around so the eggs thinly coat the bottom of the pan. Try to make it as flat and even as you can, but don't go crazy with it. Cook the egg until it separates from the pan, about 2 minutes; it will still look damp on the top side. Flip it over. I flip by jerking the handle of the pan the way you see good line cooks do in diners. (This isn't easy to do, and I don't know how to tell you to do it except *carefully*. After all the eggs I've flipped, I still hold my breath every time I go to flip them.) Cook the egg for a few seconds on the second side and then scatter the mozzarella evenly over the surface. Dot the pizza with the marinara sauce and sprinkle

it with the oregano, parsley, and salt and pepper to taste. Dust the pizza with the Parmesan cheese, drizzle lightly with olive oil, and then add the topping ingredient of your choice.

Leaving the pizza in the pan, place it under the broiler until the cheese is done to the point where you like your melted cheese. Some people like it melted but still white. Some like little brown bubbles on the surface. And some people like to go even further: They like their melted cheese really browned and crispy. My personal favorite way to eat melted cheese is when there are little dots of brown all over, just like little dots on a banana. Remove and serve immediately.

Pizza Toppings

Egg Pizza, like regular pizza, would probably taste pretty good plain, but at Shopsin's I serve every Egg Pizza with a topping. I have quite a few options, including meatballs (2 large, crumbled), Italian sausage (1 link, cooked and crumbled), ratatouille (1 cup), fried eggplant cubes (1 cup), sautéed mushrooms (1 cup), Fried Onions (page 171, 1 cup), or grilled peppers (1 cup). Use whatever turns you on.

Egg Guacamole

Serves 2 to 4

Egg guacamole might sound strange to you, but it seems pretty obvious from where I'm standing. In my kitchen I always have all the stuff to make guacamole. I have avocados and chilies. I have molcajetes (Mexican mortars) to serve it in. I have chips to serve it with. And I have customers who want eggs. Considering all those factors, how could I *not* have egg guacamole? It's almost like I'd be stupid if I didn't have it.

Ingredients

1 teaspoon Clarified Butter (page 44), regular butter, or ghee

3 extra-large eggs

½ teaspoon heavy cream

1 recipe Guacamole (page 68; about 2 cups) or any guacamole

Corn tortilla chips for serving

Salsa Roja (page 63) or any fresh chunky salsa for serving

Instructions

Heat the butter in a nonstick egg pan over medium heat. Whisk the eggs and cream together in a bowl and pour into the pan. Shortly afterward, add the Guacamole, gently fold it in with the eggs, and cook until the eggs are just done. Serve in a molcajete, if you have one, or a large bowl, with a pile of chips and the salsa on the side.

Making Tortilla Chips

1. Cut the tortillas in fourths.

2. Separate the wedges.

3. Fry till the oil stops bubbling.

4. Drain.

Guacamole
Makes about 2 cups

We make two types of guacamole: real guacamole and what we call "cheap guacamole." We use the cheap guacamole when the guacamole is a secondary ingredient, such as in Guacamole Rice (page 231) and Egg Guacamole (page 66). The only time we make real from-scratch guacamole is when someone orders guacamole and chips. Then we make sure we have really, really perfect avocados and pay careful attention at every step. To make cheap guacamole, we just mush a ripe Hass avocado in a bowl, stir in some Salsa Roja (page 63)—you can use any fresh chunky salsa—and that's it. That's your cheap guacamole. The cheap guacamole is really good, and we could probably get away with serving just that if we wanted to.

But the real guacamole is the best that guacamole can possibly be. We squish one half of the avocado and chop the other half. The squished avocado acts as sort of a postmodern binder for the chopped avocado.

Ingredients
1½ tablespoons finely chopped yellow
    Spanish onion
2 large slices of tomato, finely chopped
1 teaspoon torn or chopped fresh cilantro
    leaves
¼ teaspoon minced fresh garlic
Juice of half a lime
Minced jalapeño pepper, jalapeño relish, or
    juice from canned chipotle peppers

(see How Spicy Do You Want It? on
    page 128)
A pinch of ground cumin
2 ripe Hass avocados
Salt and pepper
Corn tortilla chips for serving

Instructions
Combine the onion, tomato, cilantro, garlic, lime juice, cumin, and jalapeño in a small bowl (or molcajete). Cut both avocados in half. Remove the pits and squish the flesh of one avocado into the bowl. Take the remaining avocado and use a table knife to cut strips across each half, and then cut in the other direction so you have squares about half the size of playing dice. Scoop the squares into the bowl, season with salt and pepper, and gently fluff it all together with a spoon so the two sizes of avocado are all mixed together. Pile corn tortilla chips all around and on top of the guacamole.

Banana Guacamole

Years ago I was reading a George Carlin book. He had a chapter titled "Banana Guacamole," and when I read those words together, I thought, "There you go! That is a *right* thing!" I got to thinking about the ways in which under-ripe green bananas are really very similar to avocados. So I took some green bananas, made believe they were avocados, and made guacamole. I kept everything else exactly the same. I even served it just like guacamole—in a molcajete with chips. I don't make it much because people don't order it, probably because they think I mix the bananas with avocado, which wouldn't sound good to me either. If people knew how good it was, they would order it. To make banana guacamole, make guacamole and substitute bananas for the avocados.

The Nairobi Trio

I never set out to invent all this egg stuff. The way I think of it, these dishes are the rewards for all the work and the focused repetition that comes from trying to do it right. By doing the reps, it's as if you get Green Stamps in your subconscious, and every once in a while, when you've collected enough Green Stamps, your subconscious gives you an idea. My ideas usually come in clusters. The day I thought of Country Scrambles, from one simple thought I added an entire category to the menu. It was really exhilarating. Although I don't do it for the rewards, those small ideas are what keep me going. To find an idea that works makes me really, really happy.

Pancakes and the Lost Art of Griddling

Something you'd find if you owned a restaurant or were a cook in one—and this must be true for those who cook a lot at home, too—is that people really like to talk about food, and they want to talk about food with *you*. This is fine with me, because I *love* to talk about food. I am not one of those cooks who try to make their food seem like some kind of magical, mystical creation that they couldn't possibly explain how to make. To the best of my ability to remember what I've done or to verbalize the process, I gladly explain how I make anything I cook to anyone who asks. I never leave out any "secret" ingredient, I never make a process sound more difficult than it is, and I never lie.

When people ask me how I make such good pancakes, I'm always sure to tell them that making pancakes is 100 percent about the equipment, meaning that the success of the pancakes is all about the way you handle the batter, not the batter itself. I tell them, If you buy a good griddle, you oil the griddle properly, you heat it as hot as it needs to be heated before you drop the batter, and you cook the pancakes for the correct amount of time, you could use boxed pancake mix or Aunt Jemima frozen pancake batter, and your pancakes would turn out just as good as mine.

Aunt Jemima 1954

But I never finish the thought. What would come next is something I am not sure I am that proud of, but writing a cookbook is forcing me to tell the truth where the truth is called for. Nobody has ever looked me in the face and asked, "What kind of batter do you use?" They ask, "How do you cook such good pancakes?" So I never have to tell them that *I use* Aunt Jemima frozen pancake batter, which in fact I do.

Kenny 1954

It's not that I couldn't make my own batter. It's just that making pancake batter is not something I like to do. Pancakes are all about physics and chemical reactions: the heat and the rising

agent working together to produce a certain light effect. Making pancake batter is like baking: You've gotta be precise. You've gotta follow the program. You've gotta do persnickety things like sift flour and make adjustments for the weather. It is for people who have patience, and it is *not* for me.

Before I discovered the frozen stuff, I tried a lot of different recipes for pancake batter, and none produced pancakes that I was totally happy with. The batters I worked with either produced puffy, diner-style pancakes, which I don't like, or produced crepes and called them pancakes. I like pancakes that are light, with a nice brown, almost fried exterior, and so airy that if you really looked closely at them, you would see that they're not really there. They're really just air bound with pancake. At some time during this process, I decided to try the frozen Aunt Jemima batter and found it produced better pancakes than any I had made up until then. The only way I imagined I might be able to make a better pancake was if I beat egg whites until stiff and then folded them into the batter, but the problem with this method is that the only thing I hate more than baking is beating fucking egg whites. I go through so much batter that I knew if I did this, I was just going to be beating those egg whites for the rest of my life. So I cut bait and started using the frozen stuff instead.

The Art of Griddling

Make sure your griddle is clean, which means there are no burnt-on pieces or small crumbs on it. To test for cleanness, run a damp oily rag over the griddle's surface. If the cloth glides smoothly with no snags, then you know the griddle is clean. If it snags or you feel bumps, use a paint scraper (or something similar) to scrape the griddle and then wipe it down with peanut oil and test it again.

Scraper

Season the griddle. To do this, first think of your griddle's surface in terms of little microscopic valleys and mountains. Your job is to fill in those valleys and coat the mountains with oil (I use peanut oil) so you have a surface that is smooth on a micromolecular level.

Heat the griddle until a drop of water bounces off the surface. This is key. The reason for the old wives' tale that the first pancake never turns out is that the griddle is never hot enough when people drop the batter for the first pancake on it. When you pour pancake batter on a griddle that is the right temperature, it will immediately puff up, not spread out.

Float a thin layer of peanut oil over the griddle. When you cook on a hot, well-oiled griddle, what you are really doing is *frying*. It's extremely shallow frying, but it's still frying.

Just before you drop the pancake batter (or bread if you're making French toast), put cold butter on the griddle and run it across the area where you're going to cook. This is one of the few instances where I use regular, not clarified, butter. The milk solids in regular butter brown, creating a nice mottled effect on the pancakes or French toast.

Butter on the griddle

Drop the batter into circles about 5 inches in diameter (or drop the saturated bread onto the griddle) and immediately turn up the heat to compensate for that lost by the introduction of the cold ingredients. While the pancakes (or French toast) are cooking, continue to turn the griddle temperature up and down as needed.

Use a thin metal spatula to turn the pancakes, and make sure it's clean. If the edge of the spatula has any gunk on it, the gunk will snag on the pancake, and the pancake will squish up like an accordion until there is virtually nothing left. Because a pancake is an illusion. When it is compressed into only its ingredients, without the air, there isn't much to it. If you had six pancakes, you now have five.

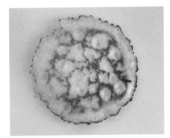

Side A

Think of your pancakes (or French toast) as a record album. There's an A-side, which is the side that cooks first, and a B-side, the side that was facing up first. Serve plain and glazed pancakes (or French toast), and pancakes that have additions stirred into the batter, A-side up. Serve all pancakes (or French toast) that you've sprinkled ingredients *onto* the batter (or bread) of with the B-side, the topping side, up. These rules are for purely aesthetic reasons, but that doesn't make them any less important.

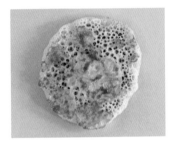

Side B

I've never used cookbooks for recipes, but I do like to read them to get ideas and to see how different cooks do things—and I especially liked doing this way back when I first started cooking. Back then, Bud Trillin used to bring me the review copies of cookbooks that were sent to him. He would bring in a stack of cookbooks, and in exchange I would give him 25 percent of the face value of the books in food credit. It was a great deal for both of us.

I consistently turned to a few of the books whenever I wanted to cook something that I had never cooked before. One was *The James Beard Cookbook*, his first, and another was Julia Child's *Mastering the Art of French Cooking*. After some time I noticed when reading both of their recipes that to make a particular dish I could use the recipe from Julia Child, which was several pages long and looked like it would take three days to make, or I could go to James Beard and find a recipe for the same dish that was half a page long and seemed easy to do. I never made the dishes side by side, and I didn't have to, to know that the James Beard recipe was the way to go—at least for me. When it comes to food, subtlety is lost on me. I probably wouldn't have noticed the difference between the two dishes cooked differently, and even if I had noticed, I wouldn't have cared.

After that, James Beard became one of my heroes. When I read his recipes, there wasn't much he did or many things he put into a dish that I couldn't figure out why. There were no mysteries. Often when I'm reading a cookbook, I get to a point in a recipe where I think, Why is he doing that? or Why is he adding *that* ingredient? And since I have no idea why, I think, What the fuck. He added it, so I had better add it or something bad might happen. But I never came to those points when I read Beard's recipes. He kept things simple and elegant, and I liked that. Whether he did it consciously or unconsciously, he subscribed to a philosophy of cooking that is "Do what you can do within the limits of what you can do, and it will all be just fine." I had a lot of respect for that, and as I started developing my own style in the kitchen, without consciously setting out to, I adopted this philosophy.

Using frozen pancake batter may seem like an exaggeration on this idea, but for me it's the same thing, because just as I don't care about the difference between a dish made from Julia Child's complicated recipe and James Beard's simple version, I can't tell the difference between pancakes made with a beaten egg white batter and those made with frozen batter. And even if I could, the difference wouldn't be significant enough to warrant the effort involved.

Plain Pancakes
Makes twelve 4-inch pancakes

There is no shame in plain pancakes. When it comes to pancakes, what is important is that they are crisp on both sides and cakey, but not *too* cakey, in the center. If what you are in the mood for is just pancakes, try to resist the temptation to add something to them.

Time to flip

Ingredients
Peanut oil for the griddle
Butter for the griddle and for serving
3 cups pancake batter (such as Aunt
    Jemima frozen batter, thawed, or scratch
    batter)
Warm Grade B maple syrup for serving

Instructions
Prepare the griddle according to the instructions in The Art of Griddling (page 71) and drop the pancake batter. When small bubbles appear on 40 to 50 percent of the surface of the B-side of the pancakes, about 2 minutes, quickly flip them using a thin, lightweight spatula. After all the pancakes have been turned, lower the heat slightly and cook the pancakes for about 2 more minutes, gently patting them down with the spatula, until the B-sides are golden brown. Carefully lift the pancakes off the griddle and flip them onto a plate, A-side up, fanned out like a hand of cards so you can butter each pancake without lifting it. Serve with butter and warm maple syrup.

Dinosaur

Lemon (or Lime or Orange) Ricotta Pancakes *Makes twelve 4-inch pancakes*

My editor, Peter Gethers, insisted on only one thing when he asked me to write this book: that I include the recipe for these pancakes. The ricotta causes them to burn more easily than other pancakes, so you need to cook them over medium-low to medium heat. If there are any pancakes that don't need maple syrup, these are them.

Ingredients

3 cups pancake batter (such as Aunt Jemima frozen batter, thawed, or scratch batter)
Zest of 2 lemons, 2 limes, or 1 orange
⅔ cup fresh whole-milk ricotta cheese
Peanut oil for the griddle
Butter for the griddle and for serving
Warm Grade B maple syrup for serving

Instructions

Stir the pancake batter and citrus zest together in a bowl. Ever so gently fold in the ricotta cheese, taking care not to destroy its texture. Prepare the griddle according to the instructions in The Art of Griddling (page 71). Drop the pancake batter on the griddle according to the instructions and cook for 2 to 3 minutes, until bubbles appear on almost the entire surface of the pancakes. Turn and very gently tap the pancakes with a metal spatula to make them uniform in thickness. Cook until the second side is golden, about 2 minutes, and serve A-side up.

Lemon zest and ricotta

Ho Cakes

Makes twelve 4-inch pancakes

Anybody who is tempted to question my use of frozen pancake batter might want to stop and think about what pancakes really are. They are flour and milk drowned in butter and some form of sugar. They're crap. As far as food value, you might as well take Crisco, whip it up with powdered sugar, and spread it on your face. I am not saying they're not delicious or that you shouldn't eat them, but they're a luxury, a recreation, like smoking marijuana or having sex. That's why I came up with pancakes with the names Ho Cakes and Slutty Cakes. These are extra sweet and decadent, but in a way every pancake is a ho cake.

When I make Ho Cakes, I use a homemade semisoft caramel. The caramel melts while the pancakes are cooking, so each pancake has a molten center, like the inside of a volcano. You can use store-bought caramels instead of making your own, but try to get ones that are good quality, which means they are made with butter, cream, and sugar, not plastic or whatever else they might be made with.

Ingredients

Peanut oil for the griddle
Butter for the griddle and for serving
3 cups pancake batter (such as Aunt
    Jemima frozen batter, thawed, or scratch
    batter)

6 small caramels, cut in half
2 tablespoons pignoli (pine nuts)
Masarepa (Hispanic cooked cornmeal) or
    cornmeal
Warm Grade B maple syrup for serving

Instructions

Prepare the griddle according to the instructions in The Art of Griddling (page 71) and drop the pancake batter according to the instuctions. Let the pancakes cook until there are bubbles around the edges and closer to the center. Place half a caramel in the center of each pancake and sprinkle each pancake with about ½ teaspoon pignoli and a thin dusting of masarepa. Cook until the A-sides are golden brown, turn, and cook until the B-sides are golden, about 2 minutes per side. Serve B-side up with butter and warm maple syrup.

Slutty Cakes

Makes twelve 4-inch pancakes

Slutty Cakes were my daughter Melinda's idea. She wanted to achieve that dry, crumbly consistency of the peanut butter in a Reese's Peanut Butter Cup inside a pancake, and she discovered, surprisingly, that she could get close by mixing canned pumpkin with peanut butter.

Ingredients

2 heaping tablespoons peanut butter
2 heaping tablespoons canned pumpkin
    puree
A big pinch of Mara Spice (page 95) or
    pumpkin pie spice
Peanut oil for the griddle
Butter for the griddle and for serving
3 cups pancake batter (such as Aunt Jemima
    frozen batter, thawed, or scratch batter)
Warm Grade B maple syrup for serving

Instructions

Mix the peanut butter, pumpkin puree, and Mara Spice in a medium bowl. Prepare the griddle according to The Art of Griddling (page 71) and drop the pancake batter according to the instructions. When small bubbles appear over 40 to 50 percent of the surface of the pancakes, about 2 minutes, drop a small spoonful of the peanut butter–pumpkin mixture in the center of each cake. Turn and cook the other side about 2 more minutes, until golden brown. Serve B-side up with butter and warm maple syrup.

Slutties

dle or a sauté pan large enough to fit the tortilla) over medium-high heat until it begins to bubble. Lift the tortilla out of the liquid and place it, wet side down, on the griddle or pan. Pour the remaining egg-cream mixture on the tortilla and spread it over the tortilla with your fingers. As soon as the underside of the crepe is light brown and mottled, which will be no more than 1 or 2 minutes, flip the crepe, moving quickly so that the egg mixture doesn't slide off. Cook the crepe for about 1 minute on the other side, until it is mottled. (I do this with my fingers, but you can use whatever tool works best for you.) Now your crepe is done. You just have to fill it and fold it. You can fill it with anything you like. We have all kinds of fillings for crepes, sweet and savory, but they are also good with just sugar sprinkled on top.

Waffles

My history with waffles is a sad story. I used to make waffles from scratch, using my frozen pancake batter with a little vegetable oil added to it. The waffles turned out golden brown and crispy on the outside, and light and puffy on the inside. I loved the process of making waffles and was very successful with them for years. Then one day I just lost it. I couldn't make waffles anymore. They would stick to the iron. They would come out too doughy or too crunchy, or they would fall apart when I took them out of the iron. I tried adjusting the batter and the heat of the iron, and I even switched waffle irons. I tried regularly to recapture my waffle technique, but I never got it back. It still hurts me to think about it, but I guess that's the price of moving forward. Some of the things you could do in the past you can't do anymore. It's like Shangri-la. After you grow up and leave, you can never get back there again.

All these "cheats" have come about in the same way: because I got sick of making something the long way, and I found that making it that way didn't make it any better. I think a lot of people out there cook from scratch because they're hoping to discover some secret that helps them make their dish the best of its kind. But I don't have the secret except to say that there is no secret. My pancakes are delicious because I know what delicious pancakes are, because my tastes, or actually Eve's taste and now my daughters' tastes, are spot-on. And I worked toward getting my pancakes to the place where they all liked them.

•

Griddling is a lost art.

Like everything I do in the kitchen, I learned to work the griddle by a process of stealing from other people followed by tons of practice. When I was young, I spent a lot of time on the road, just wandering from place to place around the country. Whenever I needed money, I would stop and work in a diner. I used to like watching the black guys in those diners work griddles, because they really knew what they were doing. But I especially liked watching a guy at a place I used to go to in White Plains, because he had Tourette's syndrome, and he would explode in a raucous stream of curses while he was making eggs. By watching these guys and by loads and loads of practice over the years, I like to think I have gotten pretty good on the griddle.

French Toast

Serves 2 to 4

A successful piece of French toast should be brown and crispy on the outside (both outsides) and creamy like custard on the inside. If the inside doesn't have a character of its own, if the French toast is just two brown sides with nothing interesting going on in the center, it's just egg-dipped bread, not French toast. I use Martin's potato white bread because it has more body than a Wonder-style white bread, which helps achieve the custardy center. You can substitute whole wheat for potato bread if you are one of those people who prefer a grainy texture to a creamy texture or because you believe whole wheat is better for your health. Once you have the right bread, the most important step in making French toast is making sure the bread is saturated with the egg mixture. It really bothers me to put a slice of bread on the griddle only to find a dry spot on it, so I go to great lengths to make sure each slice of bread is saturated. At Shopsin's, one order of French toast is four slices of bread. You can expand the ingredients here in proportion to make as many slices as you want.

Ingredients

6 extra-large eggs
¼ cup heavy cream
1 teaspoon Fox's U-bet Vanilla Syrup or
    ½ teaspoon pure vanilla extract
8 slices potato bread

Peanut oil for the griddle
Butter for the griddle and for serving
Warm Grade B maple syrup for serving

Instructions

Whisk the eggs, cream, and vanilla in a medium bowl. Put the bread slices in the bowl (no more than 4 slices at a time), press down on them with your fingers, and turn the bread in the egg three or four times, until each slice is totally saturated.

Prepare the griddle according to the instructions in The Art of Griddling (page 71) and place the bread slices on it. If you are adding a topping, sprinkle or spoon or squirt it onto the bread slices. Use a spatula to give the lightest tap so the topping becomes embedded in the bread enough that it won't go flying all over the place when you turn it. Use a pizza cutter to cut each bread slice diagonally in half (this is optional) and cook until the A-sides are golden brown, 2 to 3 minutes. Use a thin metal spatula to turn the bread, being careful that the topping doesn't fall off, and cook on the B-side for about 2 minutes, until golden. Serve plain French toast A-side up and French toast with toppings B-side up. Serve with butter and warm maple syrup.

Bread Pudding French Toast *Serves 2 to 4*

Bread Pudding French Toast is made with chunks of crusty French bread that are soaked in custard and then bound together by it. It's close to bread pudding, except that it takes just a few minutes to cook on the griddle instead of an hour and a half in the oven.

Ingredients

6 extra-large eggs
¼ cup heavy cream
1 teaspoon Fox's U-bet Vanilla Syrup or
    ½ teaspoon pure vanilla extract
1 foot of baguette, roughly chopped into
    chunks (about 1¼ inches)
Peanut oil for the griddle
Butter for the griddle and for serving
Warm Grade B maple syrup for serving

Instructions

Whisk the eggs, cream, and vanilla in a medium bowl. Add the bread chunks and use your fingers to macerate the chunks so you have atomic bread particles in with the egg. Continue adding the bread and macerating it, a handful at a time, until you have added it all. Prepare the griddle according to The Art of Griddling (page 71), dump the bread chunks on the griddle, and then pour the eggy stuff left in the bowl over the chunks. Leave it all to cook for 2 minutes to set. Take a large spatula, slide it under the bread-egg mound, and turn the thing over en masse, leaving it as intact as you can. Cook for a minute on the other side and then break it up with the spatula and toss the pieces around so the edges get cooked a bit. Get a wide-mouthed bowl (I put a little spinach in it because I like the color) and scoop the whole mess into the bowl. (I use a French fry scoop for this, but since you probably don't own one, use whatever you feel will work best.) Serve with butter and warm maple syrup.

French fry scoop

My griddle is very powerful in that it can get extremely hot and, because it's also thick (about twice as thick as any residential griddles I've seen), it stays hot even after you drop something cold, such as pancake batter or French toast, on it. Not having a griddle like mine is going to be the biggest challenge for a home cook to overcome in making really great pancakes (French toast is more forgiving). It is not impossible, but you are definitely going to have to practice.

Buy yourself as good a griddle as you can, pick up a container of pancake batter at the grocery store, and get to work. When you are practicing, make two or three pancakes at a time so you can get the feel for it without going through too much batter, and follow the steps I give you in The Art of Griddling (page 71). After cooking twenty or thirty pancakes, if you pay attention, you will start to notice some things. Using those observations, you can start to make adjustments. Once you start to gain confidence in your adjustments, you will start to develop instincts. And once you have cooked a few thousand pancakes, your instincts will take you anywhere in Pancake World you want to go.

What's underneath the griddle

Mac n Cheese Pancakes
Makes twelve 4-inch pancakes

The first time I made these was for our friend and regular customer Peter Kerwin. Every day he would have either macaroni and cheese or pancakes. One day he came in and told me to decide. At first, standing in front of my stove, I wasn't sure what I was going to do. In moments like that, I tend to just follow suggestions from my unconscious. And from somewhere a little voice said, "Do both together. Why not mac and cheese pancakes?" And it worked. Today, they are one of the most popular pancakes I make. For me the process of trial and error is like swallowing mental sand from oysters in the hopes my subconscious will give me pearls. I went out recently and spent $70 on candy because I was thinking of these pancakes and thought, What if I put Raisinets in there? I still need to find out what will happen. You should try it and find out for yourself.

Ingredients
Peanut oil for the griddle
Butter for the griddle and for serving
3 cups pancake batter (such as Aunt Jemima frozen batter, thawed, or scratch batter)
1 heaping cup cooked elbow macaroni (see Shopsin's Prep: Pasta, page 239), tossed with olive oil and warmed before using
1 heaping cup feather-shredded cheddar cheese
Warm Grade B maple syrup for serving

Instructions
Prepare the griddle according to The Art of Griddling (page 71) and drop the pancake batter according to the instructions. When small bubbles appear on 40 to 50 percent of the surface of the pancakes, about 2 minutes, drop about 1 tablespoon of the warm elbow macaroni on each pancake. Sprinkle with a thin layer of cheese (about 1 tablespoon) and use a thin, lightweight spatula to rapidly flip the pancakes. After all the pancakes have been turned, reduce the heat to medium and use the spatula to press the pancakes down on the griddle. When the undersides are golden, about 2 minutes after turning them, use the spatula in a decisive high-pressure sawing motion to lift and turn the pancakes onto a plate, B-side up. Serve fanned out on a plate like a hand of cards so you can butter each one without lifting it. Serve with butter and warm maple syrup.

Macro Mac n Cheese pancake

Pancake and French Toast Variations

You may be one of those people for whom eating the same thing, even though it sates you and makes you happy, becomes tedious. The particular food still has a pleasant memory, though, so you want to move on to something that has everything you wanted in the first place but now broadens the definition of your desire. For such people I have a long list of things that I put inside my pancakes and on top of my French toast. For each of these, start with Plain Pancakes (page 76) or French Toast (page 86) and integrate the variations below.

BACON PANCAKES and BACON FRENCH TOAST both remind me of pussy. When you press the cooked bacon into the raw pancake batter or French toast, it really likes to sink in. When you flip the pancakes back to serve them bacon side up, the bacon is *in* there, enveloped by soft walls. It's really very sexy. Press at least one slice of bacon on each round of pancake batter or bread slice just before flipping it the first time. When the pancakes or toast are done on both sides, flip them again to serve them B-side up.

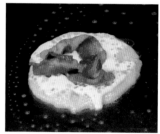

Bacon Pancake

CINNAMON-GLAZED (with or without apples or raisins) PANCAKES AND FRENCH TOAST are sprinkled with cinnamon sugar, which creates a sticky brown, brûlée-like glaze. Sprinkle a generous amount of raisins or chopped Granny Smith apples on the pancake batter or bread slices just before flipping them the first time. When the pancakes or toast are done on both sides, turn them again and sprinkle the A-side with cinnamon sugar (⅓ cup sugar to 1 teaspoon cinnamon). Sprinkle each one three times. Turn the heat up to high and turn the pancakes or toast again so the A-side (the cinnamon-sugar side) is facing down. (This temperature is too hot to cook pancakes, but the pancakes won't touch the griddle. Only the cinnamon sugar will, and the heat is essential for melting the sugar.) After about 1 minute, when the sugar has melted, flip the pancakes or French toast onto a plate and serve with the glazed A-side up.

Peanut butter

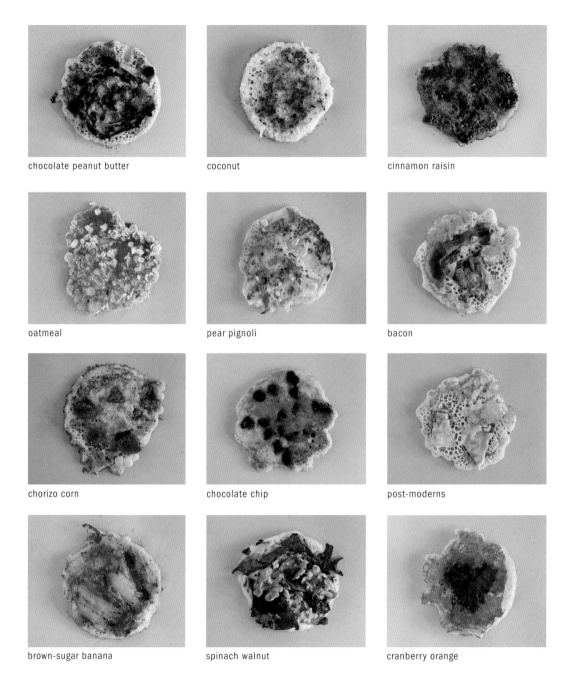

chocolate peanut butter

coconut

cinnamon raisin

oatmeal

pear pignoli

bacon

chorizo corn

chocolate chip

post-moderns

brown-sugar banana

spinach walnut

cranberry orange

PEANUT BUTTER AND JELLY PANCAKES need to cook until they are almost finished on the first side, because if you turn them too soon and have to cook the second side for too long, the peanut butter and jelly self-destruct from the heat. I use raspberry preserves, but you should use whatever you like. Wait for the entire pancakes to show small bubbles or until the French toast is almost done on one side, then squirt or spoon a small circle of peanut butter and another of fruit preserves into the center of each pancake or bread slice. Just before flipping, turn the heat up to high. After the last cake has been flipped, begin taking the first cake off the griddle. In this way they cook for only a few seconds on the delicate peanut butter and jelly side. Serve B-side up.

To shoot the peanut butter and raspberry preserves on the pancakes, we use a special gun, which we call the Peanut Butter Caulking Gun. It was originally for shooting guacamole and sour cream at Taco Bell. I found some on eBay. I also use them for shooting Nutella.

Pumpkin Pancakes
Makes twelve 4-inch pancakes

Since these pancakes take a little longer to cook than other pancakes, I finish them on low heat so they can cook longer without burning. This batter rises, so you have to gently pat the pancakes down while they are cooking to ensure that the centers cook through. The spice mixture called for in this recipe is named for my daughter Mara. It is mostly cinnamon. Both of the girls love cinnamon. They think there is no such thing as too much cinnamon. If a customer says there is too much cinnamon in some-thing, their usual response is "Impossible."

Ingredients

3 cups pancake batter (such as Aunt Jemima frozen batter, thawed, or scratch batter)
⅔ cup canned pumpkin puree
2 tablespoons heavy cream, or more as needed
A big pinch of Mara Spice (facing page) or pumpkin pie spice
Peanut oil for the griddle
Butter for the griddle and for serving
Warm Grade B maple syrup for serving

Instructions

Mix the pancake batter, pumpkin puree, heavy cream, and Mara Spice in a medium bowl. Add more cream if necessary to make a thin batter.

Prepare the griddle according to the instructions for The Art of Griddling (page 71) and drop the pancake batter according to the instructions, patting them down gently as they cook. When bubbles appear on 40 to 50 percent of the surface of the pancakes, about 2 minutes, gently turn the pancakes, lower the heat, and cook until the B-sides are golden brown, about 2 more minutes. Use a spatula to carefully remove the pancakes from the griddle and serve A-side up, with butter and warm maple syrup.

Mara Spice

This is a spice blend that Mara makes using high-quality spices from Aphrodisia, a store on Bleecker Street that sells spices and essential oils. We use it in a lot of things: oatmeal, Ashura Dried Fruit and Nut Mix (page 110), and almost anything that includes pumpkin. It is basically pumpkin pie spice, but the proportions are different and the quality of the spices is superior.

Ingredients
1 tablespoon ground cinnamon
1 heaping teaspoon ground cloves
1 teaspoon ground nutmeg
1 teaspoon ground ginger
A pinch of ground allspice

Aphrodisia, 264 Bleecker Street

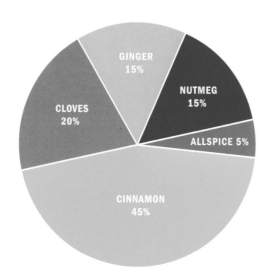

Larry's roast beef sandwich, 1977

Salads: Cooking What Clicks

One of the few advantages to owning a small business is that I can do whatever the hell I want, which means I can *cook* whatever the hell I want. Ninety-nine percent of the items I make at my restaurant I make because they are foods that "click" for me.

When I say "click," I'm talking about more than just liking the taste of the food or getting full. I am talking about being satisfied. The fulfillment I get from eating is not as strong as an orgasm, although it is similar in that there is a beginning, a middle, and an end to the experience. When I eat something that clicks, I feel satisfied and content on a multitude of levels. Eating food that doesn't click, that doesn't have that end, is like having sex and not climaxing. You are lying there afterward; you definitely had a good experience, but you didn't *finish*. The one exception to the "click" rule, as a category, is salads. I offer salads for one reason: because my customers want them.

Salads, by definition, are supposed to be light and refreshing. According to my understanding, a salad is supposed to be an ensemble of delicate, non-dense ingredients that are put together in a very deliberate way to produce some kind of special, subtle culinary effect. None of these things interests me on any level—not intellectually or conceptually, and certainly not to sate my desires as an eater. I could eat a whole pile of salad, and an hour later I would still want a roast beef sandwich.

Even though salads are very popular these days, I don't think I'm alone in my feeling about them. I think a lot of salad eaters are dishonest eaters—people who eat for reasons other than sating their true desires. I've found that more than any other category of food I serve at the restaurant, salads are the thing that is most often finished. I mean every last bite. And my salads are huge. I start my salads with piles of lettuce, enough to feed a whole family, which is coated in some kind of rich, oily dressing.

Salads have just as much protein as a main course, sometimes more when you include the auxiliary protein ingredients I toss in them, like bacon and cheese—and when I put cheese in a salad, I put in a *lot*. I don't want people to have to root around looking for a little hunk of cheese. Still, no matter how big my salads are, I find that people who order salads just keep eating until they have finished the entire bowlful. If they had ordered something that clicked, I think they would be more focused on enjoying what they were eating, and as soon as they had had enough, they would stop. Instead, they eat a salad because they think they should eat a salad, and then they go home and eat a pint of ice cream.

Serving Size
All the salad recipes are for one serving in my restaurant, but they would make two or four normal servings at home. If you want to add more chicken to a salad to make it more substantial, be my guest. It won't change the recipe at all. I find that when it comes to salads, the same recipe can serve two people, one person, three people, five people. It doesn't really matter, because no matter how much salad you serve someone, that person will eat it all.

The fact that I make salads is basically a product of evolution in terms of giving people what they want—or, rather, not giving them what they don't want. In the beginning, when I first opened as a restaurant, the most popular meal was dinner, and every dinner entrée came with bread and a side salad. The salad was a simple mix of lettuce, with maybe a little tomato or cucumber, and the customer's dressing of choice on top. They either got the salad before their main course or with their main course; the waitress just dropped the bowl at the table whenever she had time.

The restaurant was small back then, really small, so once the customer finished eating, every plate was picked up by the waitress and carried right past where I stood in the kitchen on its way to the place where the dishes were washed. I got in the habit of looking to see what people ate and what they left behind. If there was a lot of food left on a plate, I assumed that either I was serving too large a portion or there was something wrong with the food. To find out, I would usually yell out into the dining room to ask the customer if there *was* something wrong. I still do this.

Among the things I noticed as I watched the plates go by was that most of the free little salads were coming back either untouched or barely touched. This made me sad. It broke my heart to think that all that lettuce and those tomatoes and cucumbers that I or one of my cooks had taken so much time to wash and chop were just going in the garbage. It hurt me every time I saw it. The salad was good. The lettuce was really fresh. There was just *no* reason for people to leave it other than that they didn't really want a salad. After watching this for a while, I finally decided not to give people a salad unless they asked for it. I changed the menu so that it read "Salad upon request." I didn't mind giving away the salads. I just didn't want to give them to people who didn't want them. I couldn't stand to see all our hard work going into the trash anymore.

After that, my salad production dropped tremendously. Instead of making fifty or sixty salads in a night, I was making more like two, three, maybe five. Because I was making so few, I started paying more attention to the salads I did have to make. I gave more care to them, and I tried to make them special because I knew that the person who asked for it really desired it. And, naturally, I started to get more creative with them.

Around that time Eve and I were in the habit of going to a restaurant on Bleecker Street. I have no memory of what it was called or anything about it other than the fact that every time we went, we got a salad called a Brown Rice Special. It wasn't really a salad at all by conventional definition. It was warm, for one thing, and it had no lettuce. It was just rice and melted cheese drizzled with soy sauce and with a bunch of crunchy vegetables and walnuts strewn throughout. They served the salad on a cake stand: a big gooey mound of stuff all piled there on top of the pedestal. We were into it for a long time. We would share it, and every single time one of us would stick our fork in there to dig around for one of those vegetables and end up tipping the fucking thing over. It is such a stupid way to serve a salad. Still, that was the first salad that really excited me. It had some density to it.

When I set out to make entrée salads, that chewy, gooey brown rice salad was my inspiration. I knew if I tried to make them according to conventional definition that I would get either really bored or really pissed—or both. I wanted to make salads with contrasting flavors and textures and a lot of crunch. I took my heavy-handedness and bulky ideas about food and created salads that are the equivalent in heft and texture of a pastrami sandwich.

Eve painted by Sean Lennon

Brown Rice Special

Serves 2 as an entrée or 4 as a starter

This salad is what I call a "mouth food," meaning it really exists, in its truest form, only in your mouth. To get a bite you stick your fork through the rice and cheese, and the walnuts are dragged by the cheese. You then take your fork and jab through a vegetable, and you score a little lettuce along with it. You now have a bit of every ingredient in your mouth at the same time, and when you chew, all those flavors and textures transform into something that didn't exist until that moment. A new dish is created in your mouth. If you pick at it and separate the ingredients like a persnickety asshole, you are not going to have the same experience, and the experience you do have will be inferior.

Ingredients

2 cups cooked brown rice
½ cup shredded Muenster cheese
4 heaping cups chopped romaine lettuce
    (or any crispy lettuce)
½ cup walnuts, crushed lightly
A small handful white mushrooms (about
    ½ cup), sliced
1 cup cut-up vegetables such as tomatoes,
    carrots, or cucumbers, or blanched
    broccoli or cauliflower
Soy sauce to taste

Instructions

Mix the rice and cheese together in a microwavable bowl and nuke until the cheese melts enough so you can stir it into the rice. (If you don't have a microwave, find another way to melt the cheese. The oven would be the most logical solution.)

Pile the lettuce on a giant plate. Sprinkle the walnuts in the center of the lettuce. Plonk the cheesy rice on top of the walnuts and spread it out so that it sits on the lettuce like the snow on a snowcapped mountain. Place the mushroom slices and cut-up vegetables on top of the rice in whatever arranged pattern you want. Then sprinkle soy sauce all over everything. That's it. That is the dressing. It is a fucking terrific salad.

Pita Feta Salad

Serves 2 as an entrée or 4 as a starter

This salad used to be called Pita-Filia Salad. It was a joke based on the sounds of the words, but after a while I decided it just wasn't funny, so I changed the name to Pita Feta Salad. It has all the same ingredients of my Greek salad, minus the gyro meat or falafel. But it's chopped—and I think it's better that way.

The Parthenon in Nashville, Tennessee

Ingredients

8 cups mixed lettuces (We use equal amounts of all the greens we have on hand that day: Mesclun, arugula, spinach, romaine, oak leaf. We don't use iceberg but I wouldn't rule it out.)

1½ cups Tabbouleh (page 222) or any tabbouleh salad

12 to 15 pitted Kalamata olives, sliced

½ cup crumbled feta cheese (about 2 ounces)

A few thin slices of red onion

Half a round of Toasted Pita Bread (page 104)

Tahini Dressing (facing page)

Instructions

Put the lettuce in a medium salad bowl. Add the Tabbouleh, olives, feta cheese, and onion slices. Cut the pita bread into julienne, and then cut it once crosswise so that you end up with thin croutony bits. Toss to combine all the ingredients and serve with the Tahini Dressing on the side.

Tahini Dressing
Makes 1 ¾ cups

This dressing is so delicious I could eat it with a spoon. My kids love it, too. They used to eat it like crazy when they were growing up. They would take tabbouleh with this dressing to school for their lunch. I found at the restaurant that whenever customers ordered something that came with Tahini Dressing—the Pita Feta Salad (facing page) or Tabbouleh (page 222)—they would, without fail, ask for more. Now I just put a big squeeze bottle of the stuff on the table and let them go crazy with it.

The base of the dressing is tahini, which is sesame paste. Sesame paste has a texture problem. It is dry and pasty, and it sticks to the roof of your mouth for eternity. Overcoming that texture problem is the key to making this dressing. To overcome it, someone has to tell you how, because it is not intuitive. The natural tendency is to want to cut it with lemon juice or olive oil or something flavorful that you want in your dressing anyway. The secret is that nothing works except *water*. It is counterintuitive to add water to salad dressing, but that is what you have to do. It is like a miracle. When you add water to the tahini, it instantly turns from a too-thick, too-sticky substance to one that is creamy and smooth and lovely. It covers and coats like a good spaghetti sauce.

Ingredients
1 cup tahini (sesame seed paste)
3 tablespoons good olive oil
1 teaspoon ground cumin
1 teaspoon salt
½ teaspoon minced fresh garlic
¼ teaspoon sugar

Instructions
Combine the tahini, olive oil, cumin, salt, garlic, sugar, and 2 cups of water in the jar of a blender and puree until smooth. The dressing will last about 4 days.

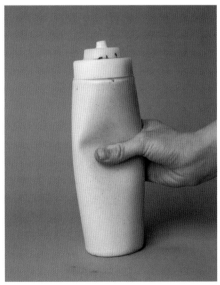

Tahini Dressing

Toasted Pita Bread

I buy only handmade pita bread, which is about a million times better than the stale, dried-out shit they sell in grocery stores. The stuff I buy is soft and velvety, and it doesn't have a pocket. It is even better toasted. To toast it, heat a light coating of olive oil on a griddle or in a skillet, add the pita, and toast until it's lightly browned on both sides.

Toasted pita

I don't eat salads, and I don't think a lot about them. As a result, most of what I make are imaginative copycat salads. I take the qualities that define the classic salads and transmute them until they become something else. The Thai Cobb (page 106) is a Cobb salad translated by a fictitious Thai guy. For the Mexican César (page 113), I took the classic and shot it through a Mexican lens. The Asian Waldorf Chicken Salad (page 108) is what you get when you cross the classic apple-mayo salad with yummy gingery Japanese salad dressing. And the Gazpacho Salad (page 115)? It is gazpacho soup, not blended.

What I am talking about is different from fusion food, which is more precious and fussy and implies the deliberate marriage of ingredients from distinct cuisines. Their beauty is like that of a half-black girl or a half-Japanese girl whose splendor lies in the delicate nature and ideal proportions of her features. My salads, on the other hand, are one thing dressed up to look like another in a way that's not really fooling anybody. They're drag queen food. But to my taste, they're very appealing.

Thai Cobb salad

Thai Cobb *Serves 2 as an entrée or 4 as a starter*

A lot of the clever names I have on my menu are things I thought of myself, but this particular one I stole. I saw it someplace during my frequent travels surfing the Web. Once I had the name, I thought about what a Thai guy in Thailand would do faced with the challenge of making a Cobb salad. I determined that he wouldn't have bacon, so he would substitute coconut, another high-fat, high-flavor ingredient. He would put some cilantro in there to give it that fresh Asian flavor. And he would use curry paste in the dressing because he probably puts that stuff in everything. I added the blue cheese because I think if you're going to make a Cobb salad, no matter where you are, you are going to have to figure out how to get some blue cheese in it or it is not going to be a Cobb.

Ingredients

¼ to 1 heaping teaspoon green curry paste (depending on how spicy you like your food)

2 tablespoons Balsamic Vinaigrette (page 107) or any balsamic vinaigrette

4 to 5 tablespoons crumbled blue cheese

3 to 5 tablespoons crushed dry-roasted pistachios

A handful of fresh cilantro leaves

¼ of a tomato, cut into 3 or 4 wedges

½ of a ripe Hass avocado

1 lime, halved

1 head of romaine lettuce (or any crunchy lettuce), cut up

One 5- to 6-ounce boneless, skinless chicken breast (see Grilling Chicken, page 127; or grill however you like)

Sweetened angel flake coconut

Instructions

To make the dressing, put the curry paste in a salad bowl that is big enough for you to toss the ingredients in it without hurting them. Add the vinaigrette, blue cheese, and pistachios. Rip the cilantro leaves into the bowl and add the tomato wedges. Slice the avocado and scoop it out so it drops into the bowl. Squeeze the juice of the lime into the bowl and stir to combine.

Add the lettuce. Cut the chicken into thin strips, throw it into the salad, and toss until the chicken and lettuce are nicely coated with the dressing. Divide the salad onto however many plates you are dividing it onto. Just before serving, sprinkle the coconut on top. You want to add enough coconut so it shows but not so much that you can't see the nice green lettuce underneath it. I want the eaters to take their forks and push straight through the thin layer of coconut as if they were eating ice cream with sprinkles on top. The reason you add the coconut right before the salad is served is that you don't want it to get wet. Wet coconut loses its delicacy and is not nearly as much fun as dry coconut when it is in your mouth.

Balsamic Vinaigrette

To dress a salad, I generally make the vinaigrette to order with ingredients specific to the salad I'm making. I keep this pre-mixed vinaigrette on hand for deglazing pans when I want something tangy. I also use it to make the Brazilian Chicken Garlic Rice Soup (page 134).

Ingredients
1 cup balsamic vinegar (better than the cheapest commercial-grade balsamic)

1 cup good, fruity olive oil
½ packet Italian Good Seasons salad dressing mix

Instructions
Mix the vinegar, oil, and salad dressing mix together and refrigerate. It will keep forever.

Brazil Chicken Garlic Rice Soup

Asian Waldorf Chicken Salad

Serves 2 as an entrée or 4 as a starter

This is an Asian permutation of a traditional Waldorf salad. The classic gets its character from a mix of walnuts, apples, and mayonnaise. I kept the apples, added bananas, and substituted a mix of dried fruits and nuts for the walnuts. To make it unmistakably Asian, I mixed Japanese salad dressing in with the mayonnaise. If you want to make this vegetarian, omit the chicken. It is unimportant to this dish. I just throw it in because my customers seem to like having chicken in their salads.

Ingredients

One 5- to 6-ounce chicken breast
½ ripe banana, sliced
¼ cup Ashura Dried Fruit and Nut Mix (page 110)
½ Granny Smith apple, peeled and chopped
A small handful of cut-up jicama (about ½ cup)
1 large bok choy leaf, thinly sliced from top to bottom
1½ to 2 cups cut-up romaine
A big handful of salad greens (Mesclun, spinach, or Asian salad greens, about 1 heaping cup)
¼ cup Japanese salad dressing (see Kamikaze Dressing, facing page)
¼ cup mayonnaise
Salt and pepper

Instructions

Grill the chicken (see Grilling Chicken, page 127, or grilled however you like).

While the chicken is cooking, take a medium salad bowl and add in this order: banana, Ashura Dried Fruit and Nut Mix, apple, jicama, bok choy, romaine, and salad greens. When the chicken is done, slice it and add it to the bowl with the other stuff.

Stir the Japanese dressing and mayonnaise together, dump it over the salad, and toss. Season with salt and pepper if desired and serve.

Melon baller is used to take out the core.

Kamikaze Dressing

Kamikaze Dressing is what I call the yummy orange-colored salad dressing they give you at Japanese restaurants. I don't know the real name for it, but I love it. I wish I could give you a recipe for it, but I can't. I spent at least seven or eight hours of my life trying to find a recipe that worked, but never did. I just can't get the proportions right. I have come close, but with certain things in the kitchen, if you've missed by an inch, you've missed by a mile. At one time I even bribed a guy who works at a little Japanese market in the East Village, Sunshine Market, where they sell an especially delicious version, to give me the recipe. But then I did something or said something—I don't even remember what it was—and he refused to give it to me. Now I just buy it from them. I use it in the Asian Waldorf Chicken Salad and also to make a Chinese Caesar in which I use sesame bread from the one-dollar dumpling places in Chinatown as croutons. Even though the store-bought version I get is good, not being able to make this dressing is one of the biggest failures in my cooking life. If you don't have an Asian market near you, I suggest you go to a Japanese restaurant and beg them to sell you some.

Ashura Hot Cereal

Ashura Dried Fruit and Nut Mix

Ashura is the name of a Turkish cereal. (It's also a serious Islamic holiday, but that is another story.) I use the name to refer to the mix of nuts and dried fruit that goes into the cereal. It has a sweet and tart quality from the range of dried fruits it contains. I like everything in the mix to be about the same size, so I cut the larger dried fruits—such as cherries, cranberries, and dates—to the size of raisins, and I crush the walnuts and pecans with the flat side of a big knife so they are not exactly chopped but not halved, either. It is easy to make this in whatever quantity you prefer because you use the same amount of each ingredient. If you were to double up on one ingredient and omit another, nothing bad would happen.

Ingredients

Equal amounts:
- Raisins (dark, golden, or both)
- Dried currants
- Dried cranberries
- Dried cherries
- Pitted dates
- Crushed walnuts
- Crushed pecans
- Sliced almonds
- Whole or crushed macadamia nuts
- Pignoli (pine nuts)

Ground cinnamon

Instructions

Mix the dried fruits and nuts together. Sprinkle the mix with a very generous amount of cinnamon—enough so that you can see the cinnamon. Shake to coat the fruits and nuts with the cinnamon and add more cinnamon if necessary. Transfer the mix to an airtight container and refrigerate until ready to use or for up to several months. I know it may seem illogical to have to refrigerate a mix of ingredients, none of which were previously refrigerated. Just trust me on this one, or you will have a kitchen full of bugs and fruit flies.

Ashura Hot Cereal

Serves 2

I did some research on Ashura, the cereal, and found recipes from countries all over the Middle East. Each one was significantly different, but all had the common characteristic of calling for a really weird mix of ingredients, especially grains. I took what I liked from each recipe and made this cereal out of it. When it comes to recipes, I am a pretty clever felon. This isn't a salad, obviously, but I put it in this chapter because I figure if you are going to go to the trouble to make the Ashura Fruit and Nut Mix for the Asian Waldorf Chicken Salad, you should have this recipe as a way to use the rest of the mix. Plus, it is a really good, really unusual recipe that I wanted to include in the book, and I don't have a cereal chapter to put it in.

Ingredients

1 cup cooked bulgur wheat (see Shopsin's Prep: Bulgur Wheat, page 222)
½ cup cooked rice (white or brown)
¼ cup canned white beans, drained and mashed (I do this between the palms of my hands.)
1 ripe banana, cut up
A squirt of rose water (¼ to ½ teaspoon)
1 cup mixed fresh or frozen fruit (see Shopsin's Prep: Frozen Fresh Fruit, page 112)
¼ cup Ashura Dried Fruit and Nut Mix (facing page)

Instructions

Combine the bulgur, rice, beans, banana, and a few tablespoons of water in a small pan over medium heat and cook, stirring occasionally, until the ingredients are warmed through. Add more water if necessary to keep the cereal from sticking to the pan, but try not to add so much that the finished product will be wet or runny. Squirt the rose water in, and give it a stir. Toss in the fresh or frozen fruit and the Ashura mix and serve.

Shopsin's Prep: Frozen Fresh Fruit

We make our own mix of frozen fruit. Our mix includes raspberries, blueberries, cherries, peaches, and mangoes. We always have it on hand in ½-cup portions to put in a few different things, including oatmeal, Frozen Fruit Iced Tea (page 246), and Ashura Hot Cereal (page 111). If you buy good-quality frozen fruit, it can be very sweet and delicious—sometimes even better than fresh fruit. And if you do have good fresh fruit, you can also portion that into baggies and make your own frozen fruit. I'm not sure it will taste any better, but for some people it might make them feel better about using frozen fruit. We like to nuke the fruit for a minute before adding it to something like hot cereal.

All hail César.

Mexican César

Serves 2 as an entrée and 4 as a starter

The principle of Caesar salad is a formula for success: crispy lettuce, crunchy croutons, and a nice tangy, cheesy dressing. Using this as a base, it is really easy to transmogrify the salad into different ethnic or regional variations. I have had as many as ten different Caesars on my menu at one time. I had one from Florida using orange juice instead of lemon, and another Asian one in which I used Asian greens, such as bok choy and mizuna, instead of romaine, sesame oil instead of olive oil, and fried bean thread noodles in place of the croutons. Mexican César seems to have struck a chord in people. It sells better than the regular Caesar.

Ingredients

1 extra-large egg
2 chipotle peppers in adobo (including a
    little of the adobo juice)
1 lime, halved
2 tablespoons good olive oil
1 teaspoon minced fresh garlic
¼ cup fresh cilantro leaves
1 heart of romaine, cut up (6 to 8 cups)
2 cups crushed corn tortilla chips
Salt and pepper

Instructions

Crack the egg into a medium salad bowl and whack it really good with a whisk. Add the chipotle peppers and juice and use a fork or whisk to crush them together with the egg. Squeeze in the lime juice. Add the

olive oil and garlic, and beat all the ingredients together soundly. You want the dressing thick but not so thick that it won't coat the lettuce; add more oil if necessary. Rip the cilantro leaves over the dressing, add the romaine, and toss to coat the leaves with the dressing. Throw in the tortilla chips and toss again gently. Season with salt and pepper if desired and serve immediately, while the lettuce and croutons are still crunchy.

Cilantro

Cilantro is really hard to keep fresh. I buy it with the roots still attached when I can find it, because I think it stays fresh longer that way. I usually rip cilantro instead of cutting it. I've heard that that's better because cutting bruises it, but I do it because cilantro sticks in the crevices left on the cutting board by knife use. This means that until you wash the cutting board really, really well, everything that you cut on it after cutting the cilantro is going to taste like cilantro, which has an extremely strong flavor. People either love it or think it tastes like soap.

Cilantro

Jicama

Gazpacho Salad *Serves 2 as an entrée and 4 as a starter*

This salad came about one year after the weather cooled down and gazpacho season was over. I had been making gazpacho, the soup, all summer long, and I wasn't ready to let it go altogether, so I thought, Why not make a gazpacho salad? Unlike cold soup, which is strictly a warm-weather food, people order salads all year long.

There are no big pieces in a gazpacho salad; everything is cut small and roughly the same size. I call for you to dice the vegetables here, but it doesn't matter what shape you cut them. Sometimes I cut the vegetables a little bigger or a little smaller. Sometimes I julienne them instead of dicing them, and sometimes I slice or shred the vegetables. The important thing is that all the vegetables are cut the same way, so once you pick a cutting theme, stick with it. The beets I use come in Cryovac packaging from France. You can use any kind of beets you want—the French ones that I use or canned or jarred. Just make sure to include the juice that comes with the beets because gazpacho salad, like gazpacho soup, doesn't taste good unless it is extremely red, and it's the beet juice that makes it that way.

Ingredients

2 cups diced crudités (blanched broccoli, cauliflower, yellow squash, and/or baby carrots)
½ large or 1 whole medium tomato, diced (about 1 cup)
1 cup seeded and diced cucumber
1 15-ounce can diced beets, including juice (about 1 cup)
½ cup frozen peas, at room temperature
1 ½-inch-thick slice of jicama, diced
2 thin slices of red onion, finely chopped
1 teaspoon minced fresh garlic
¼ cup cocktail sauce
¼ cup good olive oil
¼ cup tomato juice
1 lemon, halved
Salt and pepper
4 large handfuls of salad greens (arugula, baby spinach, Mesclun, romaine, or a mix)

Instructions

Throw the crudités, tomato, cucumbers, beets, peas, jicama, onion, and garlic into a medium salad bowl as you cut them.

Drizzle the vegetables with the cocktail sauce, olive oil, and tomato juice. Squeeze the juice of the lemon into the bowl and season with salt and pepper if desired. Add the greens and toss.

Soup, Deconstructed

When I set out to write this book, I really had to think for the first time about what a cookbook is. Who is it for? What is it supposed to accomplish? I needed to figure out what, if anything, I had to offer a cookbook audience. I know my customers like what I do and that they are satisfied with my food. But in my opinion, in terms of my cooking, I don't do anything remarkably interesting or unusual. After thinking about it for quite a while, I realized that I do have a talent. It is not in technique, and it is not in ingredients. The thing that makes my food unique is the way the dishes are constructed—or you might say *deconstructed* and then *reconstructed*.

When I go to cook anything—whether it's scrambled eggs or a bowl of soup or a meatloaf—the first thing I do is take it apart in my mind and look at all the different parts from all sides. I'm like a tech-geek who likes to take things apart and put them back together, only instead of taking apart computers and radios, I take apart food. I look to see the basic characteristics of the dish—such as the homogeneousness of the yolks and whites in scrambled eggs or the essential elements of shrimp gumbo. I look to see what characteristics give the dish its identity and what qualities I like or dislike in it. And then I take those elements and find a way to put them back together, eliminating any unnecessary ingredients or steps.

This deconstruction process is the foundation of all my cooking, and it's the reason I am able to offer as many items as I do. Newcomers to Shopsin's are always surprised by and even skeptical of the number of soups I have on my menu (I have cut back, but at one time it was close to three hundred), but that's because they're thinking in conventional soup-making terms, where the soup is made in large quantities by slow-cooking a bunch of ingredients in one giant pot. This is not how I make my soups. Not at all.

Applying my deconstruction mentality to soups, I first took the reality of soup as a finished product and broke it down into its essential elements. There is the broth, and there is everything else. The next thing I did was figure out what element takes the longest to cook and then tried to figure out how to cut that time. With soup the only thing that takes any significant time to cook is the broth, so I theorized that all I had to do was cook the broth, not the whole soup, ahead of time.

The way I now make soups is I cook whatever isn't broth—the vegetables, chicken, shrimp—and then add the broth when all that is done, so the soup takes only as long as the slowest-cooking non-broth ingredient. So my soups are actually sautés floating in broth. In this way I am able to make a chicken soup in minutes, which is how long it should take to make chicken soup. People are always amazed at the way I make soup, but I am the one who should be amazed. Taking two or four hours to make a soup just because the broth takes two or four hours to cook makes no sense whatsoever.

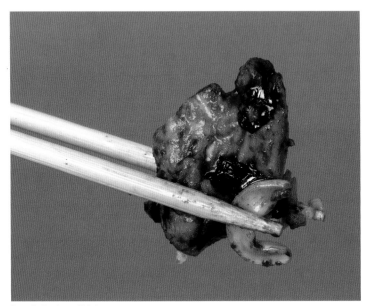

Patsy's Cashew Chicken

Patsy's Cashew Chicken *Serves 2 to 4*

Patsy was a cook at Shopsin's, a babysitter to all my kids, and a dear friend for many years until we had a disastrous argument. I said something that offended her, and she didn't talk to me for three years. During that period I tried very hard numerous times to apologize and make amends, but nothing would cool her. Later she came back and made some attempt at repairing things, but by then I wasn't interested. I don't mind having fights with people I love, but don't cut me off. How can you do that to someone you love? You can hate them for the moment; you can be angry with them; you can throw rocks and plates at them; you can punish them. But don't withhold your love. I loved Patsy. We were really, really close. She rejected my love. When she finally did come back, I didn't love her anymore. I couldn't be in a love relationship in which the love is used as a weapon.

As a cook, one of many things Patsy taught me was a dish she had stolen from somebody else that evolved into Patsy's Cashew Chicken. Its specialness lies in the fact that the chicken, which has a light flour coating, gets a velvety texture when cooked and, when finished, is covered in a sticky brown-black glaze. Patsy served it over rice, but it didn't have much gravy. The majority of people we served it to would ask, "Hey, you got any more of that gravy?" I now make it so that it has lots of gravy, and nobody needs to ask for more.

I put this recipe here because it is the same cooking concept as a soup, without the added broth. I suppose if you wanted to you could turn this into a soup by adding about 3 more cups of stock. If you do this, add the cashews at the very end so they don't get soft from the liquid. This recipe can be doubled if you like, but you may have to cook the chicken in batches to make sure it browns. Once the first batch is cooked, add the second batch to the pan.

Ingredients

Two 5- to 6-ounce boneless, skinless
    chicken breasts
All-purpose flour for dredging
2 tablespoons good olive oil
½ cup roasted cashews
4 scallions (white and green parts), cut into
    1-inch pieces
½ cup soy sauce
1 lemon
½ cup Chicken Stock (page 123), or more
    as needed, or any stock or broth
Steamed white rice for serving

Instructions

Cut the chicken into strips the size of a baby's index finger. Pour the flour on a plate or in a small bowl. Dredge the chicken in the flour and shake off the excess flour.

Heat the olive oil in a large, heavy sauté pan over high heat until it is hot but not smoking. Gently drop the chicken in the pan, evenly distributing it around the pan. (Be careful. This can be dangerous because everything is really hot. If you carelessly drop the chicken in, it will splatter on your arms and face.) Let the chicken cook, sitting in one spot, for 2 or 3 minutes. Check the underside of one piece. When it becomes medium brown, use the handle of the fry pan to toss the pan and flip the chicken pieces in the pan. It is really hard to flip every piece; just toss the pan a few times to get most of the chicken turned and then use tongs to turn the few remaining pieces so that all the brown faces up.

When all the chicken has cooked on both sides (after about 5 minutes), throw in the cashews and scallions. Add the soy sauce and squeeze in the juice of the lemon. Agitate the pan to coat the chicken with the glaze. Pour in the chicken stock, adding more if necessary to cover, and cook for another 1 to 2 minutes. Pour the chicken and gravy over the rice (preferably in a stainless-steel Chinese dome set) and serve.

The Art of Sautéing

A lot of my cooking—and all my soups—are based on the concept of sautéing. *Sauté* means to jump around (or something close) in French, which refers to what the food does in the pan. The one thing you have to know about sautéing is that in order for food to jump around in a pan, the pan has to be so hot that it is dangerous, and in order for the pan to get *that* hot, the stove has to be really, really powerful.

I have a six-burner Garland stove that my stove guy assembled from pieces from other restaurant stoves. The back right burner is covered with a heavy grate and all of the burners get hotter than probably any stove in the Western world. My stove was powerful to begin with, but then several years ago, I got the brilliant idea to take a power drill and drill out the little holes that the flame comes through. The flame that comes out of those burners is bigger and hotter than the stove's manufacturer—any of the stoves' manufacturers—ever imagined possible. I usually have the flame all the way up for sautés and soups. That's why I'm able to turn out everything I do as quickly as I do.

Sauter [sote] *vi* to jump, leap; (*exploser*) to blow up, explode; (*se rompre*) to snap, burst • *vt* to jump (over), leap (over); (*fig: ommetre*) to skip; **faire ~** to blow up; to burst open; (*culin*) to sauté; **~ en parachute** to make a parachute jump; **~ à la corde** to skip; **~ de joie** to jump for joy; **~ de colère** to be hopping with rage *ou* hopping mad; **~ au coude qn** to fly into sb's arms; **~ aux yeux** to be quite obvious; **~ au plafond** (*fig*) to hit the roof.

Painting of Kenny's stove by Sam Messer

Of course, anybody who has ever made soup before knows that my way is the antithesis of all soup theory in which the whole point is that a bunch of ingredients are thrown into one pot and cooked forever and a fucking day. The theory behind making soup the conventional way is that the flavor of the individual vegetables is leached out into the broth, creating a sort of elixir. I believe this method is futile. In my opinion, there is no special flavor that comes from taking the essence of ten or sixteen different ingredients and combining them in a liquid. In fact, I think it is just plain *wrong*.

Stock

Good stock, one that tastes good all by itself, is like a petri dish in which flavors are able to thrive. It is necessary for making any good soup, but it is *especially* important to the way I make soup because the stock won't be flavored by long-cooking the soup's other ingredients in it.

When I say that the stock tastes good, I mean that it satisfies *you*. It doesn't need to be the greatest stock ever made, and it doesn't need to satisfy Jean-Georges or Thomas Keller. If you think College Inn or another canned chicken stock tastes good, then you're good to go. But if those stocks don't taste good to you, you're going to have to move beyond that and make your own.

In good foodie restaurants, they have stockpots going in the kitchen at all times, and the cooks are constantly throwing shit in—bones and vegetables and herbs—so it gets better and better. My method for making stock is not nearly so sophisticated. I start with a paste-consistency soup base—meaning a purchased one—and then I add to it. I use commercial brands, but there is also a more readily available consumer brand called Better Than Bouillon that I hear is pretty good. (I have never tried it.) What you want to look for in a base is that it contains no MSG (monosodium glutamate) and as little salt as possible.

Chicken Stock

My chicken stock is like a guy with strong arms holding someone up so effortlessly that all you see is the person he's holding up. As a base it can take you anywhere you want to go—to gumbo, to curry, to a cream-based soup, or to a simple broth-based soup. I make a new batch every Wednesday, and I go through the stuff like water.

I generally use turkey carcasses for making chicken stock because I like the flavor better, and I find that chicken stock made with turkeys lasts longer than chicken stock made with chickens. I carve the meat off the turkeys carelessly so the carcasses have lots of meat on them to flavor the stock.

Boiled carcasses

Ingredients
A whole chicken or turkey carcass
Chicken soup base
Vegetables, cut up, or vegetable trimmings
     (such as onions, carrots, celery, celery
     leaves, parsley, thyme, mushrooms)

Instructions
Place the carcass in a large pot of water over high heat. Add the base in whatever proportions it instructs on the jar. Then add the vegetables and trimmings. Boil the stock for about 2 hours, until the meat falls off the bones. Strain, discarding everything but the liquid. This will last for several days in the refrigerator or for months in the freezer.

To make your own base, the next time you're making chicken stock, boil it for 3 to 4 hours, until it is thick and concentrated and almost jelly-like. Strain it, pour it into ice cube trays, and freeze it. Use those stock cubes instead of base the next time you are making chicken stock.

Beef Stock

Making beef stock is a real pain in the ass. You have to start by roasting beef bones, and then you have to go through the same pain in the ass you go through to make chicken stock. The good news for the cook is that people who eat beef also eat chicken. My secret to making really good beef stock is to start with good chicken stock and then I add beef soup base and a few spoonfuls of marinara sauce.

All day scraps of extra red meat get thrown into the beef stock.

Vegetable Stock

The truth behind my vegetable stock is the same as my pancake batter. I used to make my own vegetable stock using tons of regular soup vegetables such as carrots and celery and other weird things like dried mushrooms. Then this vendor I deal with started sending me quart jars of a liquid concentrated vegan vegetable stock. I was skeptical, but I looked at the label and saw that it had only good vegetable ingredients in it. I made some stock with it, and it tasted great, so that's what I use now. In addition to using it to make vegan soups, I use the stock, which is always hot and right in front of me on my steam table, to cook vegetables. When I'm steaming spinach or cooking frozen vegetables like okra, kale, or haricots verts, I put the vegetables in a Chinese strainer basket and dip them into the vegetable stock for a few seconds until they are done. This is the best way I know to cook vegetables quickly, but the added benefit is that the broth is constantly being infused with the flavor of the different vegetables. If you feel like making your own vegetable stock, be my guest, but the vegetable base has a really lovely flavor that works for me.

Chinese strainer basket

Recently I read a posting about Shopsin's on the Internet that said something like "The food isn't that great and the service sucks!" I wanted to write back, "And it's expensive, too!" But I didn't because then they would have had my e-mail address.

It's true. I get $8, $10, $15, $20 for a bowl of soup even

though not one of them—including those that contain shrimp—costs more than a couple of bucks to make. The reasons for charging so much for my soup are twofold: One is that I base the price of everything in my restaurant on the time it takes me to make it, and soup made to order takes at least four or five minutes of my (almost) undivided attention, which is a lot by my standards. The second and more important reason is based on one of the most basic tenets of my pricing philosophy: I reward myself for my cleverness. And whether you like them or not, my soups are pretty damned clever. Nobody—at least nobody I'm aware of—makes soup the way I do.

All restaurants in New York City—probably in America—make soup the same way. They make one or two vats of soup ahead of time for the day. When an order is placed for soup, they ladle out a portion, dump it in a bowl, and maybe, if you're lucky, they throw something like a crouton or some sour cream on top. That works fine for them but not for my taste. They have a different philosophical understanding of soup. Even if my soup looks exactly like the soup at the restaurant down the street that charges a few bucks for it, mine is different because it is constructed differently and the intent is different. If you can't tell the difference, then you are wasting your money on my soup. You should buy the other soup.

More important than any philosophy behind my soup-making or the speed with which I make them is that I don't *like* soup that is cooked the traditional way. I think the worst thing about most soups is that you can't taste the individual ingredients. If you were to close your eyes and take a bite, you wouldn't be able to tell what the fuck you were eating. You could take a hypodermic needle and pull from anywhere in the bowl, and it would all taste the same, because after countless hours of cooking, all the flavors have mushkied together. I understand that this is the whole point, but for me it seems like a waste of all those precious ingredients. You take a spoonful of someone else's chicken tortilla avocado soup and the tortillas taste like the chicken, the chicken tastes like the carrots, the carrots taste like everything else, and everything else tastes like the parsley. When I take a bite of soup, I want the chicken to taste like chicken—not like cabbage.

Chicken Tortilla Avocado Soup *Serves 2 to 4*

When our kids were young, Eve and I often took them to Epcot Center in Disney World in Florida. I stole the idea for this soup from the Mexican restaurant at Epcot Center. Surprisingly, the food there was pretty good. I guess you could say that is my specialty: taking pretty good food and stealing it under the assumption that if I were to do a few things differently, it could be *really* good. This is probably the most popular soup I have on the menu and one of the most popular items in general. (My co-author Carolynn orders it every time she eats here. She tries to order something else, but then she comes running back to the kitchen to change her order.) The basic flavor of the soup comes from the browned cabbage, so you have to make sure to let it brown nicely. When I'm making soup, I always add the vegetables to the pan as I chop them, so the soup and I are working simultaneously toward the same end. If you feel more comfortable cutting up all your vegetables before you get started, be my guest, but note that if you're in a hurry, my way is a lot quicker.

Ingredients

Two 5- to 6-ounce boneless, skinless
 chicken breasts
¼ cup good olive oil
3 cups thinly sliced green cabbage (about
 ½ head, cut like for coleslaw)
1 cup chopped yellow Spanish onion
Minced hot peppers to taste (see How
 Spicy Do You Want It? on page 128)
4 cups Chicken Stock (page 123) or any
 stock or broth
6 fresh cilantro sprigs
¼ cup canned black beans, drained
Salt and pepper
Tortilla chips
A ripe Hass avocado, halved and pitted

Instructions

Grill the chicken (see Grilling Chicken, facing page; or grilled however you like) on both sides for the grill marks only, not to cook it through. Cut it into strips.

Meanwhile, heat the olive oil in a large, heavy sauté pan over high heat. Add the cabbage, onion, and peppers to the pan and let the vegetables cook until they brown in places, about 5 minutes. Deglaze the pan with the stock.

Add the chicken strips, cilantro, and black beans and simmer the soup until the chicken is cooked through and the broth is warm, about 2 minutes. Season with salt and pepper if desired. To serve, put a handful of tortilla chips in each of however many bowls you are using. Pour the soup over the chips, and scoop the avocado so it drops into the bowls.

Chicken Tortilla Avocado Soup

Grilling Chicken

I don't know if anyone is actually going to grill chicken the way I do because it involves messing up your stovetop. Still, I figured I should explain how I do it because I call for grilled chicken in a lot of my recipes. If you don't have a gas stove or if you don't want to cook the chicken the way I do, I don't know what to tell you. You must have figured out some way of cooking chicken by this time in your life, and whatever that way is, you should stick with it.

For any entrée-sized meal, which is enough to serve two people at home, I start with one 5- to 6-ounce boneless, skinless chicken breast half. You can use one that weighs 4 ounces for all I care or 8 ounces; it really doesn't matter. The important thing is that it is chicken. I like to start with a thin piece of chicken because it cooks faster. To get the chicken thin, I slice it instead of pounding it. I find that pounding changes chicken's texture from appealing and spongy to tough and rubbery. To slice a chicken breast, lay the breast down on a flat surface and then, using the flat side of the blade of a big sharp knife parallel to the cutting board, move the blade through the breast toward the palm of your hand.

Meanwhile—and this is the part I think people may be reluctant to try—preheat a stove burner until the metal grid is as hot as it can get. Season the chicken with salt on both sides and throw it right on the grid, directly over the flame, and let it grill for 2 or 3 minutes, until there are nice black grill marks on the meat. Flip it and cook it until it's done.

I cook chicken all the way through for such things as salad, where it's not going to cook any longer, but I under-cook chicken slightly when it's going into something like soup where it will continue to cook in the hot broth; otherwise, it will become overcooked and dry.

How Spicy Do You Want It?

When customers order soups that have any kind of heat added to them, the waitress asks, "How spicy do you want it?" They get to pick on a scale of one to ten. Most orders come in somewhere between four and eight, with the majority of those at five or six. Depending on the level of spiciness requested, I adjust the amount of peppers I add to the dish, and I choose differently from the selection of heat sources I use, which includes (listed in the order of spiciness) fresh habanero peppers; fresh jalapeño peppers, sliced with the seeds intact; fresh jalapeño peppers, diced with the seeds removed; pickled jalapeño peppers; and chipotle peppers. I use chipotle peppers from a can, called chipotle peppers in adobo; I usually add them whole, and sometimes I just add the juice, which has the flavor of the chipotles with almost none of the heat. Since you presumably know the people you are cooking for and what they like, you can add whatever kind and amount of peppers you like.

a. habanero; b. fresh jalapeño; c. pickled jalapeños, chopped into relish; d. chipotles

I know that my way of making soup is considered radical by traditional standards, and the only explanation I can give for doing it this way or for how I came to this method of cooking is that it's a product of a lot of psychotherapy, drugs, and making chicken potpies. If Eve were alive, she might tell you differently, but the way I remember it, it started back when Shopsin's was still a grocery store and my friend Michael Clay asked me to make potpie shells for him.

Michael Clay owned Chumley's, an old speakeasy that still exists across the street from the original store. At the time, Michael and I were in the middle of a long, complicated relationship that was fueled by a mutual respect for each other's oddness. We had a good deal of fun conversing with each other on an outré, immature, macho, drug-induced level.

Chumley's was mostly a drinking place, but Michael sold a few pub-type foods, including chicken potpie. One day Michael came to me and said, "You know that asshole Lanciani? He says he's not gonna make the potpie shells for me anymore."

Lanciani was a baker who owned a little bakery called Lanciani around the corner on West Fourth Street. He was pushed

out by changes in the neighborhood and moved to a space on Fourteenth Street, where he was also pushed out due to changes in *that* neighborhood and is now, as far as I know, just plain *gone*. Lanciani sold potpie shells and potpie covers to Michael for, I'm gonna guess, $2.00 a set. Michael was selling the potpies for about $12.95—and he was selling a lot of them. So even though Lanciani was charging him a lot of money, Michael was doing really well with the potpies himself. And now Lanciani was refusing to make the shells for him at any price. So Michael said to me, "You wanna do it?"

I told him I didn't know how to work with dough or anything involving baking. I had an oven, but other than that, I don't know what made Michael think I might be able to make potpie shells. All I was making at that time were things like chicken salad and egg salad. Still, he handed me a pan—like a little Swanson's pot-pie kind of thing except made of metal instead of aluminum—and told me to give it a try.

Once Michael set me up with the challenge, I began to read up on *pâte brisée,* which is your basic flaky pie dough. Then, using a recipe for *pâte brisée* that I found in the *Joy of Cooking,* I started experimenting. This was the first time in cooking where I had to think of what I was doing outside my own immediate impulses. It was like after you've been having sex for years, actually falling in love. For the first time your feelings for the other person are not just a reflection of your essence but actual feelings *for* that person. Making the pie shells was a stretch for me. They're a pain in the ass. I had to make the dough, which was not easy. I then had to roll it out to just the right thickness and cut it into two shapes—one for the pie shells and one for the pie covers. Afterward, I had to poke holes in them all, and *then* I had to bake them.

Eventually, I got pretty comfortable with the process, and I started making the shells for Michael on a regular basis. I was making hundreds of them every week. It was the first cooking task for me that was really repetition intensive, and it was through the natural course of this repetition that I started to deconstruct the process. The biggest problem with the shells was that they took too fucking long, and they puffed up even though I poked holes in them. I later discerned that this had to do with the oven, so one day I decided to skip the oven. I turned the griddle up, threw the potpie tops on because they were flat, and griddled them as if they were pancakes. I figured—well, I don't really know what I figured. Maybe I just figured it was worth a try. Amazingly, it worked. The ambient heat of the hot griddle was close enough to the oven's blanket-type of heat, and the dough was rolled thin enough, so it cooked all the way through before it burned. And because they were on the griddle, I was able to use a bacon weight to press them down from time to time, preventing them from puffing up. They turned out perfectly and in a fraction of the time they took in the oven.

I was now making the potpie shells so fast and so efficiently that I thought: What the hell! If Michael can sell potpies, why can't I? I didn't have a restaurant yet, but I started offering potpies as a takeout dinner special. I made the shells ahead of time, froze them, and reheated them on the griddle to order, so the crust was warm and flaky when the customer got his pie. I didn't have much storage, so I also made the filling to order. I started by dredging cubes of chicken in flour and cooking them in butter. Then I sautéed some mirepoix-type vegetables like onions and carrots. (I don't use celery in potpies because I find it overwhelms the flavor.) And then I combined those and added chicken stock and cream and potpie vegetables like peas and corn.

Chicken Potpie

Serves 4

In recent years I have started to make pot-pies differently from the way I used to. The main difference is that I now use packaged puff pastry instead of making my own *pâte brisée*. Also, instead of dredging chicken cubes in flour and cooking them, I start with cooked chicken meat and just throw it into the gravy. The pastry will brown fine by itself, but if you want it to get real fancy-schmancy brown, brush it with a beaten egg yolk before baking.

Ingredients

6 tablespoons Clarified Butter (page 44), regular butter, or ghee
1 cup finely chopped onion
1 cup crumbled or chopped cooked potato (squeezed from a baked potato)
¾ cup finely chopped carrot
¾ cup sliced mushrooms
2 tablespoons all-purpose flour
2 cups or more Chicken Stock (page 123) or any stock or broth
1½ cups mixed frozen potpie vegetables, such as peas, corn, or green beans
2 cups shredded or cubed chicken meat (from half of a roasted or boiled chicken, about 1½ pounds)
½ cup heavy cream
A big pinch of ground nutmeg
1 sheet frozen puff pastry (approximately 10 × 10 inches), thawed according to package instructions (I don't have time to thaw the pastry before baking it when I get an order, so I take the pastry

directly from the freezer, with the paper still on it, and put the nonpapered side on a medium-warm griddle until it has thawed to the point where it looks like pizza dough.)

Instructions

Preheat the oven to 475°F.

Heat the butter in a large, heavy sauté pan over high heat. Add the onion, potato, carrot, and mushrooms, and sauté until the onion and carrot are soft, about 5 minutes. Add the flour and cook until it disappears into the butter but doesn't brown, about 1 minute. Add the chicken stock gradually, until you have enough to float the vegetables and the gravy has the consistency of pancake batter. Throw in the frozen vegetables and the chicken, and then stir in the heavy cream and nutmeg. The whole thing should now be the consistency of a thin milkshake. If it is too thick, add more cream; if it is too thin, cook it for a few minutes to reduce the liquid and thicken it slightly.

Pour the filling into an 8 × 8-inch oven-proof, table-worthy casserole dish (or one of equal size) or four individual casserole dishes or bowls until the filling comes ½ inch below the rim. (If there is so much liquid that it is going to overflow, don't pour it all in.) Top the pie (or pies) with the pastry and place in the oven for 12 to 15 minutes, until the crust is puffy and golden brown.

Sometime after making the potpie filling this way, I realized that I was basically making a cream of chicken soup with less liquid. By adding more stock, I could turn it into a soup.

With that realization, I thought, Holy shit! I could make five hundred soups this way! Or five million! It was a Eureka! moment. I knew right then that there was really no end to the possibilities.

At the time the only soup I made was Chicken, Mushroom, and Barley Soup (page 37), which I did in the conventional soup-making way. But now, approaching soups the way I had approached the potpies, I went crazy. It was like bossa nova time. It was just soup, soup, soup. That was all I thought about. I put something like forty soups on the menu all at once, and from there I just kept adding them, one at a time or ten at a time.

In working on my craft, I have had small ideas and big ideas. Learning how to make soup was a big idea. That moment was seeing the light. It was the first time in my life that I created something from inside me that was neither sexual nor violent. And it was a breakthrough moment in my cooking odyssey. It was the beginning of everything—not just soups but the way I cook in general.

Bacon weights: The pair on the far right are 15 pounds each, homemade with athletic equipment.

Brazilian Chicken Garlic Rice Soup *Serves 2 to 4*

A lot of times when I name a dish for a certain country—in fact, probably *most* of the time—it is not because the dish exists in that country, but because for me the dish has the telltales of that country's cuisine. This soup is the perfect example. Somewhere along the line I got the idea that the essence of Brazilian food is that the meat is marinated before it's grilled. I don't believe in marinating meat before grilling it, because I don't think it makes any difference, so for this soup I grill the chicken and then add what would normally be the marinade to the broth. I guess I also had the idea that browned garlic is Brazilian, so I included that component in this soup as well.

Ingredients

Two 5- to 6-ounce boneless, skinless
  chicken breasts
4 slices of a large yellow onion
2 slices of a large tomato
3 bell peppers (preferably mixed red,
  green, and yellow)
¼ cup good olive oil
10 whole peeled garlic cloves
2 cups cooked white rice (preferably
  day-old)
½ cup Balsamic Vinaigrette (page 107) or
  any balsamic vinaigrette
4 cups Beef Stock (page 124) or any stock
  or broth
A big handful of prewashed spinach (about
  1 heaping cup)
Salt

Instructions

Grill the chicken (see Grilling Chicken, page 127, or grilled however you like) on both sides for the grill marks only, not to cook it through. Cut it into strips.

Grill the onion, tomato, and peppers over an open flame or in a very, very hot skillet until the vegetables are charred on both sides. Take a shot at rubbing the black stuff off the peppers with a towel, but don't worry if you don't get it all off.

Heat the olive oil in a large, heavy sauté pan over high heat. Tilt the pan so the oil puddles in one area. Add the garlic cloves to the oil and fry them, keeping the pan tilted, until they just begin to brown, which should take less than a minute. Level out the pan and throw in the rice. Shake the pan; if there is not enough oil to coat the rice, add more and shake the pan again. Throw in the chicken slices and the charred vegetables. Deglaze the pan with the vinaigrette. Add the stock and the spinach, cover, and simmer the soup until the chicken is done and the broth warm, 2 to 3 minutes. Season with salt if desired and serve.

Cream of Garlic Soup *Serves 2 to 4*

The big idea behind this soup is that it is thickened with bread and redolent of garlic—and as far as I'm concerned, bread and garlic are the essence of life. This is similar to the hearty Tuscan soup ribollita, which contains cubes of bread that quickly dissolve, leaving you with a bowl of really thick mush. Unlike ribollita, though, this soup doesn't get too thick. It has a nice, fluffy texture to it, like nipples when you suck on them.

Ingredients

4 tablespoons Clarified Butter (see Clarified Butter, page 44), regular butter, or ghee
12 whole peeled garlic cloves
6 to 8 inches of regular baguette, cut into cubes
2 thick slices onion, chopped
3 cups Chicken Stock (page 123) or any stock or broth, plus more as needed
¾ cup heavy cream, plus more as needed
2 teaspoons grated Parmesan cheese
A pinch of ground nutmeg
Salt

Instructions

Heat the butter in a large, heavy sauté pan over high heat. Add the garlic and baguette cubes. Brown the garlic and bread on all sides. Add the onion and sauté for 4 to 5 minutes, until it's soft and transparent but doesn't brown. Deglaze the pan with the stock. Simmer and whisk until the bread has all but disintegrated and the soup itself is a homogenous distribution of broken-up bread and broth. Stir in the cream, Parmesan cheese, and nutmeg. Add more stock or cream if necessary for a souplike consistency. Season with salt if desired and serve.

1

2

3

Madras Soup
Serves 2 to 4

I often come up with a name that I like and then invent a dish to go with it. That's what happened here. I wanted to name a soup after a madras shirt I owned in high school. I felt really good whenever I wore that shirt. At the time I was a lifeguard, so I was really fit. For many years after I no longer had the shirt, I could still remember how good I felt wearing it. This soup has all the colors that were in the plaid: green, yellow, and cranberry. I put some Indian spices in the soup because of the name, but that is not really what the soup is about. It's really about the shirt.

There are certain soups I hold on the stove for a while to simmer before plating them; others I serve the minute the soup is assembled. This one I hold because it has sophisticated spicing, and it takes the broth a while to pick up the flavors of the spices.

Ingredients
¼ cup good olive oil
3 cups finely chopped green cabbage
1 Granny Smith apple, peeled and chopped
½ cup finely chopped yellow Spanish onion
¼ cup cooked white rice (preferably basmati)
2 tablespoons torn or chopped fresh cilantro leaves
2 tablespoons sweetened angel flake coconut
Minced fresh or pickled jalapeño peppers to taste (see How Spicy Do You Want It? on page 128)
½ teaspoon garam masala
½ teaspoon ground cinnamon
½ teaspoon ground cumin
4 cups Beef Stock (page 124) or any stock or broth
½ cup Marinara Sauce (page 236) or any marinara sauce
Salt

Instructions
Heat the olive oil in a large, heavy sauté pan over high heat. Add the cabbage, apple, onion, rice, cilantro, coconut, and jalapeño peppers. Cook for a few minutes to soften the vegetables. Stir in the garam masala, cinnamon, and cumin. Deglaze the pan with the stock, stir in the marinara sauce, and let the soup simmer until the cabbage is tender, about 3 minutes. Season with salt if desired and serve.

African Green Curry Soup *Serves 2 to 4*

This is a color soup; my intention behind the design was that all the ingredients be green. The green curry I use is actually Thai, not African, but as far as I can tell, those places use the same spices. Whether or not they actually use peanut butter in African cooking, I don't know, but the peanut butter is what makes this soup African for me.

Ingredients

¼ cup good olive oil

4 cups mixed chopped green vegetables, such as bok choy, collards, scallions, snow peas, green beans, arugula, green cabbage, spinach, and peas

4 cups Vegetable Stock (page 124) or any stock or broth

½ teaspoon to 1 tablespoon Thai green curry paste, depending on how spicy you want your soup

¼ cup creamy peanut butter

Salt

Instructions

Heat the olive oil in a large, heavy sauté pan over high heat. Add the vegetables and sauté until they just begin to soften, 3 to 4 minutes. Deglaze the pan with the stock. Add the curry paste and peanut butter and stir until both have dissolved and are integrated into the soup, and cook to warm through. Season with salt if desired and serve.

Senegalese Chicken Soup *Serves 4*

This is a really lovely soup that makes a satisfying, filling lunch. I add a lot of heavy cream to it because I really wanted it to be white. Even though it contains a lot of cream, it's not unhealthy because it is so rich that if you have it for lunch, you won't want dinner. And the combination of the spices with the sweetness of the fruit is so satisfying that you won't even feel like eating dessert. I make the same soup with shrimp instead of chicken, and with sun-dried cherries on top.

Ingredients

Two 5- to 6-ounce boneless, skinless
    chicken breasts, cut into dice-sized
    cubes
A small bowl of all-purpose flour
¼ cup Clarified Butter (page 44), regular
    butter, or ghee
1 teaspoon sweetened angel flake
    coconut
½ cup chopped yellow Spanish onion (see
    Chopping Onions, page 191)
½ cup chopped cooked potato (such as a
    leftover baked potato)
1 Granny Smith apple, peeled and chopped
1 teaspoon garam masala
1 teaspoon curry powder
1 teaspoon ground cinnamon
1 teaspoon pignoli (pine nuts)
3 cups Chicken Stock (page 123) or any
    stock or broth
1 cup heavy cream
¼ cup frozen peas

Instructions

Dredge the chicken cubes in the flour. Heat the butter in a large, heavy sauté pan over high heat. Lift the chicken cubes out of the flour, shaking off any excess flour, and then add them to the pan. Add the coconut and cook until the chicken cubes are brown on all sides but not necessarily cooked through. (Ideally the coconut will brown slightly also.) Add the onion, potato, and apple and sauté for 1 or 2 minutes to soften slightly. Stir in the garam masala, curry powder, cinnamon, and pignoli. Deglaze the pan with the stock. Add the cream and peas and simmer for 2 to 3 minutes, until the soup is warm and the chicken has cooked through.

Shrimp Gumbo
Serves 4

This is a great soup. If you order it regularly from me, it's the kind of thing that you can taste in your mouth before you get to the restaurant. The essence of gumbo is two-fold. It is all about file powder and roux. File powder is the ground leaves of the sassafras tree. Originally, the bark of the tree was used in gumbo, which acted as both a thickener and a flavor element for the soup. But today the bark is illegal because it supposedly causes cancer. So now the thing to do is use file powder to give gumbo its gumbo flavor, and roux as a thickener. You can find file powder at gourmet stores and through Internet sources for spices.

Ingredients

¼ cup good olive oil

3 bell peppers (preferably mixed red, yellow, and green), cored, seeded, and diced

1 celery stalk, diced

1 carrot, diced

1 pound small shrimp (21–26 per pound), fresh or frozen (see Shopsin's Prep: Shrimp on page 7), thawed if frozen

½ cup fresh or frozen collard greens, chopped if fresh

½ cup frozen okra, chopped if fresh

1 heaping tablespoon canned or frozen hominy, or more to taste

1 heaping tablespoon canned or frozen black-eyed peas, or more to taste

4 cups Chicken Stock (page 123) or any stock or broth

⅔ cup Marinara Sauce (page 236) or any marinara sauce

1 teaspoon file powder

1 fresh jalapeño pepper, thinly sliced, or minced pickled jalapeño peppers (see How Spicy Do You Want It? on page 128)

A hunk of Roux (page 140) or any roux

Instructions

Heat the olive oil in a large, heavy sauté pan over high heat. Add the bell peppers, celery, and carrot and sauté until the vegetables begin to soften, 3 to 4 minutes. Add the shrimp and sauté for 1 or 2 minutes, until they are barely cooked on the outside but not cooked through. Throw in the collard greens, okra, hominy, and black-eyed peas. Deglaze the pan with the stock and stir in the marinara sauce, file powder, and jalapeño pepper. Put a hunk of roux on the end of a whisk and whisk it into the soup until the soup is as thick as you want it. Once the roux is integrated into the soup, the soup is done.

File powder

Shrimp Gumbo

Roux

Roux is a mix of flour and butter that's cooked until the flour is browned and fragrant. It thickens a soup without making it lumpy. More important, it adds a unique nutty flavor. It is at the heart of New Orleans cooking, especially gumbo.

Making roux is like making napalm. Besides the fact that it burns in a split second (and if it does, you have to start over), it also splatters on your arms while you're stirring it. In over twenty years of making roux, I don't think I've made it more than twice when I didn't scorch myself in the process.

I think that traditionally, roux is made only for the particular dish it is being used in, and the other dish ingredients are added to the pot with the roux. I don't do it that way; I make big batches at a time so I always have it on hand. I'm sure that Betty Boop–type cooks (not to mention the Health Department) would tell you to put it in the fridge, but I never do. I keep it at room temperature, and it keeps for*ever*. I use roux only to thicken gumbo, but you can use it to thicken any soup or sauce. Whatever you add it to, you have to pay attention to where it is in the pot so you can whisk it in. If it doesn't get dissolved into the soup, when someone bites into it it tastes really awful, like salty marzipan. Unlike cornstarch, which takes a while to have its effect, roux does the job immediately, so the way I add it is to put the roux on the end of a whisk and then move the whisk around in the soup until the soup is the thickness I want. Then I remove the whisk and tap it to remove the excess roux.

To make roux, put the amount of clarified butter that you want to make into a roux—if you want ½ cup roux, start with ½ cup butter—in a heavy-bottomed, high-sided pan over medium heat. Throw in a small handful of flour and stir it in with a whisk. Keep adding flour by the handful until the mixture has the consistency of cream cheese.

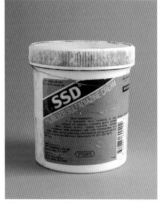

Silverdine, the best burn cream

Cook the flour and butter together, stirring often. At the point where the flour is cooked but the roux is still very light colored, it is a blond roux. This will thicken the soup without imparting a floury taste, but it won't impart a nutty flavor or any color. As you continue to cook the roux, it will become any number of shades of brown: ecru, sienna, chocolatey. I like a medium-brown roux, which will take you 20 to 30 minutes to achieve. It has a nice nutty flavor, not the crusty flavor of burnt bread that a dark roux has. When the roux is done to your liking, put it in a container and let it cool. If you have done it right, it will be a paste. If you have done it wrong, there will be a liquidy butter layer on top. In that case, just pour off the excess butter, and you'll be fine.

THE ART OF
NOEL RODRIGUEZ 3/23/79

Name Plate Sandwiches and Cooking for My Customers

If I were to give the home cook any advice, it would be to cook *with* the people you are cooking *for,* and to cook for the people you love. It may be an exaggeration, but I believe that cooking at home is at the center of any well-balanced life. If you make cooking something that everyone is involved in, not just a delivery system for the food, it can be a tremendous source of sustenance in any family unit. There is a thread there, a connection to the food that is as essential and as nourishing as the food itself.

The same thing that makes cooking together at home so important is also what makes one restaurant different from another. You can feel the difference in the generosity of serving and the obvious pleasure derived from giving. I think that in some upscale restaurants the pride in the ambience of the room, the quality of the produce used, and the expertise and finesse used to cook it take the place of that connection. But for me, having a restaurant is all *about* that connection.

When I cook, I always want to know who it is I am cooking for. This is easy in the space I'm in now because I can see everyone in my restaurant from where I'm cooking. It was the same way in the original restaurant. But even in the second space, where I couldn't see into the dining room from the kitchen, I usually knew who the food was for just by what was ordered.

If an order came in for Peanut Butter and Jelly Pancakes (page 93), no matter what else was ordered with it, I knew John and Theresa were out there because John always, *always,* without exception, orders p-b-and-j pancakes. When I put a new shrimp dish on the menu and someone ordered it right away, I either *knew* it was for Greg or *thought* it was for Greg. There are three or four dishes that I created with Greg in mind, all of which feature shrimp. I sneak them onto the menu and see how long it takes him to find them. He usually gets them on the first try. And then there is David Feige. He used to give away all of George Soros's money, and he recently wrote a book called *Indefensible* about being a public defender. David identified himself in a number of ways, but he always identified himself. He sometimes ordered a chicken cutlet, but he had me make sausage gravy, as I do for biscuits, to pour over it. When I know who it is I'm cooking for, I have that person in my mind during the entire process. And in subtle or not so subtle ways, the results will be different from the way I make the same thing for someone else.

Greg Shrimp, Spinach, Cheddar, Russian, 7-Grain
Makes 2 sandwiches; serves 2 to 4

Some customers tend to get stuck in one groove, not just in terms of a particular item but also in terms of ingredients. They might surf around the menu ordering different things and not even realize they are ordering the same ingredients in different forms. One customer, Greg, who owns a really special antiques store in Tribeca, comes in on weekdays on his way to work and on weekends after he has gone to the flea market looking for stuff for his store. Greg is trapped in shrimp land. Sometimes he will deviate from shrimp and order something else, but he has a difficult time doing it, and if I tempt him by putting a new shrimp item on the menu, he invariably won't be able to resist. He can't help himself. He just loves shrimp, and I guess he is always looking to try something new, which I commend.

If you take all the makings for this sandwich minus the shrimp—cheddar cheese, spinach, and Russian Dressing (page 155)—you get a really rich, flavorful sandwich filling by itself. This mixture has a fluffy texture, and when you add shrimp, it becomes even more bouffant. It makes for a really tall sandwich. You can also substitute bacon or chicken for the shrimp.

Ingredients
2 big handfuls of prewashed spinach (about 2 heaping cups)
¾ pound small shrimp (21–26 per pound), fresh or frozen (see Shopsin's Prep: Shrimp on page 7), thawed if frozen
½ cup feather-shredded cheddar cheese
¼ cup (or more to taste) Russian Dressing (page 155) or any Russian dressing
4 slices 7-grain bread

Instructions
Mix the spinach, shrimp, cheese, and Russian Dressing together gently. Divide the mixture between 2 of the bread slices and top with the remaining 2 slices of bread. Very gently, without squishing out the filling, cut each sandwich in half. If you want, put a toothpick in each sandwich half to hold the sandwich together, which is what we do at the restaurant. Don't press down on the sandwiches. Serve them big and let the eaters squish them down into their mouths.

Gulf Pride Shrimp, Avocado, and Cheddar Garlic Bread *Makes 2 sandwiches*

Another Greg sandwich.

Just as I have relationships with my customers, I have relationships based on mutual trust and affection with almost all my vendors. One of the pleasures of my business is my interactions with these people. The place I buy my shrimp is just one example.

Shrimp run seasonally, and getting the exact shrimp I want year-round is difficult. In the summertime it can be impossible. After many sources gave me substandard shrimp, I went to a Chinese fish market on Mulberry Street in Chinatown and found my own. For many years I took my motorcycle down there and bought a fifty-pound case of small white shrimp and brought it back to the store with me on the bike. Then one day Minda (or maybe Mara) suggested I ask the people I was buying the shrimp from if they deliver—and they did.

The man I work with there doesn't speak English, so the way it works now is I call in the morning and I say, "Fat guy with motorcycle." His response is "One case?" I say, "Thank you," and hang up. Later that day the shrimp are delivered. Just like that. No money, no receipt, no signature. When finally I feel I owe somewhere between $400 and $800, I motorcycle down to the shop. The same man who answers the phone flips through a book on his wood pedestal desk and finds my account quickly. I pay him in cash, and he takes the cash and puts it, along with all the other money he has collected that day, in an open square bin that is built into the desk. I have been doing this ritual for about ten years now without any problem or mix-ups. He knows what type of shrimp I use, and he saves some for me during the lean season.

Ingredients

¾ pound small shrimp (21–26 per pound; see Shopsin's Prep: Shrimp on page 7), thawed if frozen

⅓ cup GA BBQ Sauce (page 153)

¼ to ⅓ cup Chicken Stock (page 123) or any stock or broth

2 recipes of Garlic Bread (page 150)

½ cup feather-shredded cheddar cheese

½ ripe Hass avocado, thinly sliced

Instructions

In a small stainless-steel bowl, mix the shrimp, including any juice released from them when they thawed, in a small bowl with the barbecue sauce and a few tablespoons of the chicken stock. Add more stock if necessary to make a loose enough sauce to coat the shrimp. Heat a large sauté pan or griddle over high heat until it is very hot. Invert the bowl on the griddle, leaving the bowl to cover the shrimp until they are cooked through, about 2 minutes. (If you don't have such a bowl, cook the shrimp in a covered sauté pan.)

Make the Garlic Bread according to the

recipe on page 150, but in addition to the regular ingredients, add the cheddar cheese to the cheesy mixture.

If you are serving 4 people, cut each piece of Garlic Bread in half. Spoon the shrimp mixture in an even layer on the bottom half of each piece. Place the wedges of avocado in the spaces between the shrimp. Serve the sandwiches open-faced, with the other halves of the Garlic Bread placed parallel to those with the shrimp on them.

We do not cut this sandwich. People are forced to participate in its service by handling it at the table, and everyone has his way. Greg eats it by cutting off a piece of both baguettes and making one small sandwich at a time. He then eats some of it as an open-faced sandwich. He also has a habit of reaching over and grabbing food from other people's plates who are sitting with him and puts his findings on top of the non-shrimp-covered Garlic Bread.

Gulf Pride

I can trace the connection I have with my customers back to the pleasure I gained running the grocery store. Even when I was just selling a few basic cooked foods, I still had an essential feeding type of relationship with almost all my customers. Someone might get home from work and call up. "Kenny, can you send over some milk and eggs? And did you make anything special today? Some potpies? Okay, some of those, too. And why don't you put in some paper towels and cat food." We would put it all in a box and send it off with a delivery guy. It was a really special thing, a win-win situation. It made my customers happy to be treated this way, and I felt really good doing it.

When I opened the restaurant, I was already in this rhythmic pulse with my customers. That relationship, that thread, just continued to exist between us. I think the difference between art and craft is that in craft you care what the person consuming your product thinks. I'm a craftsman, and I believe that in many ways it is a more noble profession than being an artist. My customers are constantly giving me ideas for new dishes based on their desires. Most of what I make is the result of a true cooperative effort between what I want to cook and what my customers want to eat. Sandwiches are the perfect example. They are the evolutionary product of my listening to and trying to please my customers.

When I first started offering sandwiches, I noticed that sandwich making isn't really cooking at all. Sandwiches are assemblages of different, completely finished elements, like LEGOs. They are put together in appealing combinations with slight variations, like whether or not the bread is toasted or what kind of dressing it has on it. I put a list of breads, meats, and cheeses on my menu so people who wanted a sandwich could order a construction with their own specifications. When I became a restaurant, the list grew as the number of items I offered grew. In addition to sliced roast beef, turkey, shit like that, I also had pork loins, smoked ham, bacon, Canadian bacon. You could get roasted chicken, grilled chicken, fried chicken, red onions, grilled onions, fried onions, fresh tomatoes, roasted tomatoes, sun-dried tomatoes, fried green tomatoes. I had all kinds of lettuce, arugula, and alfalfa sprouts. It just went on and on. My sandwiches are huge. Any of them can easily serve two people.

Bridgette Chix Salad, Avocado, Tomato, and Garlic Bread *Makes 2 sandwiches*

Bridgette was a waitress at Shopsin's who now lives in San Diego. But she was more than a waitress. We were involved in her life for a really long time; I went through a lot of passages with her. Her representation on the menu, which is a sandwich she really liked, is a reflection of her significance in our lives. It is basically a regular chicken salad sandwich served on Garlic Bread.

Ingredients
Garlic Bread (page 150)
2 medium tomatoes
2 ripe Hass avocados, halved and pitted
8 to 10 ounces Chicken Salad (page 36) or
    any chicken salad

Instructions
Lay the garlic bread cheesy side up on a work surface. Slice the tomatoes and the avocados and lay the slices on the top pieces of bread, alternating the tomato and avocado so that what you see are red and green semicircles. Spoon the chicken salad on the bottom pieces of bread. If you are serving four people, cut each piece of bread in half. Serve the sandwiches open-faced.

Gidget (Tuna, Avocado, Tomato, and Garlic Bread)
I named this sandwich for this girl, Gidget, who used to come in a lot. Her real name isn't actually Gidget; she just calls herself that. I really like her because she is exciting to be around. She acts kind of slutty and stupid, but she is neither. She is bipolar like my son Daniel, so we bonded over that. I named this sandwich after her because I originally made it for her. She still orders it when she comes in. As a matter of fact, I don't think she has ever ordered anything else.

To make the Gidget, make the Bridgette, but with Tuna Fish Salad (page 152) instead of chicken salad. I guess it is also the same thing as an Edmonton, only without the cheddar or the spiciness. Looking at it now, I didn't really need to put it on the menu, but I like Gidget, and that's the real reason it's here.

Garlic Bread

Makes 2 pieces; serves 1 or 2

Ingredients

2 tablespoons salted butter, softened
1 teaspoon grated Parmesan cheese
¼ teaspoon minced fresh garlic
One 10-inch baguette, halved
1 tablespoon chopped parsley (optional)

Instructions

Preheat the broiler. In a small bowl, mix the butter, Parmesan cheese, and garlic into a paste. Smear it on the cut sides of the baguette, sprinkle with the parsley if you're using it, and stick the baguette halves under the broiler until the cheese has melted. The time will vary greatly depending on the heat of your broiler, but watch that it doesn't burn.

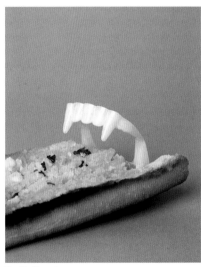

Garlic Bread

Andy's Way Grill Chix, Avocado, Turk Bacon, Blue, on Black *Makes 2 sandwiches*

This was named after Andy Hort. It is the result of one of the many requests he made of me. He and his whole family, his parents and his sister, who is now dead, came in for years. Andy was very demanding, but for some reason I never minded doing things for him. At one point he wanted his sunny-side-up eggs to have three yolks and two whites—and I even did *that* for him. I don't know why. Eve never liked him, but I liked him despite himself. He was like the little brother I wished I had.

Ingredients

Two 5- to 6-ounce boneless, skinless
    chicken breasts
4 slices black bread
1 ripe Hass avocado, halved, pitted, and
    sliced
8 or 10 slices of turkey bacon, cooked
Crumbled blue cheese

Instructions

Grill the chicken (see Grilling Chicken, page 127, or grill it however you like). Lay 2 bread slices on your work surface and put one chicken breast on each piece of bread. Put half of the avocado on top of each chicken breast, lay the bacon slices on top of the chicken, and top with a nice layer of crumbled blue cheese. Top each sandwich with the remaining bread slices, and cut each sandwich in half, being careful not to let the avocado squish out the sides.

In the early days I tried to be all things to all people. I had every sandwich ingredient known to man. I defy you to think of a sandwich ingredient that I didn't have, because, trust me, I had it. I could assemble an almost infinite number of sandwich combinations, and I was willing to do anything. All you had to do was say, "I'll have braised bacon, steamed arugula, fried okra, and some grape tomatoes on black toast—with mayonnaise but only on one slice of the bread." No matter how repulsive or weird or ordinary the combination, it was yours.

Considering how particular people are about what foods they like and don't like, you would think this system would have been really popular. But it wasn't. Nobody gave a shit. Nobody. I emphasize *nobody.* The idea was a total failure.

Looking back, I can see that it was a stupid idea. It didn't make sense on a number of levels. First, it was unfair of me to expect my customers, who are *eaters,* not *cooks,* to have the facility, much less the desire, to design their own sandwiches. And second, I know enough about the mentality of customers to realize they like to think there is something going on in the kitchen that they don't understand, something mysterious that happens to make the food they get in a restaurant better than anything they could cook themselves. If they designed their own sandwiches, that mystery aspect would be missing. So I gave up my lists of options and started offering specific sandwiches.

I had all the classics—ham and cheese, BLT, roast beef, corned beef, brisket of beef, and chicken, turkey, and egg salad. I offered a whole list of grilled cheese sandwiches and another list of peanut butter sandwiches. But I also created a bunch of sandwiches based on my own tastes as well as customer requests, and these became known as "name plate sandwiches."

I usually name the sandwich after the person who originally requested the combination or something similar that inspired it, but sometimes the sandwiches are named after the person who orders that sandwich a lot. Other times the name just comes from the fact that I like someone and was thinking about him or her at the time I was creating the sandwich.

All my customers want a sandwich named after them. They realize it is a sign of my affection. A sandwich—or any dish— with their name validates their need to feel special and be loved.

Edmonton Tuna, Avocado, and Spicy Cheddar Garlic Bread *Makes 2 sandwiches*

I make this sandwich for Alan Bleviss, a successful voice-over actor who is a regular customer and friend. Edmonton is the name of the town where he's from in Alberta, Canada. Alan likes spicy food, so when he orders an Edmonton, we make it extra spicy.

Ingredients

2 recipes for Garlic Bread (page 150)
½ cup feather-shredded cheddar cheese
A big spoonful of minced pickled jalapeño peppers or minced chipotle pepper
2 tomatoes
2 ripe Hass avocados, halved and pitted
8 to 10 ounces Tuna Fish Salad (below) or any tuna salad

Instructions

Make the Garlic Bread according to the recipe on page 150, but in addition to the regular ingredients, add the cheddar cheese and minced pepper to the cheesy mixture. Thinly slice the tomatoes and avocados.

When the bread is ready, lay it down on your work surface cheesy side up and lay the avocado and tomato slices on the bottom half of each piece of bread, alternating between the avocado and tomato so what you see is a lineup of green and red semicircles. Spoon the tuna salad on the bottom sides of the bread. If you are serving four people, cut each piece of bread in half. Serve the sandwiches open-faced.

Tuna Fish Salad

My tuna fish salad is very simple: It's tuna and mayonnaise. Period. I use Hellmann's mayonnaise, and I use solid white tuna, but you can use light tuna if you want. The government says that solid white tuna has too much mercury for pregnant women and for anyone who eats it more than once a week. I tried to switch to light, but my customers rebelled. One of the secrets to good tuna salad is to drain the tuna really well. After the tuna is drained, dump it out into a bowl and work it with your fingers to get it so that some of the tuna is solid, some is flaked, and some is crushed. Then add mayonnaise until it fluffs like a batter.

GA BBQ Sauce

We keep this tangy sauce in a catsup-style squirt jar and use it to make all sorts of things, like pulled beef, pork, or turkey sandwiches. It is a handy condiment to have around because it doesn't go bad—and it tastes really good.

The thing that gives this sauce a distinctive taste is Srirachi, which is a Vietnamese chile sauce. Its full name is Tuong Ot Srirachi. It is a bright red spicy chile sauce made by a Vietnamese immigrant family somewhere in California. These days, it is so popular that you can find it even at regular grocery stores. People who like Srirachi don't just *like* it; they are addicted to it. They put it on their eggs, their burgers. They'd probably ask us to put it in their milkshakes if they thought we would do it for them. My son Danny is one of those people, and so is Minda's husband, Andy.

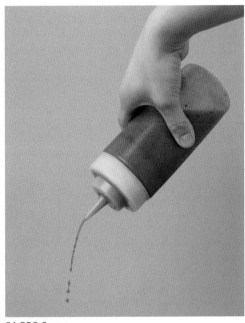

GA BBQ Sauce

Ingredients
Srirachi
Frank's Hot Sauce or whatever hot sauce
    you like
Black pepper
Apple cider vinegar

Instructions
Start with an equal amount of Srirachi and Frank's Hot Sauce and stir them together in a bowl. Add what you think will be too much black pepper and thin the sauce out with cider vinegar.

J.J.'s Way Grill Chix, Apple Stuffing, Coleslaw, & 7-Grain *Makes 2 sandwiches*

We have two customers named J.J. One we call Good J.J., and one we call Bad J.J. Good J.J. has been coming to the restaurant for a really long time. He has a physical appeal that makes you feel warmly about him and happy to be in his presence for no real reason—just because of the way he looks. He not only has that physical demeanor, but he happens to be that type of person as well. He was always just J.J. until another J.J. started coming in. The other J.J. is J. J. Abrams, who is a really aggressive, really successful Hollywood TV producer. Now that we had two J.J.'s, we had to differentiate between them, so we called the first J.J. "Good J.J." and the Hollywood J.J. "Bad J.J." The fact is that J. J. Abrams also happens to be a really good guy. In fact, he might actually be nicer than Good J.J., if that's possible.

They are both really great guys despite the fact that they are both phenomenally successful, but by the time we discovered that Bad J.J. was a really nice guy, we had already named him Bad J.J. Then it got to be funny. When we told them their names, they both enjoyed their silly monikers. This sandwich was named for Bad J.J. because he made it up. It is a really good sandwich to make after Thanksgiving when you have stuffing around. I make a few different kinds of stuffing at the restaurant. For this I use an apple stuffing, but I didn't include that recipe in the book, so you can use either the Sausage and Walnut Stuffing (page 190)

that is here, or whatever stuffing you like. It really doesn't matter.

Ingredients
Two 5- to 6-ounce boneless, skinless chicken breasts
4 slices 7-Grain bread
Bread stuffing (such as Sausage and Walnut Stuffing, page 190, or any stuffing)
Coleslaw (page 158) or any coleslaw

Instructions
Grill the chicken breasts (see Grilling Chicken, page 127, or grill them in whatever way you like). Lay two slices of bread on a work surface and place one chicken breast on each slice of bread. Put a big plonk of stuffing on each chicken breast and then put a smaller plonk of coleslaw on top of that. Close the sandwiches up and cut them in half. For sure the stuffing and coleslaw will squish out, but just do your best.

Russian Dressing
Makes about ½ cup

Eve and I had a version of this sandwich in a mall someplace. The sandwich we had was remarkable in that every part of it was bad: The bread was stale, the tomato was tasteless, the alfalfa sprouts were old, and the avocado didn't taste like an avocado; it just looked like one. And yet the idea of the sandwich, the thrust of which was avocado and Russian dressing, was so good that it ended up being a good sandwich. I like taking something like that sandwich—a good idea with bad execution—and making it great simply by paying attention to the details.

Ingredients
4 slices 7-grain bread
1 ripe Hass avocado, halved and pitted
1 tomato, sliced
Alfalfa sprouts
Russian Dressing (recipe follows) or any
    Russian dressing

Instructions
Lay 2 of the bread slices on a work surface. Slice the avocado and divide the slices between the 2 pieces of bread. Lay the tomato slices on top of the avocado and top the tomato with a pile of fresh alfalfa sprouts on each sandwich. Pour dressing over everything (how much depends on how gloppy you like your sandwiches). Close up the sandwiches with the remaining bread slices. Cut the sandwiches in half, but try not to lose too much of the insides in the process.

Ingredients
½ cup mayonnaise
1 tablespoon sweet pickle relish
1 heaping teaspoon tomato paste
A few dashes of Worcestershire sauce

Instructions
Mix the mayonnaise, relish, tomato paste, and Worcestershire sauce together in a bowl. This dressing will keep, refrigerated in an airtight container, for at least a week—probably longer.

Eve

Chaz White Turkey, Cranberry Sauce, Coleslaw, & Baguette *Makes 2 sandwiches*

This is a pretty classic sandwich. I called it Chaz after my son because I was thinking of Charlie that day, but it is really about Ellen Keely, a regular customer who taught me how to make fresh cranberry sauce.

Ingredients

A few spoonfuls of Cranberry Sauce
 (facing page) or any cranberry sauce
2 10-inch baguettes, cut in half, or 4 slices
 white bread
8 to 10 ounces sliced white-meat turkey
Two big scoops of Coleslaw (page 158) or
 any coleslaw

Instructions

Smear a generous layer of cranberry sauce on the bottom halves of the baguettes (or on the tops and bottoms if you really like cranberry sauce). Pile the turkey on the bottom halves of the baguettes, top with a big scoop of coleslaw, close up the sandwiches, and cut them in half.

Cranberry Sauce
Makes about 2 cups

Making cranberry sauce is so easy I don't know why anyone ever put it in a can. I start with frozen cranberries, which are even better than fresh cranberries because you can get them all year long. The only thing you have to do correctly to end up with good cranberry sauce is whack the cranberries in the blender for the right amount of time. It is critical that none are left whole because the skin on cranberries is too tough for the sugar to penetrate and soften them. It is also critical that you not whack the cranberries too much or you will end up with a big bowl of red crap. To get it just right, start with frozen cranberries and thaw them only slightly, so they are not as hard as little stones but are not completely thawed and soft. If you don't have a big enough food processor or blender to fit the whole bag of cranberries, you'll have to blend it in batches and then stir it all together in a big bowl. I can't make it at all when Melinda is around because no matter how big a batch I make, she'll eat the whole fucking thing.

Ingredients
1 orange, peeled and pith removed
1 cup sugar
1 12-ounce bag cranberries, semithawed

Instructions
Put the orange and sugar in a food processor or blender and process for 40 seconds or a minute or longer, until the orange is totally destroyed. You want it to have texture but not to be juice. Add the cranberries and whack them until about half the cranberries are crushed and the others are cut into about halves or thirds. Transfer to a bowl and let sit in the refrigerator for a couple of hours, until the sugar starts to work on it the way it does with fresh fruit. The cranberries will start to soften and bleed a bit so the sauce is more homogenous. This is best about a half hour after it's made, but it will last about a week.

Coleslaw

Serves 4

I use coleslaw in many ways. I serve it as a side dish with picnic-type foods like hot dogs as well as foods that feel southern to me, like barbecue sandwiches and deep-fried foods. I use it to dress sandwiches like the Chaz (page 156), a turkey sandwich with cranberry sauce, and J.J.'s Way (page 154), a chicken and stuffing sandwich. And I add different flavors to it depending on how I'm serving it. I add Srirachi (page 153) if I want a spicy slaw. I add grated green mangoes and a few shakes of curry powder to the mayonnaise to turn it Asian style. The most common variation is cranberry slaw, which is coleslaw with just enough cranberry sauce stirred in to make it pink and tasty.

To make coleslaw, I like to slice the cabbage by hand because I think it is a nice surprise once in a while to get a big chunk of cabbage in your slaw. The vinegar in the slaw dressing cooks the cabbage a little bit, so super-fresh coleslaw is different from coleslaw that has been sitting even a short while. How crisp or wilted you like yours is a matter of taste. I am just not that picky, so I like it in every stage. I give the mayonnaise amount in tablespoons rather than cups because I don't know how you would get a measuring cup in a jar of mayonnaise. I don't use either. I just reach in there and get a big glonk of mayonnaise with my hand. This slaw will keep about three days, but if you want it really crunchy, prepare the vegetables and the dressing and toss what you're going to serve just before you're going to serve it.

Ingredients

½ head green cabbage, cored and thinly sliced

1 large carrot, shredded on a box grater

6 tablespoons mayonnaise

2 tablespoons sugar

1 tablespoon salt

1 teaspoon heavy cream

3 teaspoons apple cider vinegar

Instructions

Combine the cabbage and carrots in a large bowl. Mix them together really well because once you add the dressing, they won't move.

In a separate, smaller bowl, whisk the mayonnaise, sugar, salt, and heavy cream together. It's a challenge to get these ingredients to combine, but it will happen eventually; just keep whisking. Add the vinegar and whisk to combine. Dump the dressing over the vegetables and toss to coat.

Alice's Way

Although she doesn't have a dish named after her—and I don't think she ever did—there are a number of things in the restaurant that were prepared Alice Trillin's way and a number of things in the restaurant that revolved around her. She always cared about Bud's health, and would ask me to use olive oil instead of butter. The big thing I remember doing for Alice was the NO SMOKING sign. This was back in the day when people smoked inside restaurants, and Alice didn't like to be around cigarette smoke.

Around that time, my best friend Steven Casko's son was having bad dreams. Today he is a lieutenant in the Houston Police Department but back then he had nightmares that a clown was gonna come through the window and attack him. So in a moment of what I would call brilliant parenting, Steven sat down and with his kid made a sign to hang in the window that read: CLOWN NO COME IN HERE!

Most parents would have told the kid, "Oh, you'll be all right," or bought him an ice-cream cone or some other thing that would have done nothing whatsoever to soothe the kid's fears. But Steven went straight to the source, and he solved the problem. The sign did it. The kid was cured of his bad dream.

For Alice, I took Steven's strategy and put up a sign that read SMOKING IS OK UNLESS YOU ARE SITTING NEAR: followed by a list of names, the first being Alice's. This pretty much solved the problem.

Danny

The Makings of a Great Burger

Years ago, when we were still a grocery store, every Wednesday was turkey dinner night. I made turkey dinners to go, with turkey gravy, sausage stuffing, baked potatoes, homemade cranberry sauce, the whole deal—just like Thanksgiving. Everybody loves turkey dinners, and I had a regular clientele of turkey dinner customers. Four of these customers worked at a local newspaper called *The Paper* (it's not around anymore), and they asked me if they could write up the dinners. I told them, "No! No write-ups." Even back then, I hated the media, so I made the reporters promise they wouldn't write anything. Well, they are journalists, and I guess they just couldn't control themselves. They wrote it up. In the article they wrote about how I put "buckets of gravy" on the turkey. After that, people started coming in, people I didn't even know, asking me, "Hey, you gonna put buckets of gravy on that?" I was so pissed off I quit doing turkey dinners for two years.

Among the many things I hate about the media is that they have eliminated people's ability to think and to judge for themselves. People rely on the media to tell them what is "the best"— the best vacation, the best ice cream, the best toilet paper—as opposed to deciding for themselves based on their own tastes or their own satisfaction. And not only do the media tell people what they should like, they tell them what they should like *about* it.

And the worst thing is that the media, those pricks, *they* don't even think for themselves. I get written up as a brunch place because I have been written up by someone else as a brunch place. It's the same way across the board. Every time they write up hamburgers, they name the same five or ten places. They never mention *my* hamburger, not because it isn't good, but because nobody else has written about my hamburger. Their lack of originality is insidious. Not only do I make one of the best hamburgers in the city, I make hamburgers that nobody else in the city makes. I watched *Hamburger America,* a documentary about hamburgers in little joints all across America, and I make just about every fucking burger in the movie—steamed burgers, stuffed burgers, and deep-fried burgers. You name it, I have it. But do I get a write-up about that? No...

Basic Burger
Makes 4 burgers

For me, if the meat is good and the burger is prepared correctly, a basic hamburger is enough. It is all I want. I don't even like cheese on my burgers. I like hamburgers so much that the cheese just becomes a distraction. With the exception of my Steamed Burger (page 168) and my Chicken-fried Hamburger (page 170), all my burger items start with the Basic Burger. Before making even this very basic burger, I suggest you read Burger Fundamentals (in box below).

Ingredients

1¾ pound chopped meat (20 to 30 percent fat)
Sliced cheese such as cheddar, American, or Swiss, or crumbled blue cheese (optional)
Butter for the buns
4 Martin's potato buns, or whatever hamburger bun you like
Whatever burger accoutrements you like

Instructions

Divide the meat into 4 equal, 7-ounce segments. Pat each segment into a flat patty that is the same size as the bun. (See Burger Fundamentals, below.)

Heat a large cast-iron pan with the lid on it over high heat until it is searing hot. Place the patties in the pan and cook them for 5 minutes total, turning them once halfway through cooking. If you are adding cheese, put it on just after turning the patties. Continue cooking until the burgers are the temperature you desire, but remember that they will continue to cook slightly when they are off the fire.

While the burgers are cooking, butter and lightly toast the buns. Take the burgers off the grill, put them on the bun bottoms, put the tops on top, and serve with the accoutrements of your choice.

Burger Fundamentals

The best burgers start with high-fat chopped meat. If you like a burger with a seared crust that gives way to a moist, juicy inside, you will have to start with ground chuck that is at least 20 percent fat, preferably 25 or 30 percent. I understand that some people want to reduce the amount of fat they intake, and because of the way I look, you probably won't believe me when I tell you that the extra fat in the meat is burned off in the high-heat cooking process, but it is. Whether you believe me or not, the fact is that if you don't start with the right meat, you can ignore anything else I tell you when it comes to cooking burgers, because no matter what else you do to them, you will never get anything but a dry, flavorless burger. Most supermarket chuck contains 10 or 15 percent fat, so you will probably have to ask your butcher to grind the meat for you. This is one of the side perks to using this kind of meat: You know it is ground fresh.

Seven ounces is the perfect size for a hamburger. One thing that people don't understand is that when a portion size is too big, it is just bigger, not better. When I am served an 8-ounce burger, I recognize that it is a nice idea—somebody is trying to give me a lot for my money. But the truth is that I don't really want an 8-ounce burger. It is too much. And when you are eating something that is too much, there comes a point where you're not enthusiastic about it any-more. You can't even taste it. After a lot of consideration, I have determined that 7 ounces is the perfect burger size.

When you are shaping your burger patties, don't overwork the meat. You don't want the meat and fat to be condensed into a dense patty. If you are familiar with making pie dough, it's the same thing: You want the butter interspersed throughout the dough so that when it bakes, the butter melts, forming layers in the crust. With a burger, if you keep the fat and the meat separate, it will puff up as it cooks, resulting in a robust burger that is bursting with juice.

Make the burger patties the size of a Martin's potato bun. However thick a 7-ounce patty turns out when it reaches that diameter is how thick I want it for a burger that is being cooked rare to medium. If I am cooking a well-done burger, then I pat the patty thinner. This saves me time in the kitchen because the thinner burger will cook in less time. But this is also a nice trick for a home cook, because if you are cooking for people who want their burgers cooked at dif-ferent temperatures, you can put them all in the pan together, and they will all be done at roughly the same time.

Heat the pan big-time before adding the burgers. The meat should make a loud, spattering, sizzling noise when it hits the pan. The way I see it, a hamburger is like blackened catfish. You really want the pan to be red hot so that the outside forms a crust, which acts like a casing around the inside meat. When you bite through the crust of a hamburger, it should bleed juices into your mouth.

Cook burgers for 5 minutes total, turning them halfway through, before testing. When I'm cooking steaks, I can tell by touching them when they're done, but I haven't gotten there yet with hamburgers. For hamburgers I rely on a meat thermometer to tell me how the meat is cooked inside. After 5 minutes I probe the burger right in the center, and I have a list of temperatures taped above my grill:

    120°F–125°F for rare
    130°F–135°F for medium-rare
    140°F–145°F for medium
    150°F–155°F for medium-well.

Anything higher than that is well done.

Leave a cooking burger alone. Try not to probe your burger for temperature more times than you really have to. Every time you poke a hole in your burger, juices spill out the hole, which isn't good. Also, try to resist the impulse to press down on the patties with a spatula while they are cooking. This not only presses the juices right out of them, it compresses the meat, and that combination defeats the point of everything you have done up to this point. I still do it from time to time. I can't help myself. I guess it's a lot like masturbating. I feel really good while I'm doing it, but then I feel bad afterward.

Cook burgers with a lid on the pan. With the lid on, the heat inside the pan becomes concentrated. It is like the burger is being seared and baked at the same time. Without the cover, the burger cooks too slowly, so the meat closest to the outer crust will cook until it is well done, and you end up with a burger with graduating degrees of doneness and only a thin, wafer-size bit of meat in the very center that is cooked to your desired doneness. Cooking a burger my way can be dangerous, so you definitely need a fan above your stove to do it, because once you take the lid off the pan, the flames from the burning fat go clear up to the hood.

Toast your buns. With burgers the details make all the difference. When you bite into a nice, lightly toasted bun, you will feel your teeth going through a thin layer of crisp, giving way to the soft white bread beneath. It really adds to the experience. I toast buns on a griddle, but you should toast them in whatever way is most convenient for you.

Burger Variations

REUBEN BURGER: Swiss cheese and sauerkraut

PATTY MELT: Rye toast, American cheese on both sides, and grilled onions. This burger must be cut in half before serving, which takes a lot of courage because when cut, everybody can see if the meat has been cooked correctly.

PLOUGHMAN (named after the classic British sandwich, which is not a hamburger): Branston pickle and cheddar cheese on white toast

PEEP: Sunny-side egg and American cheese

SIX-OUNCE SLIDER: A hamburger cooked like a slider (see My Sliders, page 177)

HAMBURGER SALAD: Pretty much what you'd expect except served with a bowl of greens. I cut the burger into six pieces and stick them on top of the salad like big meaty croutons. I throw French fries on top, too.

CHILI BURGER: Sometimes I serve this like a hamburger, with a thick plop of chili on top of the burger and the top bun on top of that. Other times I serve it with chili poured over the burger, bun, and all, and cheddar cheese and raw onion sprinkled on top. I love it that way because you get more chili, and the bun gets mushy like a dumpling.

THAI BURGER: Mush 2 teaspoons Thai green curry paste in with the meat.

JAMAICAN JERK BURGER: Same as the Thai Burger, only with a sprinkling of Jamaican jerk seasoning instead of the curry paste

Steamed Burger
Makes 4 burgers

There is a place in Meriden, Connecticut, called Ted's Famous Steamed Burgers. That is the only kind of burger they serve: steamed. They have these really elaborate cabinets with metal racks that they put the hamburger patties in to steam them. When a hamburger is cooked this way, most of the fat and liquid are steamed out of the meat, and what you're left with is meat that is cooked all the way through to a uniform doneness. It has a very distinctive flavor and a grayish color. It looks disgusting, but this doesn't matter because the only people who would ever order a steamed burger are people from Connecticut, and they know it is supposed to be gray. Certainly no normal person would order something called a "steamed burger" because it *sounded* tasty. If you don't have a microwave, I don't know how to tell you to cook a steamed burger. Maybe you could cook it the way you steam broccoli. If you really want a steamed burger, play with it and I'm sure you'll figure it out.

If you're making one burger, put it in a round dish. I make it in a small doggie dish made of hard, heavy plastic.

Ingredients
1¾ pounds chopped meat (20 to 30 percent fat)
Butter for the buns
4 Martin's potato buns, or whatever hamburger bun you like
Whatever burger accoutrements you like

Instructions
Divide the meat into four 7-ounce segments. Pat each segment into a flat patty that is the same size as the bun. (See Burger Fundamentals, page 163.) Put the burgers in a microwavable casserole dish with space between each burger.

Cover the dish and nuke the burgers for 2 minutes. Look at the burgers, and if they're done, take them out. Otherwise flip them and cook them another minute until done. There is only one temperature you can cook a steamed burger to: done.

While the burgers are cooking, butter and lightly toast the buns in whatever way is convenient for you. Take the burgers off the grill, put them on the bun bottoms, put the tops on top, and serve with the accoutrements of your choice.

Doggie dish used for nuking

Stuffed Burger
Makes 4 burgers

A stuffed burger is like a burger version of ravioli. It has a little treat inside with a meat casing on the top, bottom, and around the edges. Stuffed burgers are really fun to eat, because when you bite into one, there is a surprise in the center just like a jelly doughnut. They are pretty popular, especially considering that I have so many things on the menu that no one thing can be *really* popular. I've listed some stuffing options, but you can stuff anything you want inside your burgers except your finger. Or you could stuff them all differently and then everyone will be surprised.

Ingredients

1¾ pounds chopped meat (20 to 30 percent fat)

Stuffing options (8 whole chipotle peppers, 4 teaspoons minced fresh jalapeño peppers, 4 playing dice–sized cubes cheddar cheese, or 4 tablespoons chopped raw onion)

Butter for the buns

4 Martin's potato buns, or whatever hamburger bun you like

Whatever burger accoutrements you like

Instructions

Divide the meat into four 7-ounce hunks and divide each hunk of meat into 2 balls with your hands, making one half slightly larger than the other. Keeping the pairs together, roll the halves into balls, put them on a cutting board, and use the flat side of a large knife to press each ball into a flat disk with the larger of the two the same size as a hamburger bun. Place whatever you're using as a stuffing in the center of the larger disks. Slide the knife under one of the smaller disks, pick it up without breaking, and place it on top of the corresponding disk with the stuffing. Use a fork or your fingers to fold the bigger disk over the smaller one and gently push the edges to seal it well. (If you don't do it right, the stuffing inside the burger will blow out of the burger when you cook it.) Repeat.

Preheat a large cast-iron pan over high heat. Working one at a time, lift up the whole burger—again sliding your knife under it—and put each in the pan. You will probably have to do this in two batches. Whack the burgers for 2 minutes per side. These burgers are basically two skinny burgers in one, so you don't want to cook them for too long; just burn the hell out of one side, burn the hell out of the other side, and then you're done. If you like well-done burgers, you're screwed because the moist stuff in the center keeps the inner walls of the burger rare.

While the burgers are cooking, butter and lightly toast the buns in whatever way is convenient for you. Take the burgers off the grill, put them on the bun bottoms, put the tops on top, and serve with the accoutrements of your choice.

Chicken-fried Hamburger
Makes 4 burgers

This burger has a thick coating of chicken-fried crust around the meat. If you get it right, it comes up just like fried chicken, only with a hamburger inside the crust instead of chicken. It is really terrific, although, to be honest, I don't think I have ever eaten one.

Ingredients
Peanut oil for deep frying
1¾ pounds chopped meat (20 to 30 percent fat)
Salt and pepper
4 extra-large eggs
1½ cups heavy cream
All-purpose flour for dredging
Butter for the buns
4 Martin's potato buns, or whatever hamburger bun you like
Whatever burger accoutrements you like

Instructions
Preheat a deep fryer or a large potful of peanut oil over high heat to 375°F.

Form the meat into four 7-ounce patties a little flatter than for a Basic Burger (see Burger Fundamentals, page 163). Season the patties with salt and pepper.

Whisk the eggs and cream together in a shallow bowl. Put the flour in a separate bowl or pie pan. Dredge one of the hamburger patties in the flour and brush off the excess. (This is important. If you don't brush off the excess flour, it will fall off in the fryer and you will end up with bald spots on your burger crust.) Dunk the floured patty in the egg-and-cream mixture, lift, drain, and repeat, dumping the patties back in the flour and then back in the egg and cream, until you have gone through the process a total of three times. Now you should have a reasonably heavy coating, and you'll also have a hardened coating on your fingers because for some reason it sticks to your fingers even better than it sticks to the burgers.

Carefully place the burger in the oil and repeat with the remaining burgers, being careful not to overcrowd the deep fryer or pot. Cook the burgers for 3 or 4 minutes, until the crust is golden brown. While the burgers are cooking, butter and lightly toast the buns in whatever way is convenient for you. Serve deep-fried burgers like you would any hamburger, on toasted buns with whatever shit you like.

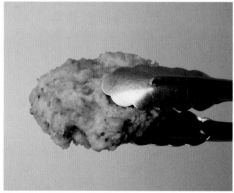

Chicken-fried Hamburger patty

Loco Moco
Serves 4

This is a Hawaiian dish—or at least it's a Hawaiian name. Actually, I have no idea about its origins. I just know what it is: a hamburger patty with oniony gravy and a fried egg on top. When you break through the egg with your fork, the runny yolk bleeds down over the patty, gravy, and rice. It's pretty special.

Ingredients

4 big yellow Spanish onions, thinly sliced
4 handfuls of prewashed spinach (about
    1 heaping cup) or other greens
4 cups cooked white rice
1¾ pounds chopped meat (20 to 30 percent
    fat)
4 extra-large eggs
Brown Gravy (page 172)

Instructions

Fry the onions (see below). Put one handful of spinach on the bottom of each of four bowls. Put a cup of rice in each bowl on top of the spinach.

Divide the meat into four 7-ounce segments. Pat each into a flat patty that is the same size as a bun. (See Burger Fundamentals, page 163.)

Heat a large cast-iron pan with the lid on it over high heat until searing hot. Place the patties in the pan and cook for 5 minutes, turning them once halfway through. Continue cooking to the temperature you desire, but remember that the burgers will also cook slightly when they are off the fire.

Meanwhile, fry the eggs (see Cooking Eggs, page 47) and make the gravy. Stir in the fried onions at the last minute so you don't lose the crunchiness. Put the burgers on top of the rice. Pour the gravy over the patties, and top each with a fried egg.

Fried Onions

An onion is like the human body. It's 90 percent water, and when you throw it in the hot oil, it just goes away. What you're left with is basically a brown-black vestige of an onion with concentrated sweet onion flavor. It's not much in terms of volume, but in terms of flavor, it's really terrific. To fry onions, start with a whole peeled onion, slice as thin as you can, and throw the slices in the deep fryer or in a small pot of hot peanut oil on the stove. Fry until the onions are charred around the edges and basically gone. Drain on paper towels.

Brown Gravy
Makes about 2½ cups

I don't know why people think that making gravy is difficult. It's not when I make it—or when you follow my recipe. I also can't figure out why restaurants make gravy in large batches and keep it on a steam table. Gravy is best when it's fresh—and it takes just a few minutes to whip up in a sauté pan.

Ingredients

1 stick butter or ½ cup Clarified Butter
    (page 44), or ghee
⅓ cup all-purpose flour
2 cups Beef Stock (page 124) or any stock
    or broth, or more as needed
Salt and pepper

Instructions

Heat the butter in a large sauté pan over high heat. Add the flour and whisk it around to break up any bumpy white shit. Cook the butter and flour together, until the flour disappears into the butter, about 1 minute. At this point you have to move quickly, or you'll end up with burned butter. Deglaze the pan with 2 cups of the stock. Let the gravy cook for 30 seconds to 1 minute to thicken to a gravy-like consistency. If it becomes too thick, add more stock or water to thin it slightly and season with salt and pepper to taste.

Zack's whisk (left) and Kenny's whisk (right)

Mirepoix

Mirepoix is a French word that refers to a mix of diced onion, celery, and carrots. It is used as the base for most soups, stews, and some sauces. Sometimes leeks or mushrooms are included in a mirepoix, but when I refer to mirepoix, I mean just the basic three. I don't measure mirepoix but I use a ratio that is about two parts onion to one part celery and one part carrot.

Hamburger Soup

Makes 4 burger soups

Hamburger soup is a dish in which I put a hamburger in a soup bowl and then pour a thin beef-stock-based soup over it. It is really not as weird as it sounds. Think about it. You have ravioli soup, dumpling soups, and meatball soup. Why can't I do hamburger soup?

Ingredients

1¾ pound chopped meat (20 to 30 percent fat)

Sliced cheese such as cheddar, American, or Swiss, or blue cheese (optional)

Butter for the buns

4 Martin's potato buns, or whatever hamburger bun you like

⅓ cup Clarified Butter (page 44), regular butter, or ghee

1 cup Mirepoix (facing page)

¼ cup all-purpose flour

5 or 6 cups Beef Stock (page 124) or any stock or broth

¾ cup frozen haricots verts or peas

4 big handfuls of prewashed spinach or arugula (about 4 heaping cups)

French fries or potato chips (optional)

Instructions

Divide the meat into 4 equal, 7-ounce segments. Pat each segment into a flat patty that is the same size as the bun. (See Burger Fundamentals, page 163.)

Heat a large cast-iron pan with the lid on it over high heat until it is searing hot. Place the patties in the pan and cook them for 5 minutes, turning them once halfway through cooking. If you are adding cheese, put it on just after turning the patties. Continue cooking until the burgers are the temperature you desire, but remember that they will continue to cook slightly when they are off the fire. Butter and toast the buns.

To make the soupy portion of the soup, heat the butter in a large sauté pan over high heat. Add the mirepoix and sauté until the vegetables begin to soften, 4 to 5 minutes. Add the flour and run a whisk around the pan to break up any lumps and incorporate the flour with the butter. (If you don't get rid of the flour at this stage, you'll never get rid of it; you'll have balls of flour in your soup.) Deglaze the pan with 4 cups of the stock, gradually adding more until you have a thin soupy consistency. Throw in the haricots verts or peas and simmer for about 1 minute, until the vegetables are no longer frozen.

To serve, put one handful of the spinach in the bottom of each of four large soup bowls. Assemble the hamburgers and place one in each bowl. Pour the soup over the burgers, dividing it evenly. If you are using them, scatter the French fries or potato chips on top and serve before the buns disintegrate and while the chips are still crisp.

the patties to keep them smashed down and cook about 2 minutes per side, until they are cooked through.

Meanwhile, butter the insides of the rolls and toast them in whatever way is most convenient for you. (I do it on the griddle.) Place the patties so they are all in a row, butting up against one another. Put the fried onions on the patties, and then top each patty with one slice of the cheese. On top of the cheese, place the tops of the buns and on top of the tops, the toasted bottoms. Then, on top of *everything,* place your bacon weight or a lid and cook for 1 minute to melt the cheese and steam the bun.

To serve, place the bun bottoms on a plate. Carefully slide your spatula under the three patties to lift them up in one piece and place them on top of the bottom buns. Serve at once.

Onion Rings

Onion Rings

I don't batter my onion rings; I just coat them in a light coating of flour. The problem with battered onion rings is that you forget they're onions. They taste good, because all fried food tastes good, but they don't really taste like onion because the batter around the onion overwhelms the onion flavor. With some commercial onion rings you can't even *find* the onions because the manufacturer chops up the onions, adds them to the batter, and then forms the batter into ring shapes. So what they are, really, is not onion rings but onion-flavored batter rings. It is homogenized and uninteresting, and it is the opposite of what I like in food, which is honesty. Truth in advertising. Some people like their onion rings thin, some like them thick—you should slice your onions however you want them because they're going to be *your* onion rings. I remember reading that Mimi Sheraton loves onion rings. Someone asked her how she liked them, and she said, "Plain." I'm with her. I don't serve them with anything, but there is catsup on all the tables, which I suspect most of my customers use with theirs.

Ingredients
Peanut oil for deep frying
Chicken Stock (page 123), Vegetable Stock (page 124), or any stock, or water
1 big yellow Spanish onion, sliced into rings
All-purpose flour for dredging
Salt and pepper

Instructions
Preheat a deep fryer or a large potful of peanut oil over high heat to 375°F.

Pour the stock or water into a small bowl for dipping the onion rings and pour the flour into a similar-sized bowl for dredging. Separate the sliced onions into individual rings. Dip the rings into the stock or water and then drop them into the flour. Toss the rings around so they are coated on all sides, then shake off any excess flour.

Drop the rings into the deep fryer and cook until they are golden brown and crunchy. Remove the rings from the fryer, drain on paper towels, and sprinkle with salt and pepper to taste.

Sterling Hayden

Flipper

Roasted Turkey

The Story of Shopsin's Turkey, or Why I Hate the Health Department

The story of roasted turkey at Shopsin's is really a story about the Health Department, and it is one of victory in the face of adversity. The Health Department has changed the way I do a lot of things in the restaurant, but the saddest of all is the way they changed how I cook my turkey.

For a long time turkey was the star of Shopsin's. Starting back when I was still a grocery store, I used to roast a whole turkey every day. On a busy day, if I sensed we might run out, I would make two. I learned how to cook my turkey from an Italian lady named Rita Grippo, who lived across the street from the store. She told me, "You know how I do it? I wrap the whole thing in foil and cook the turkey for three and a half hours. Then I take the foil off and cook it until it's brown." So that's exactly what I did. I cooked the turkey until it was done or very nearly done. Then I took it out of the oven, got a paintbrush, painted the whole thing with melted butter, and then put it back in the oven until it got nice and brown.

Let me tell you, that turkey was *beautiful.* When it first came out of the oven, the smell would be all over the place, and nobody, not one person who happened to be in the store at that moment, would be able to resist it. For the rest of the day the turkey sat on a stainless-steel shelf like something out of a Norman Rockwell painting—a fresh, brown, juicy turkey tempting every customer who walked in. It still crackled from the heat for an hour or two after it was out of the oven. My customers loved those turkeys. They would buy some to take home, turkey dinner style, they'd buy it as sandwiches, or if they knew us, they might just reach in and rip off some of the skin or beg me for the pope's nose. Joe Brodsky, who used to be the Poet Laureate of

America and was a regular customer for years, would come in and get the neck, which I can only assume is a Russian proclivity because nobody else begged me for the neck. I usually sold the entire turkey (or two) by the end of the day, and whatever was left over I would just throw out because tomorrow would be another day and would yield another fresh roasted turkey.

That beautiful turkey was everything fresh food could be. It was like a girl in her twenties: vibrant, alive, athletic, and gorgeous. Sadly, it is now a thing of the past, because one day, some prick from the Health Department came in, looked at the turkey sitting up there on its shelf, and said, "Is it 140 or 40?" meaning over 140 degrees or under 40 degrees. That's the law. Everything in a restaurant has to be either super fucking hot or super fucking cold. Well, it wasn't either. It was sitting out at room temperature as it did every day. Nobody ever got sick from my turkey or anything else in my restaurant. But the Health Department doesn't care about that. All they care about are their rules and their fines. They took the turkey—that gorgeous brown juicy Norman Rockwell bird—threw it in the trash, and poured Palmolive on it. That is what they do: They put dish soap or bleach on what they throw out so you can't just take it out of the trash after they leave and try to serve it. It was such a waste.

Today I still make turkeys, but I don't even bother to baste them. There's no reason to, because nobody sees them. They go straight from the oven, after they have cooled enough, to the refrigerator. When the turkey is sliced for sandwiches, I leave lots of meat on the carcass, which I boil. From that process, I get gorgeous pulled turkey that I use for the High School Hot Turkey Sandwiches (page 186); I mix it with GA BBQ Sauce (page 153) to make barbecue sandwiches. And the carcass makes a really rich, delicious stock. Those assholes aborting its most vital and beautiful stage couldn't stop me from utilizing turkey in its secondary and tertiary stages and beyond. In fact, having been robbed of that first phase of my turkey's life, I think I am *more* inclined to get use out of its other stages. I like to think I won my battle with those Health Department pricks, because I am still doing what I like to do.

•

In my business, the food you get from your vendors is no better than your ability to discern its quality. Vendors are always trying to slip you something that is not as good as what you asked for, hoping that you won't notice and they'll make more money. I could give you an example of this on a daily basis. It is really criminal.

I used to buy my turkeys from two brothers who owned a butcher store in the neighborhood. Their names were Morris and Sidney; they were from Genoa. Sidney only had fingers on one hand because the fingers on his other hand were chopped off when someone accidentally turned on the meat grinder.

Illustration by John Tenniel

Despite all my idiosyncrasies, I like to think that thanks to a combination of psychotherapy and drugs, I am pretty together. Pretty sane. Morris, on the other hand, was out of his fucking brains. I used to go in there a few times a week to pick up my turkeys. He did all his transactions on a manual cash register with a paper receipt. One day I noticed that he didn't tear the tape after each transaction. He ran it all the way through one way, and when he got to the end of the tape, he ran it through the other way. And after that, he flipped the tape and ran it through on both sides. So every roll of adding tape was, in Morris's world, *four* rolls of adding tape. He would tell you it was to save a few pennies, but the *real* reason he did this is that he was nuts.

One day Morris was bragging to me that he had been on that corner for fifty years. Way back in the '40s, he said, chicken was really rare. When he couldn't get it, he used to take veal cutlets and sell them as chicken cutlets. He said nobody ever noticed the difference. I don't know how he expected to inspire trust in me by telling me he sold veal for chicken. He was telling me the story to show me how times had changed, but what I got from it was that he was a liar and a crook.

When it comes to turkey, I believe that frozen is okay, but I only buy turkeys that are noninjected and naturally fed, so the only turkeys I ever bought from those guys were Norbest non-injected turkeys. At some point, though, I noticed that on the Norbest turkeys Morris was sending me, someone had taken nail polish remover and erased the part where it said the turkey was injected. I got in a huge fight with Morris over this, and then I went and found myself a butcher I could trust.

Roasted Turkey

Throughout my years of experience, I have done all the tricks that people do when they cook turkeys. I've dotted the turkeys with butter, basted them, and turned the heat up or down while they were cooking. While basting gave it a nice brown crust, none of those tricks made any difference to how the turkey tasted. Since the turkeys I cook now are kitchen turkeys, not display turkeys, I don't give a shit about their looking brown and beautiful. I just want them to taste delicious, so I don't do any of those tricks. No butter, no salt, no pepper, no nothing—just really good turkey. The only secret I have to cooking a delicious turkey is not to *overcook* it.

Longtime favorite butcher

The reason most people overcook turkeys is that they are under the impression they have to cook turkey to something like 180°F—another piece of crap propagated by the Health Department. In actuality, you don't want to cook turkey past 140°F. Anything more and the entire turkey, even the dark meat, is going to be dry. In what is a ludicrous cycle of stupidity, to compensate for the dryness caused by overcooking it, commercial turkeys are injected with whatever it is that they have to be injected with to keep them from drying out past the point where you can eat them.

The way I cook turkey is a variation on the Rita Grippo way. I preheat the oven to 425°F, then I take heavy-duty aluminum foil and tear off a big piece. I put the turkey on the foil at a 60-degree angle with the legs pointed toward the upper-right corner. I then fold the ends of the foil over the turkey so the entire ass end of the turkey is covered completely and the legs are sticking out of the foil. And then I stick the turkey in a pan and bake it. A 25-pound turkey, which is the only turkey I ever make, takes exactly 3½ hours to reach 140°F, which is where I want it. If you are cooking a smaller turkey, you will cook it for less time, but follow the same rule for temperature: Cook it to 140°F. No matter what size turkey you're cooking, if you have not cooked a lot of turkeys, it's a good idea to use a meat thermometer to check for doneness. Probe the deepest place in the breast.

If you want your turkey to look pretty, before wrapping it in foil, dot it with butter. When the turkey is about half an hour from being done, take the foil off, brush the whole thing generously with melted butter, and stick the turkey back in the oven for another half hour, until the skin is brown and crackly, and the internal temperature is 140°F.

Due to the high temperature of melted butter, it is best to use a brush with real hair bristles for basting. I use a paintbrush.

High School Hot Turkey Sandwiches *Serves 2*

When I was in high school in White Plains, the women in the kitchen didn't just dish out prefabricated food, they really *cooked*. And the food they cooked was really delicious. Every Thursday they served hot turkey sandwiches, and I loved them. This is my rendition of those sandwiches. I serve them closed and then smother the whole thing with warm, glistening brown gravy so that they look like big petit fours. The best part for me is the way the bread on top disintegrates into a heavy wet dumpling.

Ingredients

1 stick butter or ½ cup Clarified Butter (page 44), or ghee
½ cup Mirepoix (page 172)
¼ cup sliced white mushrooms
⅓ cup all-purpose flour
2 cups Beef Stock (page 124) or any stock or broth, or more as needed
Salt and pepper
½ pound pulled (shredded) turkey (or sliced turkey g'schmushed into bits with your fingers)
4 slices white bread

Instructions

Heat the butter in a large sauté pan over high heat. Add the Mirepoix and mushrooms and sauté until the vegetables begin to soften, 4 to 5 minutes. Add the flour and whisk it around to break up any bumpy white shit. Cook over really high heat for about 1 minute, until the flour disappears into the butter. Deglaze the pan with the stock. Let the gravy cook for 30 seconds to 1 minute to thicken to a gravy-like consistency. If it becomes too thick, add more stock or water to thin it slightly and season with salt and pepper to taste.

Put the turkey in a bowl. Add enough gravy to bind it. Lay 1 slice of bread on each of two plates. Divide the turkey over the two pieces of bread. Top each sandwich with another piece of bread and pour the remaining gravy over the sandwiches. Eat with a knife and fork.

Turkey Cloud

Makes 8 to 10 10-ounce patties

A Turkey Cloud is turkey stuffing, with the emphasis on *turkey*, meaning it is not stuffing *for* a turkey. It's stuffing *made* of turkey. It is basically a bread *boudin*, which is a Creole-Cajun sausage made with rice as a filler. Only this is made with turkey instead of pork, and bread instead of rice. You can also think of it as turkey hash. Whatever you call it, it is a way to take meat and extend it with a starch into something savory and delicious. I make it in big batches, shape it into individual-sized patties, and freeze it in baggies. I use them for the Tom Tom (page 188) breakfast plate, where the patties are wrapped in scrambled egg. But its most popular use on the menu is as a cheap side dish for eggs: turkey hash patties. To make the hash patties, nuke the Turkey Clouds just enough to defrost (about 30 seconds) and then sauté them in hot butter or olive oil so that the outside gets crunchy like hash.

Ingredients

2 extra-large eggs
3 cups stuffing mix or croutons
3 tablespoons Clarified Butter (page 44), regular butter, or ghee
½ big yellow Spanish onion, chopped
½ pound pulled (shredded) turkey (or sliced turkey g'schmushed into bits with your fingers)
2 cups warm Chicken Stock (page 123) or any stock or broth

Instructions

Whisk the eggs in a large bowl just to break up the yolks. Add 3 cups stuffing mix or croutons and mix them together.

Heat 1 tablespoon of the butter in a large sauté pan, add the onion, and sauté until it is soft and pleasant but not browned. Stir in the turkey and the stock. Pour into the bowl with the bread and eggs, and mix all together. At this point, if the mix is too dry, gradually add more stock until the mixture is the mushy consistency of cooked stuffing that comes out of a turkey. (Try not to go too far with the stock, but if you do, you can dry it out by adding more stuffing mix or bread crumbs.)

Form the stuffing into 10-ounce patties about ⅓ inch thick. Heat the remaining 2 tablespoons of butter in a sauté pan over medium-high heat; place the patties in the butter and cook 2 to 3 minutes per side, until they are browned on both sides.

To freeze, let the patties come to room temperature, and then place each patty in a plastic bag. Close the bag and freeze. When you are ready to use the cloud, nuke it or put it on the counter to bring to room temperature, and then sear it as described above.

Sausage and Walnut Stuffing *Makes about 8 cups*

The biggest hurdle to making this stuffing is to find sagey breakfast sausage that is not in a casing. Whether the casing is made of plastic or of natural skin, you could cook it forever, and it will *never* disappear. If you get a bite, it will ruin your meal. It is just an unpleasant reminder of the last time you gave a blow job using a prophylactic. You have to find sage sausage with no casing or else big sausage, not the teeny-peenie kind that will take you forever to squeeze the meat out of when you're talking about 4 pounds. Look in Hispanic-type stores and butcher shops, or if you don't mind squeezing the teeny-peenies, go ahead—have a good time.

After you have found the sausage, the next big hurdle comes when you cook it. As you brown the sausage, you are going to discover that it is probably 70 percent fat. It is *loaded.* The fat just pours out of it when it cooks, but you have to leave the fat in the pan. You can't drain it no matter how tempted you are to do so. And here is the clincher: Just as you start to feel a really strong impulse to drain some of the fat, not only do you have to leave the fat there, but you have to add a stick of butter to the pan. You *have* to do it. The fat is what makes the stuffing taste good. When people order something with stuffing, no matter that the stuffing is supposed to be an accoutrement, what they really want to do is eat stuffing. So whenever I give stuffing, I give a lot of it. It's like bacon: No matter how much I put

on a plate, the one thing I can count on is that it will all get eaten.

Ingredients
2 extra-large eggs
12 ounces stuffing mix
¾ cup walnut halves, broken with your fingers (I find that walnuts are not the sturdiest of travelers; they go bad quickly. If I buy them in halves, rather than pieces, and then crush them as I use them, they are less likely to be stale.)
2 to 3 fresh sage leaves, crumbled or chopped
1½ pounds sage sausage, meat squeezed out of the casing if necessary
6 tablespoons butter
1 big yellow Spanish onion, chopped (about 2 cups)
2 stalks celery, diced (about ½ cup; more if you really like celery)
2 to 3 cups warm Chicken Stock (page 123) or any stock or broth

Instructions
Whisk the eggs in a large mixing bowl. Add the stuffing mix, walnuts, and sage leaves. Set aside.

Cook the sausage in a large sauté pan over high heat, mushing it around in the pan to break it up while it cooks. Cook until the sausage is browned all over and looks done but is not quite cooked through. Add the butter, cutting it up in the pan with a spatula to make it melt faster. When the butter has melted, add the onion and celery, and cook until the onion is soft, 5 to 10 minutes. Stir in 1½ cups chicken stock; add more if necessary to obtain the consistency of a thick soup.

Pour the sausage mixture into the bowl with the stuffing mix. G'shmush it around and add more chicken stock, until you get the consistency of stuffing scooped out of a turkey.

To freeze, divide the stuffing into individual 10-ounce (or larger 1-pound) portions and put each portion in a plastic bag. Press down on the stuffing with the palm of your hand until it is about 1 inch thick. Before using, nuke the stuffing to warm, or bring it to room temperature on the countertop and heat it up in a saucepan over medium heat with a little butter or chicken stock until it's the temperature at which you want to eat it.

Teeny-peenie sage sausage

Chopping Onions

To chop onions, cut a cleaned onion in half on the axis so when you lay the onion down the stem is sticking straight up. Cut each onion half in half. Lay the onion so you see semicircles, and then cut to the thickness that you want the onions chopped. For finely chopped or minced onion, slice the onion as thin as you can. This isn't the conventional way to cut an onion. I like doing it this way not just because it's easier, but because when you chop things too much, the chopping squishes the molecular structure and takes away the crunch.

Shopsin's six-page menu, actual size

eggs with any toast

scrambled or fried	4.95	cheese	
poached on toast	5.95	melted over the	
six egg whites	6.95	eggs +$2	
soft boiled eggs (3min)toast soldiers 6.95			

egg special   8.95
2 eggs (scrambled or fried)
toast (white, wheat, rye)
three slices of bacon
thin french fries

pizza omelet, one topping 13.95
western ham omelet /cheese 14.95
western bacon omelet /cheese 12.95
chorizo open omelet   14.95
egg flop (plain flat omelet)   7.95
omelets-toast 6.95 (all egg whites+2.25)

fillings-anyside order@$1.25 each

crunchy hash, eggs, toast $14.95
1. bbq beef brisket 2. corned beef 3. smoked pork 4. pulled pork bbq 5. hopple popple 6. white trash chicken hash 7.pastrami 8.red flannel

MEAT-   SIDE ORDERS $3.95
bacon (maple glazed +$2), merguez (lamb or chicken), chorizo, turkey sausage, livermush* sausage (links or patties), beef chili, spam,virginia ham, turkey bacon, turkey kielbassa, thai chicken sausage, turkey hash patty, turkey, smoked pork butt, chicken, turkey, bbq brisket, ga pulled pork, sweet bbq pulled chicken, pulled turkey, pork scrapple,

VEGETARIAN-
vegan sausage, grilled bananas, cheese grits (+$2), grits, steamed spinach (+$2), acorn squash, grilled tomatoes, steamed vegetables, okra, fried onions, fried potatoes, artichoke, plantains, roast pepper, kashajalopaeno cheese grits *. +2, fried mushrooms, salad, corn, guacamole. corn, haricot vert, corn, collard, mixed vegetables, vegetable hash patty, beets

POTATOES
hash fried cubes, petal fries , mashed, cajun cubes* french fries, yam, garlic cheese potato skins (+$3), potato & onion puffs (+5), mashed yam, spanish fries* (+3)

CHEESES   (in eggs or omelets $2)
ricotta, swiss, cheddar, feta, american, jack, mozzarella, cream cheese, goat cheese, gruyere, gorgonzola, blue

toast - any of these with egg entrées: (2.95 for side order)
rye, black, wheat, sullivan squares, bagel, pita, baguette, corn bread, matzoh, efse, crumpets, flour tortilla, biscuits, ciabatta, corn tortilla, sourdough,1/2 garlic bread, sesame triad,muffins (blueberry, corn, banana, english),lwhite, farle, pizza bianca
butter; preserves: vegemite; sour cream, crm cheese, peanut butter, fluff, nutella

HIGHSCHOOL
creamy mushroom, sausage gravy, egg open sandwich 13.95

HIGHSCHOOL
creamy mushroom, sausage gravy, egg open sandwich 13.95

moon over miami
plain toast 5.95
grilled cheese

three sunnys on rice & cuban(ham) beans   8.95
(or vegan black beans)

CHILI & EGGS
meat 12.95
cubed meat 14.95
cheese, tortilla chips (beans or rice + $1)

huevos
motulenos 16.95
corn tortilla, bean puree, sunnys, red salsa, pulled pork bbq, melted jack, peas, plantains*

MEXICAN EGG DISHES

chorizo open omelet	14.95
egg burrito	8.95
ropa egg burrito (pork or beef)	12.95
sloppy joe egg burrito	11.95
egg burrito cheese melt	9.95
hash brown egg burrito	10.95
egg quesadilla	8.95
egg nachos (beans?)	9.95
huevos rancheros	11.95
migas (casserole)	12.95
egg enchiladas chipotle	12.95
chilequilles	12.95
egg guacamole	11.95
ropa vieja huevos (pork or beef)	15.95
egg encacahuatadas*	12.95
guacamole fried rice	15.95
taco basket chili, eggs	12.95

3 EGG ENCHILADAS (mix and match)   14.95
chicken,cheese,avocado,bean, spinach, chorizo, turkey bacon,fried onions,mushrooms, artichokes, haricot vert, chili, bbq turkey, pork bacon, vegan sausage, cuban

BLISTERS ON MY SISTERS   full-9.95 small-6.95
(corn tortillas, bean, rice/vegetable mixture, covered with 2 fried eggs, broiled with cheese until it bubbles and browns)
special blisters on my sisters full-12.95 small-9.95
1. vegan sausage,vegan black beans
2. bacon hoppin' john, black-eye peas
3. chorizo, cuban black bean,ham
4. all meat chili, onion, ranchero veg
5. chicken,avocado,gumbo veg

Sweet Potato Latkes 13.95
"gotta" sauce or apple sauce

Country Scrambled   12.95
(eggs & add-ins mixed while cooking)

BLISTERS ON MY STUFFING   10.95
(2 sunny side eggs over stuffing, lite melted cheese)

apple pecan	bbq pork black bean
cornbread gumbo	beef brisket tomato
sausage walnut	turkey sage

BLISTERS ON MY CASSEROLE   10.95
(2 sunny side eggs, bechamel vegetables, browned crust; choose one) bacon + 2.25
artichoke hearts, haricot vert, okra, asparagus, mushrooms, onions, peas, spinach, corn, potato, bell peppers, chipotle peppers, broccoli, cauliflower

corn / cheddar / chorizo
avocado /gruyere/spinach
sausage/ potato/ jack cheese
bacon,chicken,avocado,bleu
macaroni/cheese/broccoli
chicken/ mushrooms/ onions
tomato/mozarella/ricotta
chicken/jack/fried onions
turkeybacon/tomato/spinach
gorgonzola/avocado/arugula
artichoke, goat cheese, tomato
chicken/cheddar/bacon
vegan sausage/ corn/ jack
chicken/potatoes/blue cheese
halloumi/spinach/pignoli
turkey sausage/cheddar/tomato
chipotle/fried onions/avocado
bbq pork/ pecans/ cheddar
spaetzel, chicken, gruyere
pastrami, swiss, mushrooms
haricot vert, goat cheese,peas
cx merguez,irish beans,tomato

EGGS CORDON BLEU 9.95
(eggs & cheese in a crepe, breaded, fried)
special cordon bleu 12.95
ham and swiss
sausage and jack
bacon and cheddar
chicken gruyere
mushrooms, onions mutzi
merguez, feta
bbq beef brisket and cheddar
bbq pulled pork and jack

---

3 Tiger Paws 7.95
mini egg-cheese buns, fries
add 2.95 for:
bacon
tomato
avocado
fried onions
turk. bacon
mushrooms
sausage

I'll scratch your back if you scratch min

asian vegetable dumpling
bulghur mint tomato
stage coach (wagon wheel pasta, beans)
ham, butter dumpling split pea
cream of crisped onions
shrimp tomato gumbo
chicken and sausage cream

-Pete Variations- 3 poached eggs on:
"pete" - jalapaeno, jack, garlic baguette 8.95
sneaky pete - "pete"+ bacon crumbles, tomato, scallions 11.95
pete moss - "pete" + vegan sausage, tomato, scallions 11.95
pete's sake - cilantro chutney, jack, garlic sour dough; 12.95
chicken, pignoli, scallions on top
pedro-chipotle, cheddar; jicama, chorizo, onion, cilantro top 13.95
pasquale - arugula, mozzarella, olive oil, garlic sullivan street
square bread; shrimp, tomato, parsley on top 14.95

BLUES BROTHERS SPECIAL 13.95
three eggs, cubed cheese fried potatoes, greens + one:
vegan sausage; bacon; sausage; turkey bacon; pork
sausage; fried onions; fried mushrooms, all meat chili;
Georgia bbq* (brisket, chix, turkey, pulled pork, sliced pork)

SAVORY PAIN PERDU** (with sour cream) 9.95
1.cilantro 2.chipotle 3.jalapaeno 4. ga bbq 5.habanero 6.sesame

Britters 13.95
Gibraltar oatmeal farle, lamb merguez, eggs, fried onions
London tomato,Branston beans, crumpets, cheddar scrambled
Irish black toast, kippered herring, tomatoes, bacon fried eggs +3

ROLL YOUR OWN ROCKETS 12.95
steamed corn tortillas, sour cream, salsa. and any 3 (three):
eggs, bacon, sausage, avocado, chili,cheese, chicken, beans,
fried onions, haricot vert, fried mushrooms, bbq beef brisket
chicken merguez, chorizo, pork bbq, smoked turkey, fries,
steamed vegetables, gumbo greens, vegan sausage, beets

cereals
oatmeal- 6.95 dried fruit & nuts 7.95 fresh fruit 8.95
ashura - dried fruit, nuts, rice, fruit, white beans,
rose water, bulghur wheat 9.95
granola - plain- 5.95 dried fruit & nuts 7.95 fresh fruit 9.95
grits- plain- 3.95 dried fruit & nuts 5.95 fresh fruit 7.95
polenta plain- 4.95 mushroom/onion cream 7.95 pecan chicken 9.95

---

cantaloupe 3.45
grapefruit 2.45

breakfast menu

grilled tomato, goat cheese, bagel 7.95

toasted bagel, nova. cream cheese 7.95

NYPOUTINE 12.95
french fries, rich gravy, cheese curds plus:
1. ga bbq pork , onions
2. bbq brisket chili, onions

new pancakes 9.95
brown sugar banana

empanadas 9.95
1.cheese & eggs
2.chili & cheese

EGG SANDWICH 8.95
three scrambled eggs
melted cheese on seven
grain toast with:
ham;bacon; sausage;
chicken; turkey, chili
extras: tomato, avocado,fried
onions or mushrooms + 2.25

---

rules- 1. limit four people per group 2. no cell phone use 3. one meal per person minimum

PANCAKES OR FRENCH TOAST

plain	$6.95
almond smoothie	8.95
almond crunch	10.95
almond butter	11.95
apple cinnamon	11.95
blackberries	12.95
bacon	10.95
banana	8.95
banana, chocolate, nut	10.95
berries and flowers	11.95
black & blueberries	12.95
blackberry blues	12.95
blueberry	9.95
blueberry lavender	12.95
blueberry & raspberry	11.95
charoset	10.95
cheese & eggs	10.95
cheddar french fry	11.95
chipotle corn *	9.95
chocolate almond butter	12.95
chocolate cashew butter	12.95
chocolate chip	7.95
chocolate coconut	10.95
chocolate peanut butter	10.95
chorizo, corn	10.95
cinnamon	8.95
cinnamon raisin	9.95
coconut	7.95
coconut sweet rice	9.95
cranberry orange	9.95
cream cheese & banana	10.95
dates & almonds	11.95
dried fruit nuts	10.95
french toast filled crepe	11.95
french fry cheese toss	12.95
granola	9.95

major pancakes 14.95

*ho cakes-corn meal, pignoli,caramel hearts
*slutty cakes-pumpkin / pbutter, pistachio, cinn
*giant glazed apples, nuts crisp kake
*ga bbq chicken, monterey jack cheese, masa
*turkey pumpkin with vegetables, cran/maple
*belgian 4 berry fruit stack, whipped cream

matzoh brei 9.95

dutch pancake (one large thin) 9.95
open dutch pancake with: 12.95
mixed fruit; apple cinnamon;
coconut; pineapple; banana;
black & blueberry; goat cheese;
artichoke, tomato/arugula;
mushrooms & onions;
tomato/pesto/cheese;
banana, mixed chocolate chips;
turkey, mushroom gravy (+$2);
eggs, bacon, hash fries (+$2)

pancake /french toast glazes: 1.95
maple ; caramel; cinnamon, sugar,
brown sugar, cream cheese frosting,

burrito french toast 12.95

fried cornflake bananas
blackberry sweet ricotta
fried granola plantain
sweet lime chevre pignoli
raisin pineapple banana
mango cream chse
fried crunchy avocado

WAFFLES 6.95 toppings - 2.25 each

banana, cinnamon apple, mango,
peach, raspberry, blueberry, raisins,
cranberry, maple walnut, grapefruit,
coconut orange, pineapple, ice
cream, lemon ricotta, pecan caramel,
fried chicken, lime ricotta, sundried
cherries, strawberry topping, custard
blackberry, raspberry

broiled mushrooms
stuffed with eggs,
bacon, fried onions,
cheddar   12.95

12" non-dairy chutney crepes

coriander	8.95
mango	9.95
fresh spinach	11.95
peach	10.95
raspberry	10.95
fresh arugula	11.95

bread pudding french toast

regular (cubed baguette)	11.95
cowboy (sausage &cheese)	14.95
nowboy(vegan sausage &cheese)	14.95
ohboy! (fried mushrooms, onions)	12.95
ahoy boy (shrimp, avocado, jack)	14.95
chowboy (chicken, pecan, spinach)	14.95

potato, egg, cheese boats

bacon, gucamole,
chicken, chili, 11.95

BRUNCH COMBINATION PLATTERS 18.95

A. Acorn squash, chicken salad, spinach pancakes . scrambled eggs. toast

crepes

plain	6.95
cinnamon	7.95
fruit (pick1or2)	9.95

mango, pineapple,
dried cherry, peach,
banana, raspberry,
blueberry, apple
lingonberry, lemon
lime, blackberry,
cranberry, pear,
orange, grapefruit
8.95
white chocolate
dark chocolate
fluffernutter
fluffernutella
chocolate coconut
spinach, ched, rice
10.95
ham & cheese
chicken gruyere
chorizo bean
chili, cheese
sausage, cheese
bacon & eggs
8.95

Waffle french toast 10.95

lime ricotta pancakes 12.95
macaroni & cheese 11.95
macadamia 10.95
macadamia white choc 12.95
mango 9.95
mint chocolate 11.95
mixed berries 12.95
mixed fruit (in & on top) 12.95
oatmeal (toasted) 10.95
orange ricotta pancakes 12.95
peach 10.95
peach raspberry 11.95
peanut 7.95
peanuts, chocolate 10.95
peanut butter and jelly 10.95
pear pignoli 11.95
pecan 9.95
peppermint smoothie 8.95
pignoli 8.95
pineapple coconut 11.95
pistachio 9.95
pistachio white chocolate 11.95
plantain,cinnamon, parm 12.95
post modern 12.95
potato pancakes (fried) 13.95
pumpkin 11.95
raspberry 10.95
red rose blackberry 12.95
silver dollar pancakes 12.95
spinach walnut 10.95
sundried cherry 9.95
sundried cranberry 9.95
walnut 8.95
white chocolate almonds 11.95
white mint chocolate chip 12.95
whole wheat french toast 10.95

F. Macaroni 'n cheese, 3 cinnamon raisin pancakes, vegan sausages, salad
G. Blackberry pancakes, pecan french toast, turkey bacon, turkey sausage
H. Oatmeal cakes, branston tomato salad, Heinz beans, eggs
I. Egg burrito adobe, coconut pancakes, vegi-sausage, cranberry salsa
J. English muffin, eggs, bacon, cheese, maple sour cream, mini blues
K. 1/2 banana pancakes, 1/2 cinnamon raisin french toast, bacon, sausages
L. Krakatoa-scrambled eggs, sausage potato volcano, lava sauce, toast
M. Poached eggs, english muffin with ham/tomato/scallion, cinnamon currant pancakes, pumpkin butter, french fries
N. Ropa vieja huevos, tortillas, coconut/choc pancakes, guacamole
O. Open spinach, string bean, jack burrito omelet, mini coconut pancakes, spinach tortillas, spinach fried mushroom salad
P. Jambalaya-chicken, shrimp, chorizo, eggs, corn muffin, slaw
Q. fried shrimp guacamole, chili/egg quesadilla, caramel roll-up
R. Turkey, mushroom sage gravy, sausage walnut stuffing, cranberry sauce, scrambled eggs, seven grain toast
S. Lite fried chicken and vegetables, three cinnamon raisin pancakes, scrambled eggs, rye toast
T. Three black & blueberry pancakes,1/2 white chocolate french toast, steamed baby spinach, vegan sausages
U. Catfish hash** poached eggs, corn fritters, toast
V. Peach chutney nondairy crepe, vegan sausage, mufeletta chopt salad
W. Cranberry ricotta pancakes, fried artichokes, cumbak sauce, eggs
X. Fried mac'n cheese, comeback sauce, sausage cakes, eggs, toast
Y. Shrimp, bacon, sausage cheese hash mountain, eggs, toast
Z. Sausage & egg slyders, chili french fries, bacon french toast (+$2)
AA Smoked sliced pork bbq*, corn fritters, cranberry ricotta, eggs
BB Turkey kielbassa, fried pickles, blackberry pancakes, fried eggs
CC Grilled chicken, sauteed greens, poached eggs, pizza bianca
DD Mac'n cheese hamburger, egg poutine, salad
EE Guacamole BLT, cinnamon sundried cherry pancakes, banana grill
FF Vegan sausage poutine, peppermint french toast, cheddar scrambled
GG Mashed potato, boudin noir onion gravy, eggs, toast, haricot vert
HH 3 Sliders, chili frech fries, chocolate chip pancakes
JJ Banana burrito french toast, potato nik, blackberry chutney, eggs
KK chicken & lamb merguez, egg tabbuleh, tahina, zatar nan

ORANGE JULIE

5.95

DRINKS 2.25
7-up
apple juice
cranberry drink
pepsi / diet pepsi
ginger beer
iced coffee
iced tea
plain
lemon tea
green tea (splenda)
peppermint (syrup)
sweet tea (sugar)
with frozenfruit (3.95)
limeade
lemonade
lavender lemonade
lime rickey
poland water
red birch beer
tropicana oj
tomato juice
pommegranite juice
hot coffee or tea   3.50
red bull   3.50
all beer   4.50

nondairy slushy 5.95
(ice, juice, fruit, syrup)
pina colada, lime, lemon
pineapple,apple, peach
coco lip flip, raspberry,
strawberry, cranberry,
blueberry, orange almond,
banana,peanut butter,
pumpkin, avocado,mango,
grapefruit, mamey, jicama

iced tea- frozen peaches, raspberries 4.95

fresh squeezed juices
orange- smll 1.95 med 3.95 lge 4.95 grapefruit-5.95
fresh squeezed citrus sodas 3.95
grapefruit;lime;orange; lemon (juice, seltzer, syrup)

fruit smoothies
(yogurt or milk,or soy milk
ice, fruit juice , syrup) 5.95
coconut
pina colada
cranberry
peach
pineapple
blackberry
cherry
lingonberry
banana

milk shakes/ malteds
(ice cream,milk,syrup) 5.95
almond
avocado
banana
banana mint
blackberry
blueberry
blue raspberry
butter pecan
butterscotch

BREAKFAST NAME PLATES
ABRAHAM well cooked pastrami and eggs, rye toast $10.95
ALTA COCKER well cooked brisket and eggs, pumpernickel toast $11.95
ALABAMA- grilled spam, onion, cheese in scrambled $9.95
ANDRÉ- cream of garlic goat cheese poutine, scrambled eggs $11.95
ANGUS- kippers, rice, rolled tomato eggs, english muffin $14.95
AUNTIE scrambled eggs, blue cheese, avocado, spinach $9.95
BAYOU   scrambled eggs okra, salsa, cheddar $10.95
BILLY-BOB poached eggs, white toast, livermush, gravy $11.95
BON AMI- bacon, cheddar creamed corn over eggs, cubed baguette $11.95
BRUCE- Jersey bacon & cheese flat omelet, toast $8.95
BUTCH- beef stew over eggs on toasted english $13.95
CAIN & ABEL- corned beef, pastrami, eggs, cheese, rye toast $13.95
CAPOTE- chunky beef gumbo, corn bread, poached eggs in a bowl $12.95
CHAVA-eggs, alfalfa, cheddar, avocado, russian, on 7 grain toast $10.95
CHE cuban rice, guacamole, poached eggs, chili tomato cream $11.95.
CHIC-maple glazed squash, poached eggs, chopt veggies and vegan sausage $13.95
CHICKADEE- scrambled, chicken, bacon, avocado, toast $10.95
CITY ISLAND- onion saute, nova lox, scrambled eggs, toast $10.95
CLOUDY seared egg jalopaeno jack roll up, corn tortillas $8.95
COLUMBUS- arugula, walnut, gorgonzola crostini, poached eggs $11.95
CYPRUS- halloumi, well scrambled pork & eggs, sour dough toast $12.95
DAVE scrambled cheddar, cooked together, any toast $6.95
DEBORAH vegetables, bulghur wheat, tahina , zatar pita $11.95
DIANE poached eggs on garlic, cheese baguette $8.95
DIEGO poached eggs, poutine (fries, gravy & cheese curds) $10.95
DIXIE biscuits, eggs, white gravy $9.95
DIXIE SUE-"dixie"with pork or vegan sausage; pork or turkey bacon; $12.95
DIABOLIQUE- 3 chocolate chip pancakes, 1/2 cinnmon raisin french toast $10.95
DOMINIQUE- 4 plain pancakes, bacon or sausage $8.95
EMILIA- egg salad, bacon, grilled tomato, toast sandwich $10.95
ESTHER nova lox, scrambled eggs, cream cheese, toast $11.95
FAIRIE oatmeal pancakes, bacon fried eggs, flat biscuits $11.95
FELLINI tomato, garlic bread, ricotta & egg casserole $10.95
FLACO chili and eggs over tortilla chips, shredded cheddar $8.95
GAINESVILLE- hash browns american cheese, over easy eggs $9.95
GARY scrambled eggs, peas, mozzarella $8.95
GERALD scrambled eggs, fried spaetzle, bacon, peas $13.95
GOLDIN HAZE sunnies, cheddar, bacon, grilled baguette $10.95
GRAVEYARD STEW mushroom mire poix gravy, eggs, cubed toast $11.95
HUSSEIN- foul muddamus, pita panni, cheese kurds, tahina sauce $11.95
ILIANA mango salsa, avocado, eggs, refried rice*, corn chips $10.95
JAZZ- scrambled, asparagus, truffle butter, gorgonzola $10.95
JULES- grilled chicken merguez, arugula, goat cheese eggs, toast $12.95
JOEL-3 granola pancakes, eggs, fried mushrooms, peach chutney $12.95
JOSE fried white bean, jalopaeno arepas,+ eggs, salad* $10.95
JUAN FLOP seared eggs, cheese, chili, toast $8.95
JUANITA chicken, cilantro, cabbage, avocado over eggs, tortilla chips $12.95

raspberry
strawberry
blueberry
morir sonando
(oj, cream, lime juice, vanilla)
horchata
banana julio
(cinn, cream, banana,ice)
grapefruit lassi

choc. peanut butter
coconut
coffee
cranberry
fluffer nutter
grape
grapefruit
green tea
lavender
lemon lime
lemon ricotta
lingonberry/banana
mamey
mango
mango-raspberry
maple walnut
nutella mocha
orange
orange mint
peach
peach-raspberry
peanut butter
pina colada
pineapple
pistachio
pomegranate
pumpkin pie
raspberry
strawberry
three berry
vanilla
white chocolate
white chocolate mint

egg creams 3.95
chocolate, vanilla,
cherry,strawberry
(syrup,seltzer, milk)

floats 3.95
red cow, purple cow,
brown cow, green cow

fountain sodas
(syrup,seltzer) 2.25
lemon,grape,cherry,
lime,mint,lavender,sour
cherry,orange, maple,
vanilla, chocolate,
strawberry, almond

DESSERTS 7.95
baby banana split
cajaeta crepe
choc chip crepe
cinnamon donuts
ebelskivers
nutella fluff crepe
ice cream sundae
bread pudding
crunchy bananas

MALTHOUSE 3 poached eggs & cubed toast $7.95
MACON- eggs, turkey bacon, corn bread $8.95
MARA scrambled, truffle butter, cream cheese $8.95
MARBLEHEAD soft scrambled, corn, cheddar $8.95
MARCELLE- scrambled tofu, vegetable curry, basmati rice $10.95
MASSIMO-eggs, grilled zucchini, cheddar, tomato,on ciabatta $11.95
MONDO GAMBA scrambled, shrimp, jack salsa,flour tortillas $12.95
MONTY black & blueberry pancakes, chicken merguez, cranberry sour creme $11.95
MR. OSE english muffin, turkey panchetta, egg whites, cheddar $9.95
MURPHY bacon, sweet beans, over easy, fresh tomato, garlic farle $11.95
MT FUJI poached eggs, grits, steamed asian vegeables $13.95
MUSTAFAH- falafel, eggs, tahina, pita, lettuce,tomato, onion $11.95
NOAH Irish beans, onion, spinach, tomato, black toast $10.95
NORWEGIAN CREPES lingonberry preserves, egg, ricotta, $12.95
OLAF potato crepes with eggs, arugula and gruyere $11.95
PIERRE- fried onions & mushrooms, vegan sausage, goat cheese omelet, toast $13.95
PIAF eggs, gruyere sauce, fried onions on toast $10.95
PILAR grilled lamb merguez in hard scrambled eggs, pizza bianca $11.95
PIPERADE mixed peppers, onions, garlic, tomato, eggs on ciabatta $11.95
PLOUGHMAN eggs, cheddar, blood pudding, Branston pickle, ww tst $11.95
POTATO NIKS- niks, banana sour cream, scrambled eggs $12.95
RAJAH gyro meat, tahina, tabulleh, eggs on pita $13.95
RED- garlic, spinach mashed sweet potato wrap, tahina sauce $11.95
RISA three poached eggs, cubed buttered toast, grilled tomato $9.95
ROBBIE scrambled eggs, jack,corn,jalopaenos, corn tortillas $8.95
ROCKET- arugula, scrambled, gruyere, avocado $10.95
SABU poached eggs over curried chicken and spinach fritters $12.95
SAM - eggs, bacon, tomato, grilled cheese sandwich $11.95
SARASOTA well scrambled pulled pork and eggs, corn muffin $11.95
SERGIO spinach, eggplant, tomato, shrimp frittata, toast $14.95
SHAKSHUKA- garlic, tomato, eggs, parsley, parm casserole, lefse* $10.95
SHAWN chicken fried eggs, gumbo rice, 7 grain toast $11.95
SHIRLEY poached eggs over cubed BLT sandwich $11.95
SHRIMP LEFSE-avocado, jack, salsa, jalopaeno, parsley, garlic $13.95
S.O.S.- eggs, creamed chipped beef, on buttered toast $11.95
SQUAW EGGS-bacon, peppers, cheese, hominy $11.95
SVETLANA open face kielbassa potato blue cheese omelet $12.95
SWAN- maple glazed pumpkin, cheese quesadilla $11.95
SILLYCYBIN wild mushroom cream over poached eggs, 7 grain toast $12.95
TOM -TOM seared eggs filled with turkey patty stuffing, any toast $9.95
TONY- italian vegetable frittata with mozzarella $13.95
TWAIN- huckleberry Finnish crepes $11.95
TOULOUSE- boudin noir blue cheese cubed potato poutine, eggs $12.95
VIVA ZAPATA- chunky beef fried onion mole, sunnies cuban rice $13.95
UPTOWN- poached eggs, southern fried chicken cutlet, corn bread $14.95
WHITLEY seared eggs, chipotle, corn tortillas $8.95
XRATED- meatloaf, fried pickles & onions, gravy, eggs, toast $13.95
YOGI- rutabaga stuffed yam, salad, cup of tomato gumbo soup $12.95
ZACK-scrambled, cheddar melted on top, toast $6.95

all sandwiches
with salad or potato chips, french fries + $1.95

warm sliced meats 9.95

pastrami	smoked pork
chicken	corned beef
turkey	beef brisket
virginia ham	chorizo

salad sandwiches 8.95
egg; turkey; tuna, chicken

grilled cheese 5.95

meat balls 8.95
beef, vegan, turkey, meat loaf

reuben on rye toast 10.95
pastrami, corned beef, pork

shrimp po' boy 12.95

grilled chicken 9.95
plain, ga bbq, sweet red bbq,

peanut butter & jelly 5.95

blt on toast 8.95
bacon, lettuce, tomato (avocado +$2)

israeli on pita choose one: 8.95
falafel; gyro; tabbuleh

karmine killer 12.95
batter fried chicken, onions, peppers, mushrooms, ricotta cheese topping, on a toasted sesame bun

turkey cloud * 9.95
ga bbq hash patty on a bun

southern meat on a bun 8.95
livermush;scrapple; spam; fried turkey pull; chicken fried ham; pulled southern bbq*-
pork, chicken, turkey, brisket

beets, goat cheese 8.95

open sandwiches;gravy 14.95
Turkey, sausage stuffing, cranberry,mushrooms
Chicken, cornbread stuffing

NAMEPLATE SANDWICHES

algiers cx merguez, quinoa, spinach garlic bread** 12.95

amarillo- pulled pork, red salsa, monterey jack, garlic bread 12.95

andy's way- grilled chicken, avocado, turkeybacon, blue, black 12.95

audrey- eggs, tomato, avocado, swiss, white toast 10.95

booty taco fried eggplant, jack, garlic baguette ** 12.95

bridgette- chicken salad, avocado, tomato, garlic bread   11.95

bud curried greens, asian veggie, sesame bun *   9.95

candice - virginia ham, cheese, dill sauce, black bread   10.95

champ -grilled chicken, bacon, avocado, chipotle mayo, lett & tom   13.95

chaz - white turkey, cranberry, coleslaw, baguette   10.95

cheeseburger club - triple decker with bacon, lett, tomato 14.95

cobb- poached chicken, avocado, bacon, blue cheese   13.95

cuban- smoked pork, jack, ham, salsa, pressed sandwich* 12.95

daniel- grilled chicken, chili, jack, rye toast   12.95

danny diner beef stew sandwich 11.95

dickey- fowl ball (crunchy turkey) parmagiana   12.95

edmonton- tuna, cheddar, avocado, spicy garlic bread   11.95

eve - avocado, tomato, alfalfa, russian, 7 grain   8.95

fat darrell-chicken fingers, french fries, mutzi, marinara, club roll12.95

fandango vietnamese tabbuleh, falafel crumbles, zatar pita **   10.95

food fairie fried beets, turkey, goat cheese on ciabatta   12.95

Gallant- warm turkey, bacon, avocado, cranberry mayo, ciabatta 13.95

gidget- tuna, avocado, tomato, garlic bread   10.95

golda- knish, pot roast, mushroom/cherry gravy, cheddar 14.95

good boy fried baby artichokes and okra parmagiana   12.95

gregg- shrimp, cream cheese, cocktail sauce, garlic 7 grain 13.95

gulf pride- shrimp, avocado, cheddar garlic bread 14.95

gussy fried pickles, spinach, goat cheese, "come back" sauce* 12.95

high school hot turkey sandwich; mushroom gravy 11.95

homeboy blue cheese fried potato/chicken salad   12.95

hot brown- chicken, turkey bacon, american, gravy, toast 13.95

hyatt- tomato, avocado, salsa, cheddar,jack,cilantro 10.95

Indian summer-warm turkey, cran/mayo, spinach, avocado, ciabatta 13.95

irish-spinach, grilled tomato, beans, black toast 9.95

jj's way-grilled chicken, apple stuffing, slaw,7 grain 12.95

jewboy** -bbq brisket, grilled onions, swiss cheese 13.95

jolly smoked pork tenderloin, branston pickle, cheddar, crumpets   12.95

joseph - grilled turkey, jack, mexican garlic bread 11.95

kate-triple decker; turkey, bacon,swiss,lettuce, tomato 14.95

kenneth -turkey, ham, swiss, russian, slaw, pumpernickel 12.95

Kerwin- pulled pork, arugula, cheddar, fried onions,, cranberry 12.95

open face melted cheese 14.95
1. Chicken salad, bacon, sliced egg, jack
2. Chicken, mushroom, mustard sauce mutzi
3. Avocado russian,tomato, bacon, cheddar
4. Grilled eggplant, tomato basil, pignoli,mutzi
5. Chicken, grilled peppers, pesto, mutzi
6. Turkey, bacon, cranberry sauce, cheddar

turkey dinner special
light/dark, mushroom gravy, cranberry sauce, stuffing, potato 15.95

croque monsieur 10.95
gruyere & ham sandwich
bechamel sauce - (egg +$2)

triple deckers 14.95
(toast,lettuce,tomato)
1. fried shrimp, bacon, jack, tartar sauce
2. grilled chicken, swiss, guacamole, bacon
3.merguez, gruyere, bacon, blue cheese
4. poach chicken, turkey bacon, goat cheese

FAKES

bread choices-
baguette, rye, bagel, whole wheat, white, english muffin, crumpet, pita, black, ciabatta, sour dough, sesame bun, pizza bianca

3 hamburgers $6
3 cheeseburgers $7
2 double hamburgers $8
2 double cheeseburgers $9
french fries + $2.65

---

mecca II lamb merguez, tahina, fried onions, lettuce wrap* 12.95
mecca III daikon chicken, arugula, pignoli, lettuce roll 10.95
minda - chicken salad, turkey bacon, garlic rye, slaw 12.95
monte cristo- turkey, ham, swiss, battered meat and melted cheese 13.95
nuclear melt down - warm mixed meat and melted cheese 13.95
nuclear sub -sliced deli meats, swiss, hot peppers, herbs 13.95
oprah mashed and fried potatoes, horse radish, white toast 12.95
pan bagnat- tuna, egg, onion, tomato, vinaigrette, arugula 10.95
rooster - chicken salad,spicy cheddar garlic bread, avocado 12.95
savannah - pulled turkey, gumbo gravy, 7 grain toast, cran 11.95
sexy- warm chicken, ciabatta, swiss,capers, arugula, dijon,tomato 12.95
suny- mango chutney, avocado, chicken, lime j, cilantro whole wheat 11.95
tango sirracha chicken salad, bacon, 7 grain toast** 12.95
taos bean paté, guacamole, lettuce onion, jack, toast 10.95
t.bruno - turkey, tomato, sausage stuffing baguette 11.95
tamara - avocado, tomato, salsa, cheddar, jack, lime, 7 grain 9.95
turkey dinner- triple decker, stuffing, cranberry, sweet potato14.95
yetta knish grilled cheese 8.95
yucca- chunky sirloin beef and chicken chili, toast, cheddar 13.95

SALADS

arugula, turkey, gruyere-avocado, cranberry dressing 14.95
brown rice special- crudités, walnuts, cheesy rice 13.95
caesar- with or w/o anchovies 9.95
cheeseburger- what you'd expect, but cut up with greens 12.95
chef's- julienne cold cuts, sliced egg 11.95
chicken 10 ways 13.95
1. steamed 2. grilled 3. mayonaise 4. thai curry 5. daikon 6.asian cx waldorf 7.cobb 8. thai cobb 9. merguez acorn squash 10. mother and child reunion
gazpacho- finely chopped vegetables, tomato dressing 12.95
greek falafel- pita, feta, calamata, tahina, tabbuleh 13.95
gyro (beef)- pita, feta, calamata, tahina, tabbuleh 14.95
mexican caesar-chipotles, tortilla chards, cilantro, lime juice 9.95
mexican chef's- tortilla basket, meats and cheeses, avocado 14.95
pita feta, bulghur 13.95
tuna niçoise 13.95
turkey,bacon, swiss club cut up with greens 12.95
vegetable garden 11.95
waldorf 10.95

---

corn muffin, cuban gravy

sinwiches 5.95
fluffernutter, banananutter fluffernutella, maplenutter

sausages on a bun 9.95
chicken merguez*
lamb merguez*
thai chicken*
boudin noir
pork patty
turkey
grilled onions +2

spanish fried potatoes -
fried onions, jalopasnos 6.95

danish fried potatoes-
fried mushrooms, blue cheese 7.95

CHEESE STEAKS- 10.95
grilled onions, cheese baguette
1. philly- thinly sliced rib eye steak
2. texas- smoked bbq pulled beef brisket*
3. georgia- bbq pulled pork*
4. mott- thinly sliced chicken
5. LES- thinly sliced pastrami

SPECIAL GRILLED CHEESE 9.95
bacon,tomato, american
pork bbq, onions, cheddar*
eggs, bacon, american
guacamole, monterey jack
chicken, cheddar
fried onions, swiss
beets, gruyere
fried mushrooms, mozzarella
virginia ham, gruyere
chorizo, chipotle, cheddar*

african avocado tomato* V   11.95
african green curry V   9.95
apple butternut squash V
asian dumplings + vegetables   11.95
  pork, chicken , vegetable V
avocado cheese tortilla V   10.95
baked bacon garlic cream V   11.95
beef barley   10.95
beef pepperpot*   12.95
blackbean vegan sausage V   11.95
bok choy bop V   9.95
brazilian chicken, garlic , rice   14.95
burnt garlic tomato zucchini V   10.95
cabbage, apple curry V   9.95
carrot ginger orange V   10.95
cabbage, potato, pea V   9.95
cashew tomato, cream V   10.95
cat fish gumbo   12.95
cheeseburger soup (french fries) 12.95
chicken soups 10.95
curry, gumbo, angelhair,broccoli dijon, burrito, cheddar bacon, feta spinach, mushroom marsala creme, asian vegetable, cambodian chicken cream, pesto cream, spaetzel vegetable,spinach blue cheese, asian vegetable, tortilla avocado, vegetable, wild barley, coconut rice, bananas 12.95
cilantro,spinach thin dumplings 11.95
jambalaya + shrimp, chorizo 14.95
chili tomato V 11.95
chorizo 10.95
wild rice, black bean garlic, gumbo, chunk beef gumbo 12.95
corn chowder V   9.95
cream of any vegetable   10.95
cuban bean polenta melt   11.95
danbury chowder (bacon?)
  clam, shrimp, or catfish   11.95
eggplant caponata V   10.95
feta tomato tortilla V   9.95
florida peanut V   8.95
fried burrito chicken; shrimp; beef   12.95
fried asian dumpling   12.95
  chicken,pork,vegetable V
ginger scallion, broccoli, cauliflower 10.95

yin/yang soup combination 14.95

choose soup here
szechwan shrimp*
mango chicken lime
nigerian beef stew
grilled cilantro chicken
rutabaga pumpkin cream
plaintain pulled turkey
turkey meatball stew
corn, masa, mushroom
asparagus blue cheese
sausage and peppers
patsy's cashew mushroom
macadamia chicken, cherry
jamaican vegetable gumbo*
sweet potato cream curry
chorizo cabbage potato
vegan sausage black bean
thai chicken pistachio curry
GA pork bbq ranchero
cuban chorizo bean
cream of tomato
manhattan clam chowder
smoked beef brisket bbq

choose rice here
tofu/pea/peanut
mixed fresh fruit
fried onion
cuban black bean
guacamole
gumbo dirty rice
dried fruit, nuts
spinach coriander
pea, peanut, curry
hot vegan sausage
coconut banana
artichoke tomato
pistachio ricotta
beef sloppy joe
eggplant caponata
fried mushrooms
mango chutney
string bean tomato
salsa refried cheese
artichoke curry
spinach green bean
goat cheese pesto

burgers burgers

7oz hamburger, toasted bun 6.95
american cheeseburger 7.95
deluxe cheeseburger, fries 10.95
bacon burger 9.95
bacon cheeseburger 10.95
chili burger 9.95
chili cheeseburger 11.95
6 oz slyder
steamed cheeseburger 9.95
chicken fried burger 11.95
Reuben burger 9.95
Ciabatta- (gruyere, capers,arugula, dijon) 11.95
Ploughman (Branston pickle,cheddar) 9.95
Loco moco-rice, onion gravy,egg 11.95
Maco loco- mac'n cheese sauce 12.95
Frenchburger(bleu, dijon, baguette) 10.95
Patty melt (rye toast,onions,cheese) 10.95
stuffed burgers 8.95
chipotle**
raw jalopaeno**
cheddar
other 8.95
thai beefburger**
jamaican jerk**
thai chickenburger**
turkey burger
vegetarian burgers 6.95
thai falafel burger*
jamaican falafel*
falafel burger
vegan burger
vegan black bean

bun/ess   10.95
hamburger smothered mushrooms and onions on spinach

**KEN'S IDEA 11.95
3 fried chicken parmagiana on mini buns, french fries**

jack's idea 8.95
fries +3 mini grilled cheese sandwiches

slyders grilled onions, french fries
3 mini-cheeseburgers 9.95
3 mini-bacon cheeseburgers 11.95
3 smoked bbq pork, cheese 11.95
  (also beef brisket, chicken, turkey)
3 mini-sausage cheeseburgers 10.95

french fries and.........
cup 3.95   bowl 5.95 cheese +$2
bacon & cheddar 9.95
chili & cheese 10.95
buffalo sauce * 6.95
poutine (curds and gravy) 9.95

lunch specials lunch

with soup or salad or fries
sandwiches on a bun
7.95
tuna salad

lunch special soups
cups 6.95 bowls 9.95
arugula tomato
asian dumplings-

...red tomatoes (corn bak sauc) 5.55
mac'n cheese puffs 8.95
potato puffs 9.95
fowl balls 10.95

2 hot dogs, fries (one toping) 9.95
kraut, chili, cheese, coleslaw, beans, guacamole, fried onions, onion relish

kid's menu $3.95
hamburger, eggs, pasta, blt, mac-cheese, PB&J, tuna, hot dog, pancakes, taco, grilled cheese, fluffernutter

grilled cheese sandwich 6.95
american, swiss, gruyere, cheddar, mozzarella, goat, crm cheese, montery jack
1.95 for- bacon; tomatoes; avocado; grilled onions or mushrooms

ATKINS STYLE FOOD
11 oz burger, salad 8.95
large bacon cheeseburger 12.95
chili cheeseburger, baby spinach 14.95
chicken cutlet parmagiana 16.95

LUNCH

served wednesday thru friday only
on Saturday and Sunday please ask
your wait person if it is available

chicken & rice
chicken wild rice
cuban black bean
chili con carne
garlic bean
gumbo
jamaican gumbo*
mushroom barley
hot pierogie
lite lentil
pea-leek
pesto tomato
potato curry
quinoa coriander
ranchero
sesame udon
spinach bean
spinach wild rice
stage coach
string bean tomato
tomato ravioli
tomato rice
turkey gumbo
turkey meatballs
vegan black bean
vegan meatball

veggie burger
falafel burger
vegan blackbean burger
mr.softee
hamburger
turkeyburger
veggie meatballs
grilled cheese
chicken salad
tuna melt
bronx pulled turkey
italian blt
9.95
ga bbq pork or beef
ga bbq chicken
jamaican falafel**
turkey kielbasa
grilled chicken
beef sloppy joe
turkey sloppy joe
cheese burger
jerk chicken**

10.95
lunch BLT
meat loaf parm
chicken bbq cranberry
turkey in the straw
pastrami reuben
corned beef reuben
chicken(pulled) parm
shrimp parmigiana
crisp beef tacos (2)
chicken cheddar reuben 11.95

burritos 11.95
beef, shrimp, chicken
vegetable, pork
turkey curry
cashew sweet rice
vegan black bean
tuna noodle casserole

hot broccoli, dijon* v 8.95
lentil 9.95
madras chicken or shrimp* 12.95
manhattan chowder (bacon?)
  clam, shrimp, or catfish 11.95
minestrone 9.95
  vegetaria, cacciatore,genovese
mojo cactus, parmesan v 11.95
matzoh ball 7.95
  chicken & vegetables 12.95
mulligatawny chicken or shrimp 11.95
wild mushroom cream v 10.95
oxtail turnip 12.95
new england chowder (bacon?)
  clam, shrimp, or catfish 12.95
nigerian dumpling curry v 10.95
pastina vegetable v 9.95
pea, bacon, ham, mire poix 10.95
pea-leek butter dumplings v 9.95
pear walnut spinach v 10.95
peruvian shrimp avocado* 12.95
pistachio red chicken curry* 15.95
portobella cashew v 9.95
potato leek (creamy?) v 9.95
quesadilla cabbage v 10.95
ray's chicken garlic angelhair 11.95
roasted eggplant tomato basil v 10.95
saigon shrimp, bacon, threads 13.95
sausage (vegan) mushroom v 10.95
senegalese chicken or shrimp 12.95
sesame turnip barley v 10.95
shrimp 11.95
bisque or cheddar corn chowder
southwest corn chowder* v 10.95
spanish garlic and egg 11.95
spicy pea vegetable* v 10.95
spicy pumpkin tomato* v 9.95
spinach potato leek creme v 10.95
stew soups- 12.95
  beef, chicken,shrimp,vegan sausage
sweet potato vegetable v 10.95
Thai * 11.95
  lettuce thin noodle, chicken thin noodle, spinach cream curry, coco rice, fried dumpling cream chicken
macadamia chowder
tomato 11.95
  mushroom basil, cream + cheese
  croutons, vegetable
wild mushroom cream v 11.95

TEX-MEX

NACHOS (beans?) 8.95
extras+3
artichokes, philly steak, chorizo, mushroom, eggs & bacon chicken, guacamole, chili,

no rice burrito bags 6.95
cheese hand held burrito, + one item: beef, cuban bean, eggs, chicken, vegan black bean, spinach, chicken, arugula

burritos - flour tortillas filled
with rice, cheese, beans and greens
8.95
beef chili
vegan black bean
cuban black bean
vegetable curry
9.95

avocado, spinach
vegan meatballs
mushroom arugula
turkey curry
11.95
sloppy joe
chorizo
steamed chicken
huevos ranchero
pulled bbq pork
corn, yam, pumpkin(no rice)
12.95
pecan chicken wild rice
cashew, spinach brown rice
shrimp; or chunky beef
grilled chicken or smoked pork

burrito cheese melt
1.95 extra

make it a potato burrito
(potato instead of rice, potato flour tortillas 2)
2.95 extra

THE DANNY BURRITO- fried onions, black beans, jack, avocado, spinach, basmati rice, fried mushrooms 14.95

TACOS 10.95
crisp corn tacos (3)
soft corn tacos (3)
flour tacos (2)
chili, turkey, chicken, shrimp, egg; cheesy steak, pulled pork, sloppy joe, spinach-black bean

---

ENCHILADAS
carmine st beef 10.95
carmine st cheese 9.95
steamed chicken 10.95
grilled chicken   12.95
asparagus cheese 12.95
bbq pork black bean 11.95
corn, yam, pumpkin 11.95
spinach collard wild rice 13.95
pecan cx wild rice creme 14.95
shrimp encacahuatadas 16.95
avocado, spinach, jack 13.95
string bean tomato salsa 10.95

ENCHILADA SPECIAL
choose any 3 $12.95
(chicken, mango, eggs, cuban bean, avocado, turkey, spinach, vegan bean, cheese, beef chili, asparagus, peas

mexican main courses 15.95
baja bbq turkey (peppers, jack, chili, mashed potato)
chicken wild rice fiesta
confetti fried spaghetti with chorizo
chicken Fajitas
moon pie meatloaf, mexi-rice, guacamole
taco fried chicken, avocado slaw, refried rice
taco fried shrimp, avocado slaw, refried rice
chicken, chili, cheese, pecan rice, baked bananas

queso cremoso wraps 10.95
(cream cheese, lettuce shred, flour tortilla)
chicken, cocktail sauce
smoked pork salsa rojo*
bacon guacamole
turkey, salsa verde*
chorizo, cilantro chutney

---

quesadillas
cheese 8.95 beef chili 10.95
steamed chicken 10.95
grilled chicken   11.95
turkey black bean 12.95
chorizo or shrimp 11.95
black bean   9.95
pecan cx wild rice 13.95
ga pork bbq   11.95
pizza   12.95
haricot vert garlic 9.95
beef cheesy steak 11.95
chicken mango chutney 12.95
7 layer chicken 16.95

BEEF CHILI
(all meat, served with cheese and home made corn tortillas)
cup 7.95 bowl 10.95

cheese 8.95
empanadas

---

pot pies in a bowl 15.95
(15min)
chicken, beef, turkey, mushroom vegetable, cheese with bacon or ham and eggs

appetizers   8.95
kush (vegetable salad)
foul muddames
burmese hummus
Thai green curry puree
4 mac'n cheese pancakes

2 jamaican beef patties* 9.95

stew pot 14.95
beef, chicken, turkey, vegan meatball, oxtail, hot dog kraut, catfish

· buffalo wings 10.95
· buffalo fingers 9.95

macaroni & cheese 8.95
american, cheddar, jack, blue, gorgonzola, swiss, mozzarella, gruyere
2.25 extra-spinach, haricot vert, bacon, fried onions or mushrooms, ham, smoked pork butt

cheese garlic bread	6.95
pesto garlic bread	4.95
sundried tomato, basil	7.95
garlic, basil,cheese	6.95
chicken, pecan, jack	9.95
pear, prosciutto,pignoli	8.95
fresh tomato, basil	7.95
fried mushrooms	9.95
bacon, avocado	9.95
texas chili, cheddar	8.95
shrimp, shallot, dijon	12.95
chipotle cheese	7.95
pistachio pesto	6.95
asparagus pignoli	9.95

PARTY OF FIVE   Robert Hershon

you could put a chair at the end
or push the tables together
but dont bother
This banged-up little restaurant
where you would expect no rules at all
has a firm policy against seating
parties of five
And you know you are
a party of five
It doesn't matter if one of you
offers to leave or if
you say you could split into
a party of three and a party of two
or if the five of you come back tomorrow
in Richard Nixon masks and try to pretend
that you don't know each other
It won't work: You're a party of five
even if you're a beloved regular
Even if the place is empty
Even if you bring logic to bear
Even if you're a tackle for the Chicago Bears
it won't work
You're a party of five
You will always be a party of five
A hundred blocks from here
a hundred years from now
you will still be a party of five
and you will never savor the soup
or compare the coffee or
hear the wisdom of the cook
and the wit of the waitress or
get to hum the old -time tunes
among which you will find
no quintets

---

with grilled chicken 10.95

taco tray specials
served with refried rice, avocado, sour cream, black beans, salsa roja

A 2 crisp or soft tacos (chicken, beef, turkey, chorizo)12.95
B 2 crisp or soft tacos (shrimp, pork, merguez) 13.95
C 3 large tacos in a super bowl platter 14.95

chili potato boats 10.95

Q-TII s (two mini buns, wet onions, pickle) 9.95

turkey, chicken, pulled pork,
pulled beef, virginia ham,
chili, chorizo, sausage,
kielbassa, lamb merguez,
pork bacon, smoked pork
tenderloin,vegan sausage,
chicken merguez

toas-tites

cheese	5.95
egg-cheese	6.95
bacon-cheese	7.95
fluffernutter	6.85
chili-cheese	7.95
smoked bbq- beef brisket;	
pork; chicken; turkey*	10.95

shepherd's pies 12.95
chicken, beef, vegetable
mexican beef, chorizo,
turkey, shrimp, merguez
*toppings: grits, yam, rutabaga,
mashed potato, masa*

chili with
fried 9.95
crushed
potatoes

SPAGHETTI $11.95
marinara; butter, cheese, garlic; carbonara;
meat sauce; pesto; chorizo black bean;
clam sauce (red or white); puttanesca;
prima vera (red or white); wild mushroom creme;
cream chicken pesto; cincinnati (chili);
alfredo; NY beef sauce; meat balls

LUNCH PLATES 14.95
batter fried catfish fingers, french fries
cajun meatloaf-okra gravy
catfish picante, pesto vegetables
chicken apple sausage au gratin
chicken cacciatore, pasta
chicken chow fun
chicken mushroom marsala, ravioli
chicken parmagiana, spaghetti (+4)
chicken and sausage dirty rice
chicken mushroom pastry dumpling
chopped steak sizzle- mushrooms, peppers
corn fried catfish- gumbo au jus
eggplant parmagiana, spaghetti (+3)
stuffed eggplant- merguez & cashews
stuffed eggplant- vegetables & pecans
hanoi hoppin john with shrimp
grilled chicken, coconut rice, pistachio
  curry vegetables, fried bananas (+4)
brisket, kasha bow ties, fruited gravy
jambalaya,chicken,shrimp,sausage (+2)
krispy lemon chicken- cranberry slaw
Lizzy's okra snow pea chicken
louisiana hot chicken fingers- fries
glazed virginia ham, mashed yam
meat loaf mushroom vegetable gravy
patsy's cashew chicken
cashew wild mushroom wide noodles
chicken mushroom dijon risotto
shrimp maque choux
southern fried chickencutlet-gumbo au jus
thai grilled chicken, pistachio wild rice
turkey ala king, toast points
turkey- corn bread stuffing, pumpkin gravy
turkey mushroom gravy, sausage stuffing
turkey veggie curry, coconut rice
waffles with crisp fried chicken fangers

Mexican Food Fiction

I am addicted to the Internet. Among other things, I like to see what people are saying about me, but I also like to see what people are saying about food in general. One of the sites I visit regularly is Chowhound, where food-obsessed people like to talk about what they ate last night or where they are going to eat or where they can go for a specific food. It seems as if the majority of the entries read something like "I'm going to such-and-such restaurant. What's the best thing on the menu?"

When I read that, I think: Why would you give a shit what the best thing on the menu is? Maybe you don't like the best thing on the menu. Maybe the so-called best thing is deep-fried yak brains, and maybe, just *maybe,* deep-fried yak brains don't appeal to you. Why don't you just order what sounds good to you? Well, I already know the answer. It is because people are afraid of being mediocre, of being ordinary.

It wasn't that way twenty or thirty years ago; it was easier to be satisfied. People didn't have cell phones. There were no flat-screen televisions. They didn't feel the need to indulge in eighteen-course dinners that some jerk-off restaurant reviewer described as "orgasmic." They didn't have any of the media hype we have now that it is supposed to make us happy or even contenders for happiness. People were more content with their ordinary lives and with their mediocre desires.

Even today most people's taste—whether it pertains to food, art, drama, or sex—if they are really honest with themselves, is just not that highly evolved. The difference is that people are not happy with that simplicity. When it comes to food, which is the only subject I know anything about, they reach higher than they have the palate to appreciate; sometimes they reach so high in terms of what they order or go to cook at home that I am not sure they even know what they're eating, much less like it. And they definitely reach higher than anything they could achieve in terms of their own cooking skills. No wonder they are daunted by cooking. They have no idea what the fuck they're eating. How can they expect to know how to make it?

I have a lot of character defects, but reaching above myself in terms of my own desires is not one of them. I don't pretend to like things or try to like them because someone told me to or because I think I should like them. I have no problem with my lack of sophistication when it comes to anything and certainly when it comes to food. It is not necessary to tickle my palate with subtle nuances and exotic hidden ingredients. With food, I don't like subtlety. What I like is gusto. I think that is why I like Mexican food so much. You take a bite of good Mexican food, and it just explodes all over your mouth.

The fact is that Mexican food can be sophisticated and subtle and it can use all kinds of exotic ingredients, but that is not the Mexican food I am talking about. The kind of Mexican food I like is the kind I was introduced to in my twenties at a place called the Chili Parlor on Tenth and Bleecker Streets in the Village. It is Mexican food based on a foolproof combination of melted cheese, spicy peppers, and greasy red meat. The owner, Kendall, was a stage director on Broadway, and he had all these black tootsies working for him. They weren't really drag queens, but they were very gay, like prancing gay, at a time when the only place you would find prancing gays was in the Village. When your order arrived, a guy would prance over with one of those little handheld graters where you turn the crank and the cheese comes out the other end, and ask you if you wanted cheese. If you did, he would grate it with great fanfare and shake his fanny in the air to the rhythm of his grating.

There was no back kitchen at the Chili Parlor. Everything was prepared right behind the counter in plain sight of the dining room. I loved to sit at the counter and watch all the plates being assembled. I always ordered the same thing, beef enchiladas, and after I ordered, I would watch as one of these guys made them. They would dip the corn tortillas in the deep fryer, fill them with ground beef, roll them up, grate fresh cheddar on top—with their ass shaking—and then put them under the broiler. The enchiladas came to the table bubbly and hot, with chopped raw onion on top. I loved those enchiladas so much that I would try to find different ways to eat them, the way some people find different ways to eat Oreos, eating the filling first or eating the edges around the filling. Sometimes I would cut up five or six pieces of enchilada so I could eat the bites continuously without being disrupted by the cutting. Other times I would break off a piece of the tortilla and dip it into the cheese with my fingers.

Carmine Street Enchiladas *Serves 2*

These are based on the enchiladas I loved at the Chili Parlor. I call them Carmine Street Enchiladas because I always name my favorite items on my menu—the ones that bring me great pleasure and cause me no difficulty—after the store, and until our recent move, we were on Carmine Street. I have one customer, Gary Goodrow, who has the same disease with these that I did at the Chili Parlor. He has been ordering them ever since he met me, more than twenty years ago. It seems he can't order anything else.

This is really more of an assembly than a recipe. It takes me less than three minutes to make them, including melting the cheese under the broiler. It may take you a little longer, but not much. You can double this recipe if you like, or you can make a huge pan of them if you have enough of the necessary ingredients.

Ingredients
Good olive oil for frying the tortillas
6 corn tortillas
½ cup My Chili (page 233) or any meaty
    chili
1 cup feather-shredded cheddar cheese
Chopped onion (optional)

Instructions
Preheat the broiler.

Pour a thin layer of olive oil in a small skillet and heat over medium-high heat. Put each tortilla in the oil one at a time and turn to coat both sides with oil. Add more oil to the skillet when it becomes dry. Lay the tortillas on a cutting board or any flat surface and spoon 2 heaping tablespoons of chili in the center of each. Roll up each tortilla and lay them seam side down in a casserole dish with the enchiladas touching each other slightly to help keep them closed. Sprinkle the enchiladas with the cheese and place them under the broiler until the cheese is melted and bubbly, 2 to 3 minutes. Remove from the oven and sprinkle with the raw onion if desired.

Those enchiladas made me so happy. I was totally addicted to them. I went to the Chili Parlor at least once a week, sometimes three or four times. I don't know if I ever tried another thing in that place. I could taste my enchiladas before I even sat down. I didn't actually cook Mexican until about ten years later—after I had had my breakthrough experience making soup and had started to sow my oats in terms of cooking—but when I did, Chili Parlor was the inspiration. And the flavors I got from those enchiladas were the flavors I was after.

In the beginning of my Mexican food adventure, I tried some exotic ingredients, like huitlacoche, which is this slimy black fungus that they use in authentic Mexican cuisine, but none of them did anything for me. Today I'm pretty happy in my Mexican *Goodnight Moon* room. I stick with a simple palette of basic ingredients that include spicy meat, chili, cheddar and Jack cheeses, tortillas, avocados, cilantro, sour cream, fried plantains, chiles, cumin, tomatoes, and corn.

Best taco holder
(tacostandup.com)

For the same reason that I don't use exotic Mexican ingredients, none of my Mexican food is authentic Mexican food, either. You could call my Mexican food ps'Mexican, like "pseudo-Mexican." When I am creating individual dishes, I often get ideas from something I ate in a restaurant or from the Internet. Someone on Chowhound might ask if anyone knows where they can get, say, migas. I'll do a search to find out what the hell migas is, and if it looks as if I have the ingredients and the skills necessary to make it, I'll give it a try. Other times I'll take a name I like, such as Huevos Rancheros, and invent a dish that I think fulfills that name. I never consult a recipe or worry if I am getting it "right" according to some traditional Diana Kennedy version of that dish. That is not what cooking is about for me. Think of my Mexican food as culinary fiction. If any of the dishes here resemble an authentic Mexican dish, it is a total coincidence.

Huevos Rancheros
Serves 4

Huevos Rancheros means rancher's eggs. I know that Huevos Rancheros is a *specific* Mexican dish, but this isn't that. I don't even know what real Huevos Rancheros is. When I came up with this dish, I envisioned a rancher out on the plains, cooking over a big open fire behind a chuck wagon, one of those things with the wooden wheels and the big canvas top. I pictured him making eggs and figured he would want some kind of sauce to go with the eggs. He would have a big iron stew pot and just start throwing stuff in: peppers, onions, tomatoes. He wouldn't have a chef's knife, just one of those flip-open kind, dulled from use, so he'd cut everything really chunky. Naturally, he would eat it with tortillas to sop up every last drop of sauce and egg yolk. The sauce is enough to serve four people; cook as many or as few eggs as you like.

Ingredients
¼ cup chopped or crumbled cooked potato (squeezed from a baked potato)
½ big yellow Spanish onion, chopped
½ each yellow, red, and green bell pepper, cored, seeded, and chopped
½ to 2 teaspoons minced jalapeño, habanero, or chipotle pepper (depending on your taste; see How Spicy Do You Want It? on page 128)
3 tablespoons good olive oil
A big handful of fresh or frozen collard greens (about 1 cup)
½ cup canned black beans with juice, or more if you really love beans
1 whole roma tomato (fresh or from a can of San Marzano tomatoes), chopped
½ cup Chicken Stock (page 123), or any stock or broth, plus more as needed
8 extra-large eggs
½ cup feather-shredded cheddar cheese
8 warm corn tortillas

Instructions
Preheat the broiler.

Heat a large, heavy sauté pan over really high heat until it's really hot. While the pan is heating, chop up your vegetables. Carefully pick up the red-hot pan, bring it to the cutting board, and brush the onion and peppers into the pan. Return the pan to the stove and pour in the olive oil. Give the pan a quick flick so the oil distributes over all the vegetables. Add the collard greens, black beans, and tomato and cook for about 1 minute. Add the chicken stock, cover the pan, leave it on enormously high heat, and let it sit and sizzle for a few minutes.

In the meantime, cook the eggs sunny-side up (see Cooking Eggs, page 47), or however you want your eggs, in an oven-proof pan. (You may have to do this in batches.) When the eggs are done, transfer them to the plates, sprinkle with the cheese, and put them under the broiler until the cheese melts and bubbles and browns to your liking. (You need to act quickly so the eggs are still runny when you serve them; runny eggs are key to this dish.)

Take the cover off the ranchero stuff and flip the pan a couple of times. It should be thick but not wet. If there is not enough liquid for the stuff to flip easily, add more chicken stock. If there is too much liquid, tilt the pan and pour off the extra. Spoon the ranchero stuff next to the eggs, dividing it evenly, and serve with the warm tortillas on the side.

Zack

Taco-fried Chicken

The coating on this chicken consists of two parts: the crushed tortilla chips it is "breaded" with and the vinegary Spicy Buffalo Wing Sauce it is coated with after coming out of the hot oil. Served with an avocado-based salad and refried rice, it is one of many dishes always cooked by Zack.

Ingredients

Peanut oil for deep frying
All-purpose flour for dredging
3 extra-large eggs
1½ cups heavy cream or milk or water
1 to 2 cups crushed tortilla chips
4 5- to 6-ounce boneless, skinless chicken breasts
Salt and pepper
Spicy Buffalo Wing Sauce (facing page)

Instructions

Preheat a deep fryer or a large potful of peanut oil over high heat to 375°F.

Put the flour in a bowl big enough to fit one of the cutlets. In another similar size bowl, whisk the eggs and cream together. Put the crushed tortilla chips in a third bowl.

Using a large knife, with the flat side of the blade parallel to your cutting board, slice the chicken through the middle to form cutlets about ⅝ inch thick. Salt and pepper both sides of each cutlet.

Dip a cutlet into the flour and turn it so that it is uniformly coated. Shake off any excess flour and dip the cutlet in the egg-cream mixture and then in the crushed tortilla chips. Repeat the dipping process with as many cutlets as will fit in your deep fryer or pot without touching one another.

Drop the cutlets in the oil and cook for 4½ to 5 minutes, until the crust is a nice golden brown. Make sure the chicken is submerged while it is frying. Place on paper towels to drain. While the chicken is frying, repeat the dipping process with the remaining cutlets and fry them after the first batch is out of the oil.

Pour the Spicy Buffalo Wing Sauce into a bowl. Dump the sauce over the chicken just before serving.

Ready to be covered in sauce

Spicy Buffalo Wing Sauce

Here is a very straightforward recipe for traditional Buffalo wing sauce. It goes like this: Mix equal parts of Frank's Hot Sauce (or another hot sauce you like) and melted butter—period. For what it's worth, I got it straight from the horse's mouth. Many years ago Bud Trillin did a really long story for *The New Yorker* on the woman who invented Buffalo wings at the bar she owned in Buffalo, New York, and one day he brought her into my place. She was a very sweet lady. The story she told me about the wings was that she had teenage kids who, along with their friends, were always hungry. To satisfy their enormous appetites without spending too much money, she used the part of the chicken that didn't get used in the restaurant: the wings. She cooked the wings for the kids on a regular basis until she finally came up with something they really loved, which is what we now know as Buffalo wings.

Buffalo sauce

Migas
Serves 2 to 4

As with almost everything I cook, I add the ingredients of this dish to the pan as I cut them. By the time I have added everything, the peppers and onion are soft or at least soft*ish*. In a rustic, gaucho-like dish like this, I don't really care how soft the onion is, if it is browned or translucent, or even if it is still a bit raw. It is all going to taste good. Besides, the real flavor of Migas is the texture and flavor of the browned, chewy corn tortillas.

Ingredients

3 tablespoons good olive oil
3 corn tortillas, halved and cut into thin strips
1 each red and yellow bell pepper, cored, seeded, and julienned
½ big yellow Spanish onion, chopped
½ large tomato, chopped
1 jalapeño pepper, thinly sliced into rings (see How Spicy Do You Want It? on page 128)
1 teaspoon minced fresh garlic
1 teaspoon ground cumin
½ bunch scallions (white and green parts), thinly sliced
2 roma tomatoes (fresh or from a can of San Marzano tomatoes)
½ to ¾ cup Beef Stock (page 124) or any stock or broth
Extra-large eggs (2 per person)

Instructions

Heat the olive oil in a large sauté pan over high heat. Throw in the tortilla strips and fry until they are crispy. Throw in the bell peppers, tomato, onion, and jalapeño pepper, adding them to the pan as you finish cutting them. The peppers and onion should be nice and soft by the time you add the last vegetable. If they are not soft enough for your liking, cook for another minute or two. Add the garlic and cumin and stir. Add the scallions and roma tomatoes and cook for another minute. Add ½ cup of the stock. Lower the heat and simmer until all the stock has been absorbed and the tortilla strips are soft. Add more stock if necessary; you want enough so the vegetables don't burn while they cook, but not so much that the stock doesn't cook off after a minute or two. This is a dry, not saucy, dish.

Meanwhile, fry the eggs (see Cooking Eggs, page 47). Divide the Migas among individual serving plates and serve with the fried eggs on top.

Tortillas in pan

Pecan Chicken Wild Rice Enchiladas *Serves 2 to 4*

This was Eve's favorite dish at Shopsin's. It isn't made with typical Mexican flavors; the only thing Mexican about it is that it is enchiladas. Eve liked to recommend it to her customers so she could eat whatever they left on their plates. When she was running the store, we got about three orders a day, which is a lot in a restaurant with as many options as I have. Now, without Eve there to guide people, it hardly ever gets ordered, which is too bad, because it's delicious. You can double or triple this recipe if you like and make it in a big casserole dish. I char the chicken over an open flame to get a bit of that charcoal flavor. If you don't want to bother grilling, you can cook the chicken in the pan (make sure it's really, really hot) before cooking the vegetables, but you won't get that charcoal flavor.

Ingredients

2 5- to 6-ounce boneless, skinless chicken breasts
Salt and pepper
¼ cup good olive oil, plus more for frying the tortillas
½ large head green cabbage, cored and thinly sliced
½ big yellow Spanish onion, chopped
A big handful of fresh or frozen collard greens (about 1 heaping cup), chopped if fresh
2 jalapeño peppers, thinly sliced into rings (see How Spicy Do You Want It? on page 128)
1 tablespoon minced fresh garlic
1 teaspoon ground cumin, or more to taste
1 cup Chicken Stock (page 123) or any stock or broth
1 cup pecan halves or pieces
½ cup cooked wild rice (see Shopsin's Prep: Wild Rice on page 217)
⅔ cup heavy cream
8 corn tortillas, warmed
1 cup shredded Monterey Jack cheese (about 4 ounces)

Instructions

Preheat the broiler.

Grill the chicken (see Grilling Chicken, page 127) just enough to sear and get grill marks but so that it is still slightly raw in the center. Cut the chicken breast into bite-sized pieces. Salt and pepper the pieces and set aside.

Pour the olive oil into a large skillet over high heat. Add the cabbage, onion, collard greens, jalapeño peppers, garlic, and cumin. Sauté until the cabbage begins to brown and the onions are soft, about 5 minutes. Deglaze the pan with the stock. Add the cooked chicken pieces, pecans, wild rice, and cream. Cook for 4 or 5 minutes, until the chicken is cooked through. If there's too much liquid, simmer a few more minutes to cook off the excess.

Pour a thin layer of olive oil in a small skillet and heat over medium-high heat. Working one at a time, turn each tortilla in the oil to coat both sides and add more oil to the skillet when it becomes dry. Lay the tortillas on a cutting board or any flat surface and spoon 2 heaping tablespoons of the chicken mixture in the center of each, leaving any remaining liquid in the pan. Roll up each tortilla and lay seam side down in a casserole dish with the enchiladas slightly touching each other to help keep them closed. Cover the enchiladas with the cheese and any remaining liquid from the chicken mixture. Place under the broiler until the cheese has melted, about 4 minutes.

Pecan Chicken Wild Rice Enchiladas

Ché Cuban Rice, Guacamole, Poached Eggs, and Tomato Chili Cream *Serves 2 to 4*

This egg dish is really more of an assemblage of different elements, most of which are already prepared in my kitchen. When I get an order, all I have to do is smush up some guacamole, poach some eggs, mix up the already cooked rice with the already cooked beans, and then make the sauce, which I also do from premade ingredients. If you have some of my staples prepared or similar items available to you in cans or jars (such as canned black beans and jarred marinara sauce), it will be an easy recipe for you, too. If not, this recipe will be a lot of work, and you should probably make something else.

Ingredients

1 cup cooked white rice

1 cup Cuban Black Bean Soup (page 224) or any black bean soup, warmed

½ cup My Chili (page 233) or any meaty chili

2 tablespoons Marinara Sauce (page 236) or any marinara sauce

2 teaspoons heavy cream, or more as needed

Extra-large eggs (2 per person)

Guacamole (page 68) or any guacamole

Instructions

Mix the rice and soup together in a bowl and set aside.

In a separate bowl, mix the chili, marinara sauce, and cream, adding more cream if necessary for the sauce to go from brownish to pinkish in color. Set that aside, too.

Meanwhile, poach the eggs (see Cooking Eggs, page 47).

Divide the black beans and rice among however many plates you are using. Carefully slide the eggs on top, and pour the chili cream sauce over the eggs, draping it the way a dress designer would drape a piece of cloth, so the eggs are only semicovered and some of the egg whites peek through. Top each egg with a dollop of Guacamole (page 68) and serve.

Shopsin's Prep: Wild Rice

We buy long-grain Canadian wild rice, cook it until it's done, and let it cool. Then we divide it into 5-ounce portions, bag it, and freeze it. When I need wild rice, I just nuke it until it is thawed out. If you don't have a microwave, thaw it at room temperature or make your rice fresh.

The Building Blocks of Creativity, or How I Do What I Do

Because my menu is as large as it is, a question I get asked often is how I am able to offer as many items as I do and as quickly as I do. Except for one or two items, everything I make comes to the table, if I don't have a backlog of orders, within five minutes from the time it was ordered—and usually a lot sooner. And what people who ask the question probably don't know is that I make every one of those items—from start to finish—to order.

But I still think it's a stupid question. Or at least it's stupid to be quite so amazed. I could put five thousand items on my menu, and it would be the same story. My classic response is "If *I* can do it, how hard can it be?" The way I cook is just not that special. It's not as if I'm Beethoven and writing beautiful music even though I'm deaf. There is nothing, I mean *nothing*, I do that a monkey couldn't do.

What it takes to cook the way I do is not talent but *intention*. The real question is not *how* I can make nine hundred or five thousand items to order, but *why* I make all those items. And the answer essentially is that I do it because I want to. And because I am neurotically obsessed in a way that, luckily, is not unhealthy and doesn't hurt anyone. The fact that this obsession produces something serviceable to other people is a positive effect, but it is also a total coincidence.

Cooking, for me, is a creative process, and I believe that people who are creative are creative for one of two reasons: Either they are going for truth and beauty, or they create as a way to dilute the venom produced by their subconscious minds. I cook for the second reason. When I cook, I am in a cathartic, recuperative process that calms me down and brings me from a neurotic state to a relaxed, functioning state.

Sometimes, by around twelve or one o'clock, after cooking really hard in the morning, I don't feel the need to cook anymore. I did what I had to do. Since the real reason I was in the kitchen was to take care of my emotional instability, not to make food, I'm done. When that happened in the old days, I used to just close. I would tell Eve, "I don't feel like cooking anymore. I'm going home." And I would take off my apron and leave. I do that less often now, but not because I don't feel like leaving. I just have more self-control than I used to. And also Melinda won't let me. She is much stricter with me than Eve was.

On my days off, when I am not cooking, I usually don't do anything. I'm immobilized. I can't wait to go to the restaurant the next day. That's the thing about anxiety that derives from childhood: Whatever is wrong with you reinvents itself every day. The trick is to turn the torment into something positive in your life, which for me is food. The result of this cycle is that I am constantly creating new things. Not only have I had as many as nine hundred items on my menu at one time, but I am constantly adding new things and taking off those that don't sell or that I don't like to make.

•

In terms of the operational aspect of offering so many items, I have developed systems and production regimes over the years that allow me latitude to do what I do. I have shortcuts available to me because of all the equipment I have: a fryer, a microwave, a griddle, a salamander, and really powerful stovetop burners, all of which I could reach with my feet nailed to the ground. And I have loads of prep literally at my fingertips.

I am not an Alice Waters type of cook who is inspired by ingredients and builds from there. The inspiration is mine—it comes from within me. But as a creative person, ingredients are the tangible medium I work with, so when I *am* inspired, when I am in the therapeutic, creative process of cooking, I start looking around, and the more ingredients I have, the more creative I can be.

In the freezer, which is to my left, I keep a long list of breads that I serve with breakfast or sandwiches. I have open canisters of really good frozen blackberries, huckleberries, pineapple, peaches, peas, blueberries, raspberries, and mango, and baggies of mixed fruit that we put together ourselves. I keep a variety of frozen vegetables on hand: collard greens, corn, peas, okra, and a few types of green beans. I have shrimp, chopped brisket, chopped lamb, pulled beef, pork, and turkey. And then I have ingredients I have cooked ahead of time and frozen in individual portions: polenta and pasta, bulgur wheat for making Tabbouleh (page 222), and cooked wild rice for the Pecan Chicken Wild Rice Enchiladas (page 215). I have mashed rutabaga, mashed sweet potatoes, mashed regular potatoes. I have puff pastry squares for Chicken Potpie (page 132). And that's just the tip of the iceberg.

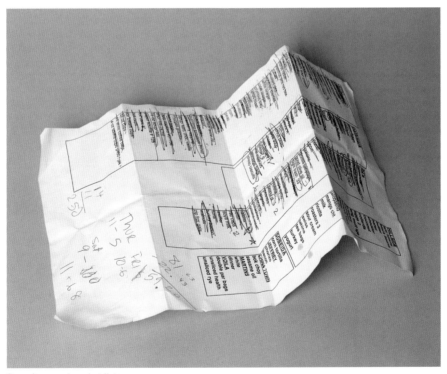

One of many shopping lists

Tabbouleh
Serves 2 to 4 (makes about 1½ cups)

If you ask me, I make the best tabbouleh salad in the city—maybe anywhere—and I'll tell you why: because I'm the only one I know who makes tabbouleh salad *fresh*. Every other tabbouleh I have ever seen was made ahead of time. The only thing that takes any time to cook is the bulgur wheat, so I make that ahead of time and freeze it. Then I can prepare the rest of the tabbouleh—the herbs and tomato and lemon juice—to order. It is such a simple solution, and it makes so much sense. I'm not sure why everybody doesn't do it my way.

I use Tabbouleh in a lot of different dishes. I spoon it on top of a Greek salad, and I toss it into the Pita Feta Salad (page 102). But it is also good on its own: just a mound of Tabbouleh served with Toasted Pita Bread (page 104), with Tahini Dressing (page 103) on the side. The other key to good Tabbouleh is a lot of lemon juice. I make sure I have enough by putting in however much I think I need, and then when it looks as if it has enough, I add more. If you think your Tabbouleh could use more lemon juice than I've called for here, add more.

Ingredients
8 ounces cooked bulgur wheat (see
    Shopsin's Prep: Bulgur Wheat, below)
1 tablespoon good olive oil
1 medium tomato, finely chopped
⅔ cup finely chopped fresh parsley
2 tablespoons thinly sliced scallions
A big pinch of crushed dried mint
Salt
2 whole lemons, halved

Instructions
Put the bulgur wheat in a large bowl. Add the olive oil, tomato, parsley, scallions, mint, and salt to taste. Squeeze the juice of both lemons over everything. Toss all the ingredients together and you're done.

Shopsin's Prep: Bulgur Wheat
I make bulgur wheat in big batches and freeze 4-ounce portions in plastic baggies, which I reach for whenever anyone orders something that calls for bulgur, such as Tabbouleh (above) or Ashura Hot Cereal (page 111). This recipe is enough to make two recipes for Tabbouleh, so you can divide it in half and freeze one half for next time. I add turmeric to the water I cook the bulgur in. Turmeric is a yellow spice common in curry powder. I don't use a lot, so it

Tabbouleh

doesn't add much flavor, but what it does do is give the grains of wheat a rich golden color.

Boil 1½ cups water in a large saucepan over high heat. Stir in 1 teaspoon turmeric and 1 cup bulgur wheat. Lower the heat, cover the pot, and simmer the bulgur until all the water has been absorbed, 10 to 15 minutes. Turn off the heat, let the bulgur sit in the pot for a few minutes, and then fluff it with a fork as you would with rice. If you are going to freeze the bulgur, let it cool first. Divide it in half and save one half for another batch of tabbouleh. Or divide it into 1-cup portions if you plan to use it to make Ashura Hot Cereal. Put it in plastic baggies and freeze.

On the steam table next to the freezer I have various soups and sauces and three types of stocks, all of which I prepared ahead of time, with the exception of vegan black beans, which come from a can. I use these precooked sauces and soups as if each was an ingredient. As I add each ingredient, I am really adding a whole subset of ingredients, and I am also adding the time it took to cook them. In addition to the vegan black beans from a can I have a really good, really rich Cuban Black Bean Soup (page 224) that is made with ham. I have vegan gumbo, Ranchero Sauce, My Chili (page 233), and Marinara Sauce (page 236).

Ham hock

Cuban Black Bean Soup *Serves 6 to 8*

The important thing about this soup is that when I make it, it starts with a ham bone. The ham I use in the store is a smoked ham from North Carolina, similar to a Smithfield ham but not as salty. When I need ham for sandwiches and other things, I carve it directly off the bone, but I do it carelessly. This sloppiness is intentional: I want lots of meat left on the bone to flavor this soup. When I make it with a ham bone, I make a huge batch using 4 pounds of beans. After it has cooled, I transfer it to big plastic bags and freeze it. If you have a ham bone and a pot big enough to cook 4 pounds of beans, I suggest you do the same because this soup is really good, and you can do a lot of things with it. If you don't have a whole ham bone, go to your butcher and ask for a smoked shank, which you can use for cooking 1 or 2 pounds of beans, depending on how much meat you want in them. In a pinch you can substitute two ham hocks; they give you some of the ham flavor, but they don't have any meat on them.

I serve this soup on its own, topped with sour cream and cilantro. I also use it to make a Cuban black bean burrito, which is basically a Chili Burrito (page 238) but with this soup instead of the chili. This soup is also the base of the Cuban Bean Polenta Melt (recipe follows), and it's used to make Blisters on My Sisters (page 227) and a breakfast plate called Ché (page 217). I suppose you could make any of these using canned black bean soup if you wanted.

They may not taste *as* great, but sometimes just *good* is enough to satisfy.

Ingredients
1 pound black turtle beans, soaked for at least 12 hours
1 smoked pork shank, or ham bone or 2 ham hocks
½ big yellow Spanish onion, chopped
1 tablespoon ground cumin
1 tablespoon garlic powder
1 tablespoon good olive oil
2 teaspoons red wine vinegar
¼ to 1 teaspoon minced pickled jalapeño peppers, depending on taste (see How Spicy Do You Want It? on page 128)

Instructions
Drain and rinse the beans three times and then put them in a large pot with the pork shank, onion, and enough water to cover. Add the cumin, garlic powder, olive oil, vinegar, and jalapeño peppers. Simmer for 4 hours, or until the beans are the proper texture for your taste. (Personally, I am not an al dente bean guy. I like my beans so that when I bite into them, the texture is pleasantly creamy and tender, like a piece of cake.)

Remove the pork shank, pull the meat from the bone, discard the bone, and put the meat back in the pot. If you are freezing some of the soup, let it cool before portioning it into plastic bags.

Cuban Bean Polenta Melt *Serves 4*

This dish is black bean soup with a polenta and cheese crust. It is the same concept as the crouton that sits on top of French onion soup. The proper menu name for this is Cuban Bean Polenta Melt, but in the restaurant we refer to it as Jim's Polenta Soup, because Jim Lally, one of our regular customers, is the only one who orders it. Jim Lally is a wonderful guy. He is probably my favorite person in the world besides my kids. I don't know what it is about him, but when I'm with him, I get a really good, right feeling. If he were a woman, I would marry him.

Ingredients

4 servings of Cuban Black Bean Soup (facing page) or any black bean soup

1 serving of Polenta (page 226), or any polenta, hot

4 small handfuls of feather-shredded cheddar cheese

Instructions

Preheat the broiler or the oven to as hot as it will go.

Ladle the soup into 4 single-serving heat-proof bowls so that it comes to just below the rim. Top each serving with a ½-inch-thick layer of hot polenta. Cover each serving of polenta with a small handful of the cheddar cheese and put the bowls under the broiler or in the oven until the cheese melts.

The Kitchen Dance

I have an athletic obsession with efficiency. I work rigorously and with great dedication, like an athlete in training, at trying to find the fastest, most time- and energy-efficient method to produce a particular result. Once this method is developed, it is repeated and rehearsed hundreds or thousands of times both individually and as a team with whomever I am cooking with. The result is that we are able to do multiple things at once, and we almost never even touch each other. We move in synch, at once chaotic but totally fluid, like a graceful modern dance.

Polenta

Makes 4 servings

The main thing you need to know when cooking polenta is that the water has to come to a boil for the polenta to soften, but after it comes to a boil, you need to turn down the fire *immediately*. You must be really careful not to let it boil over the top. It happens in a matter of seconds, and it doesn't give you any warning. It looks as if it is sitting there, and all of a sudden it's all over your stove. Over the years it has gotten to be a game with me to see if I can catch it.

The other thing you need to know is that no matter how tempting it is, you cannot stir polenta. It is like rice that way: It needs to be left alone. This recipe is for the way I like polenta, which is a little more solid than grits but not so solid that it can be sliced like a piece of pie. If you like your polenta more liquidy, like hot cereal, add more stock. If you want to slice it, add less.

saucepan over high heat, and cook until it just begins to bubble. Lower the heat to the lowest possible simmer and let the polenta cook, covered, until it softens, about 45 minutes. Be careful not to let the polenta burn on the bottom; if it does, you have to throw the whole pot of polenta out because the burnt flavor goes through the polenta like a rocket. If it is cooking too quickly and you think it is going to burn before it is cooked through, stir it—and turn the fucking heat *down*. If you are going to freeze the polenta, let it cool to room temperature, then put it into baggies in whatever size portions you like. I freeze it in 3-ounce portions, which is one serving in my restaurant. Press down on the bag of polenta with the palm of your hand so you are freezing a disk about ½ inch thick.

Ingredients

3 cups Chicken Stock (page 123) or
    Vegetable Stock (page 124) or any
    stock or broth
½ cup heavy cream
1 cup plus 2 tablespoons cornmeal
4 tablespoons (½ stick) butter
Grated Parmesan cheese (however much
    you like; I just throw the shit in. I don't
    know whether it's 2 tablespoons or half
    a cup.)

Instructions

Mix the stock, cream, cornmeal, butter, and Parmesan cheese in a heavy-bottomed

Adjust liquid to reach preferred density.

Blisters on My Sisters *Serves 2*

This name came from a Frank Zappa song called "Jewish Princess" where he says: "I want a dainty little Jewish princess with a couple of sisters who can raise a few blisters." I decided to make something called Blisters on My Sisters, and when I went to the kitchen to make it, this is what I came up with. I make the rice and beans mixture in a bowl because all my ingredients are hot all the time, but since you are probably starting with cold ingredients, I gave you directions for mixing the ingredients together over heat.

Ingredients

6 corn tortillas, warmed
2 cups cooked white rice
1 cup Cuban Black Bean Soup (page 224), or canned black bean soup or black beans, drained
2 roma tomatoes (fresh or from a can of San Marzano tomatoes), chopped
Minced jalapeño or chipotle peppers (see How Spicy Do You Like It? on page 128)
2 extra-large eggs
2 big handfuls of arugula

Instructions

Heat the tortillas on the griddle or in whatever way you like to heat tortillas. In a sauté pan over medium heat, combine the rice, soup, tomatoes, and jalapeño peppers. Mush it all up together.

Meanwhile, cook the eggs sunny-side up (see Cooking Eggs, page 47). To serve, put 1 handful of arugula in the bottom of two plates. Put the tortillas side by side on top of the arugula, and the rice-beans mixture on top of the tortillas, dividing it evenly. Carefully slide the sunnies on top of that, and serve.

In order to keep as many things on hand as I have, the restaurant runs on a constant, cyclical rhythm with ingredients. In addition to our daily cooking, we are involved in a constant cycle of preparation. I roast a fresh 25-pound turkey every other day in addition to boiling two or three whole chickens every day. Once a week, I cook a brisket, and every two weeks I cook a whole leg of lamb. This system works like a cycle in nature in that it is very intricate and everything relates to everything else. A lot of my cooking has to do with finding ways to cycle through ingredients that I already have. And most of the ingredients have multiple uses and functions.

Whenever I make anything with beef brisket or pot roast, I take the ends or the scraps left over and throw them in the beef stock. Also, the brisket that isn't used by the end of the week is put into the stock overnight. The next morning I take it out, trim off the fat, and pull the beef. This process has two benefits: It makes for a richer stock, and it makes the beef taste beefier by locking in the flavor. After the beef is pulled, I add a little stock to it to moisten it. Then I put it in the freezer in bags, and when I need pulled beef to make barbecue beef with GA BBQ Sauce (page 153), I just nuke it up, mix in the sauce, and I'm finished. After, I strain the stock and throw any bits of meat in the chili.

If I notice a vegetable that will soon be in the freezer too long, I use that vegetable instead of what I would normally have used because I don't want to throw anything out. (I guess I am like Alice Waters that way, only instead of using the freshest vegetables I can find, as she does, I use the oldest vegetables I can find.) I came up with almost all my turkey items as a way to try to use up the parts of the whole turkey that would otherwise have gone to waste. And I invented an entire category of foods, the Yin/Yang Special Rice Variations (page 231), as a way to use yesterday's rice.

Cooking like this is not just a financial issue for me. It is an emotional issue. I have a relationship with everything I cook, and finding new ways to use these foods at different stages of their existence represents a desire in me to continue those relationships. After cooking and carving a whole turkey, for instance, I am not ready to break up with the turkey just yet, so I boil the carcass as a way of prolonging our bond.

Coconut Rice
Serves 2

All of the Yin/Yang Special Rice Variations (page 231) came from this rice dish. I
started serving it as a side to a grilled
chicken dish, but it became so popular that
my customers started ordering the chicken
dish without the chicken. They just wanted
the rice. My evolution as a cook has had a
lot to do with following my customers
wherever their desires take me. This recipe
can easily be doubled.

Ingredients
2 cups cooked white rice (preferably day-
    old)
⅓ cup heavy cream
½ cup Chicken Stock (page 123) or any
    stock or broth, or more as needed
½ cup sweetened angel flake coconut
    (more if you really love coconut)

Instructions
Preheat a griddle or large sauté pan over
high heat until very hot. Add the rice,
cream, and stock. You want the liquid to
cover the rice but not so much that a lot of
liquid leaks around the sides of the mound
of rice. Sprinkle the coconut on top of the
rice, cover, and steam until the rice is warm
and the liquid has been absorbed. If there is
too much liquid, remove the lid to cook off
the excess.

Yin/Yang Divided Bowls

The inspiration for the Yin/Yangs came from two places: First was a desire to use up the rice left over at the end of the day the *next* day. We make fresh rice every morning as part of our prep, and we always have some left over. I wanted to see if I could put the leftovers to use, so I started making Coconut Rice, but I still had more rice left over. The second need was to make use of Melmac bowls that I found on the Internet. The bowls are divided by a curved line down the center, so if you were to look down on the bowl, it looks like a yin/yang symbol. The bowls are from the 1950s, and I think the idea was that you put your mashed potatoes in one side and your string beans or whatever overcooked vegetable you were serving that night in the other. I found the bowls on eBay, and I bought them all up. I bought so many that I actually changed the market price of them on eBay because I made the demand look so strong.

Tofu, Peas, and Peanut Rice

I love eBay. For me it's like Disneyland with a phone cord. I am always buying stuff on the Internet. My daughters get really pissed off when they see more packages come in, but a lot of items on the menu have come about as a result of the stuff I buy. When it arrives, I think up something to make with it. The way I look at it, you have to be prepared, because you never know when creativity is going to strike. Sometimes I find uses for the things I buy, and probably more often I don't, but I wouldn't be creating anything if I didn't give myself the freedom that I do.

Beef Sloppy Joe Rice

The way Yin/Yangs work is that I have a list of soups (which are separate from my normal soups but are not categorically different; you can use whatever soup you like) and a list of "special rices," and customers get to choose one from each list. At the time I bought the bowls, I had already learned to use yesterday's rice from a Julia Child book. She said that the reason fried rice tastes so good is that the Chinese use day-old rice to make it. The old rice, because it is dried, becomes an incredibly friendly vehicle for fat and develops a texture that is quite different from the rice in its first run-through.

Mango Chutney Rice

Yin/Yang Special Rice Variations *Serves 2*

The Yin/Yang Special Rice is really a formula. You start with 2 cups rice for two people, add some cream and stock to loosen the rice up a bit, and then add whatever other ingredients you like. Here are some from my menu, but you can use this formula to make Yin/Yang–type rice out of whatever you have around and like to eat.

Ingredients for Special Rice Variations

2 cups white rice (preferably day-old)
2 tablespoons heavy cream
¾ cup Chicken Stock (page 123) or any
    stock or broth

Plus variations ingredients:

Tofu, Peas, and Peanut Rice

Half a small package of firm tofu, a handful of frozen peas, and a handful of crushed peanuts. Follow the instructions for Coconut Rice (page 229), but add the tofu, peas, and peanuts instead of the coconut.

Guacamole Rice

1 recipe Guacamole ("cheap" or regular, page 68), or any guacamole. Follow the instructions for Coconut Rice (page 229), but fold in the guacamole when the rice is done.

Beef Sloppy Joe Rice

¼ cup My Chili (page 233) or any meaty chili, and ¼ cup Marinara Sauce (page 236), or any marinara sauce. Follow the instructions for Coconut Rice (page 229), but stir in the chili and marinara sauce instead of the coconut.

Pistachio Ricotta Rice

A handful of pistachios and ¼ cup fresh whole-milk ricotta cheese. Follow the instructions for Coconut Rice (page 229), but add the pistachios instead of the coconut and fold in the ricotta when the rice is done.

Artichoke Tomato Rice

½ cup frozen artichoke hearts, thawed, and ¼ cup Marinara Sauce (page 236) or any marinara sauce. Follow the instructions for Coconut Rice (page 229), but stir in the artichoke hearts and marinara instead of the coconut.

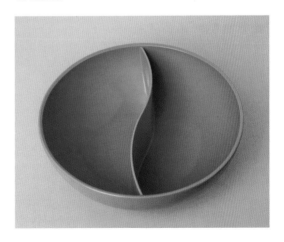

Rules of Prep and Leftovers

The same method I use to make hundreds of soups from scratch I use to make nine hundred items in five minutes: I parse a dish into its individual components and look at how those elements might be put back together in a way that takes less time and attention or fewer steps. My rule of thumb is anything that takes less than five minutes is made from scratch, and anything that takes more than five minutes is made ahead of time and either refrigerated or frozen. I cook a big load of whatever it is, divide it into individual-sized portions, put each portion in a small plastic baggy, and put the baggies in the freezer. This is something the home cook does without thinking. What these packages really are is leftovers. Below are my basic tenets regarding leftovers:

Everything you cook is a potential leftover ingredient. If you make something once, assume that you're going to make it again—so make more than you need and freeze the rest.

Freeze your precooked items in the size you are most likely to use them—or half that. You can always use two, but you can't divide a frozen block in half.

When you are freezing dense foods such as mashed potatoes and polenta, press down on the bag with the palm of your hand to form a ½-inch-thick disk. It thaws most efficiently this way.

If you do not have a microwave, you can bring frozen items to room temperature by putting them on your kitchen counter until they thaw out. Or if you sealed the bag they're in really tightly, drop them into a pot of simmering water.

Keep a mix of salt and pepper in one container. Mine is a ratio of 80 percent salt to 20 percent pepper. Usually if I'm adding salt to something, I'm adding pepper, too. And this way I only have to pick up one container instead of two. It is not salt now, and it is not pepper; it's saltandpepper.

My Chili

Serves 6 to 8

My chili changes from day to day. I start with a base of chopped beef, tomatoes, and onions. Chili needs to have a tremendous amount of onions in it. You cook the crap out of the onions, so you don't really know they are there, but they are the secret to the chili's tasting good. From its base, my chili is in constant motion. If at the end of the day I have hamburger left over, I cook it on the griddle and throw it in. The same thing with brisket or roast beef or lamb. I don't even have a routine way of spicing my chili. I add more of this or that as I go along, depending on the way it tastes.

I serve my chili on its own, topped with melted cheddar. But I also use it as a base or accoutrement for a number of other dishes. I use it to make a Chili Burrito (page 238), Sloppy Joe Burrito (page 238), chiliburger, chili fries, Chili Mac (page 237), and Bolognese sauce (see Spaghetti Bolognese, page 240). The list goes on and on. I love my chili. I don't think there has been a single day in the last thirty years that I haven't tasted it, and I usually have an entire bowlful at least.

Ingredients

2½ pounds chopped meat (20 to 30 percent fat)

2 big yellow Spanish onions, chopped

1 to 2 tablespoons minced pickled jalapeño peppers, depending on your taste (see How Spicy Do You Want It? on page 128)

1 tablespoon minced fresh garlic

2 teaspoons salt

1 teaspoon pepper

1 teaspoon ground cumin

1 teaspoon dried oregano

3 cups Marinara Sauce (page 236) or any marinara sauce

½ cup brewed black coffee

Masarepa (Hispanic cooked cornmeal) or cornmeal

Instructions

Heat a large high-sided sauté pan over high heat until it is so hot that a drop of water will bounce when it hits the surface. Throw on the chopped meat. Spread it out flat with a heavy spatula using a random chopping motion to disperse the meat evenly and break it up into small clusters. Add the onions and cook for 10 to 20 minutes, until the meat is brown all over and the onions have softened and begun to melt away. Sprinkle with the cumin, jalapeño peppers, garlic, salt, pepper, and oregano, and sauté for a few more minutes. Add the marinara sauce and the coffee, and cook for about 15 minutes to burn off some of the liquid.

Turn off the heat and leave the chili alone for about 20 minutes so that the fat will rise to the top. Sprinkle with a thin layer of masarepa; this helps absorb the oil. Once you can see that the fat has been absorbed, stir the masarepa into the chili. Simmer the chili over low heat for another 20 minutes (or longer if you like; you can't cook it too much). Add water or more coffee to the chili if it gets too thick, and season with additional salt and pepper to taste.

Note: If you have time, refrigerate the chili or freeze it before serving. This softens the texture of the meat, which is nice. If you serve the chili on more than one day, certain factors have to be adjusted every day you serve it. Add beef stock, water, or coffee if the chili becomes dry, more masarepa if it is too fatty, or more chopped meat (or any cooked meat that you have around) if the chili seems lifeless. Let your chili evolve.

Cream of Tomato Soup (with Garlic Bread croutons)

Cream of Tomato Soup *Serves 2*

I do a lot of things with marinara sauce, but this soup, which is basically a puree of tomatoes enhanced by some cream and cheese, is probably the simplest and cleverest. What happens is that the tomatoes, by being left whole, are prevented from giving out their true vitality, so when they blow apart in the blender, they give the soup a really intense, fresh tomato taste. To make a reduced-fat soup, use less (or no) cream and substitute the same amount of chicken stock. I serve it with a giant crouton on top because I think it is ideal to have something crunchy in everything I eat. To make croutons, follow the recipe for Garlic Bread (page 150) and then cut the bread into cubes after it is done.

Ingredients

2 cups Marinara Sauce (page 236) or any
    marinara sauce
1 cup Chicken Stock (page 123) or any
    stock or broth
¼ cup heavy cream
1 tablespoon grated Parmesan cheese
½ teaspoon minced fresh garlic
½ teaspoon butter
Salt

Instructions

Pour the marinara sauce (including a few big chunks of tomato if you have them in your sauce) into the jar of a blender. Add the stock, cream, Parmesan cheese, garlic, and butter. Whack it all together. It should be a souplike consistency. If not, add more chicken stock or cream, whichever you want more of. Pour the mixture into a pan, heat it up, and add salt to taste. You now have a really good cream of tomato soup.

Marinara Sauce
Makes about 4 cups

Marinara sauce is a staple building block in my cooking. I make it using whole canned San Marzano tomatoes. I use only one brand: Nina's. They're probably all good, but I've been using Nina's for thirty years, so I *know* they are good. If my supplier suddenly can't get Nina's tomatoes, I don't switch tomatoes, I switch suppliers. I leave some of the tomatoes whole so that the sauce has a dual function: It serves both as a sauce and as a source of warm, seasoned, whole peeled tomatoes. I add tomato paste, which gives the sauce the same richness that long cooking does.

Ingredients
¼ cup good olive oil
½ big yellow Spanish onion, chopped
1 teaspoon minced fresh garlic
½ cup burgundy wine
One 28-ounce can whole peeled tomatoes (preferably San Marzano), including juice
1 teaspoon to 2 tablespoons sugar (depending on how sweet you like your sauce)
One 6-ounce can tomato paste
A small handful of whole fresh basil leaves
Salt

Instructions
Heat the olive oil in a large pot over high heat. Add the onion and garlic, and sauté for about 5 minutes, until the onion has softened, not browned. Lower the heat if the onion or garlic is browning. Add the wine and cook for 1 or 2 minutes to burn off the alcohol. Add the tomatoes and sugar, and lower the heat. Break the tomatoes up with a wooden spoon to help them break down, but leave a few whole. Simmer the tomatoes for 30 minutes to 1 hour until the broken-up tomatoes have cooked down to the consistency of marinara sauce. Stir in the tomato paste and basil, and season with salt to taste.

Chili Mac
Serves 4

This is a popular American dish made of tomatoes, elbow macaroni, and chopped meat. It is basically a Sloppy Joe with pasta instead of a bun. It is a cafeteria staple that I think was invented at Horn and Hardart's, a now defunct chain that used to have locations all over New York City when I was growing up. Chili Mac is one of the foods developed for poor white people. Even today you can buy a 1-pound bag of elbow macaroni for 39 cents and half a pound of chopped meat for around a buck and a half. Another 89 cents for a can of tomatoes, and you could feed a family of four for cheap.

I make my Chili Mac with my already made chili, already made marinara, and already cooked elbow macaroni, so the whole thing takes about one minute longer than the time it takes to defrost the elbows in the microwave. Traditionally, Chili Mac is made without cheese because it is a poor man's dish, but you can top it with Parmesan or a melting cheese, such cheddar or Monterey Jack, instead of bread crumbs. If you are making this using frozen precooked pasta, start the sauce first because the pasta will take only a few minutes to warm up. Timing is key when it comes to any pasta. However you do it, from scratch or frozen, you want the pasta hot when it hits the sauce.

Ingredients
½ pound elbow macaroni
1 cup Marinara Sauce (facing page) or any marinara sauce
1 cup My Chili (page 233) or any meaty chili
Bread crumbs

Instructions
Preheat the broiler or the oven to as hot as it will go.

Cook the pasta to al dente, or warm the cooked frozen pasta.

Mix the marinara sauce and chili in a saucepan and warm them together over medium heat until bubbling. Stir in the hot macaroni. Dump the mixture in a casserole dish, cover it with a thin layer of bread crumbs, and put it under the broiler until the bread crumbs are brown.

Chili Burrito
Serves 2

I'm giving this recipe to demonstrate the kind of thing that I make in no time, because it consists of all premade ingredients that I have in front of me. It goes out of the kitchen in literally less than one minute. And it tastes great. It will take you a little more time.

Ingredients
2 cups cooked white rice
⅓ cup My Chili (page 233) or any meaty chili
⅓ cup Cuban Black Bean Soup (page 224) or any black bean soup
A few spoonfuls of Salsa Roja (page 63) or any fresh chunky salsa, plus more to serve on the side
½ cup feather-shredded cheddar cheese
2 large flour tortillas
Guacamole (page 68), or any guacamole, to serve on the side
Sour cream to serve on the side

Instructions
Put the rice on a hot griddle or in a hot sauté pan over high heat. Plop the chili, black bean soup, and salsa on top of the rice and stir it all together. Sprinkle the cheese on top. Take a smaller pan or lid or anything flat and heat-proof and put it on top of the mound of ingredients. Cook until all the ingredients are hot and the cheese has melted. Heat the tortillas in whatever way you like to heat tortillas. Take the cover off the chili-rice mound, and, using a spatula, toss it all together so it is a homogeneous mixture. Pick up half of the glop and lay it down in a line down the center of one of the tortillas. Repeat with the other half of the glop. Fold the sides of the tortilla in on top of the filling and then roll the burrito away from you to close. Serve with the salsa, guacamole, and sour cream on the side.

Sloppy Joe Burrito
Make the Chili Burrito, but don't add the rice. I prefer this version. I don't like rice in a burrito, but as a cook, I can't avoid it. Most people who order a burrito expect an enormous schmonster-sized thing stuffed with rice.

Sloppy Joe Sandwich
Make the Sloppy Joe Burrito, but pile the chili mixture onto an open-faced toasted hamburger bun instead of a tortilla.

The secret ingredient to chili

Shopsin's Prep: Pasta

I keep all different shapes of pasta precooked in the freezer: elbows, bowties, ziti, penne, spaghetti. The one we use the most is elbow macaroni, whose first use is Mac n Cheese Pancakes (page 90), followed by kid's spaghetti, followed by Chili Mac (page 237). When we cook pasta, we taste it three times: once before it is done, a second time when it is not *quite* done, and a third time when it is probably done. We undercook our pasta slightly, just enough so that if you got it in a restaurant, you'd say, "Gee, they could have cooked it fifteen seconds more."

Boil 1 pound of pasta in salted water until al dente. Drain the pasta and rinse it under cool water. Drizzle the pasta with olive oil and toss it so that it doesn't stick together. If you are not using the pasta immediately, let it cool to room temperature, divide into 4 portions, and freeze each portion in a separate plastic baggy. When you need pasta, bring it to room temperature either on the counter, in the microwave, or in a pot of simmering water before using.

Spaghetti Bolognese
Serves 4

Bolognese sauce usually requires a long time to cook to meld the flavors. But not my version. I start by sautéing meat with some onions, but then I add just a touch of chili. The chili gives the Bolognese the depth of flavor you get from long, slow cooking because it *was* cooked long and slow. I also add cooked meat, such as leftover pot roast or brisket, at the end. Meat that is cooked too long in sauce loses its happiness. I made this optional in this recipe because I realize you may not have it at home, but I always add it, and I think it's what makes my Bolognese sauce superior to others I've tasted. I finely chop the mirepoix for this so it is basically cooked when it hits the pan. No matter how you cook the pasta—from scratch or reheated frozen—you want to time it so it is hot when you add it to the sauce.

Ingredients

1 pound spaghetti (or other pasta shape)
¼ cup good olive oil
½ pound chopped meat (20 to 30 percent fat)
½ cup finely chopped Mirepoix (page 172)
½ cup Marinara Sauce (page 236) or any marinara sauce
½ cup My Chili (page 233) or any meaty chili
1 cup cooked meat, such as leftover steak or pot roast, chopped (optional)
2 tablespoons heavy cream, or more as needed
½ cup grated Parmesan cheese, plus more for serving
A pinch of ground nutmeg

Instructions

Cook the pasta to al dente, or warm the cooked, frozen pasta.

Heat the olive oil in a large skillet. Add the chopped meat and Mirepoix and cook for a few minutes to soften the vegetables. Stir in the marinara and chili and cook until the sauce is warmed through. Add the chopped cooked meat if you are using it. Stir in the cream. You want just enough cream to take the sheen off the tomato sauce, but not so much that the sauce turns pink. Sprinkle the cheese and nutmeg over the sauce. Add the spaghetti and toss the spaghetti and sauce together with tongs. If the spaghetti was not hot when you added it to the sauce, cook it for a minute or two to warm through. Serve with additional Parmesan on the side.

Spaghetti Bolognese

As you can imagine, I constantly have to reprint my menu. In the early days before everyone had computers and good printers, I used to have to take it to a copy place in the Village to be printed, so I didn't change it as often as I do now. Then my son Charlie got a computer and a laser printer, and started to design and print the menu for me. We had a few different menus back then. We had separate breakfast, lunch, and dinner menus, and we also had a separate one for Colin, who cooked for me on some nights in the original store. Colin couldn't make all the stuff I could, so his menu was a limited version of mine.

Now I do my own menu. My daughter Mara says the worst thing she ever did was teach me how to use Quark, and the second worst thing was teaching me how to kern, which is when you adjust the spacing between letters. I do this a lot because it allows me to cram more words onto a page. The morning after I print a new menu, Minda or Zack stuffs the new menus into the plastic holders. This happens anywhere between once and four times a week, depending on how creative I've been.

Selling Water, or the Secret of the Restaurant Business

One thing I find really sad about the direction that New York City—and maybe the whole country—is going is that it is becoming harder and harder for a small place like mine, a true family business, not one that just *looks* like a family business, to operate. I work hard, my food is good, and I have a really steady clientele, but none of these factors is enough to make it as a restaurant in Manhattan anymore. It seems like the only way to make a good living, and to keep up with all the fines and fees the city government wants me to pay them on a regular basis, is to run a business that is about making money.

This doesn't work for me because, for better or worse, I've made a conscious choice *not* to pursue money. This was a decision I made early in my life as a businessman. When I first started running Shopsin's as a grocery store it didn't take me long to discover that there were "hot" shelves and "cool" shelves. If I put something on a "hot" shelf, I was as much as three times more likely to sell it than if it were on a "cool" shelf. I started manipulating these "hot" spots. I would put slow sellers and high-profit items on the "hot" shelves, and on the cooler shelves I would put more marginally profitable items and staples— things like dish soap and toilet paper and flour, stuff that people were either going to buy because they needed it or they weren't going to buy no matter *where* I put them.

At one point I found myself spending a *lot* of time manipulating the shelves in an effort to maximize my profits. Then one day I just stood up and said to myself: This is a bad place to go. I am focusing on marketing and on making money instead of what I enjoy doing, which at the time was a little bit of simple deli-style cooking and a lot of interacting with my customers.

In that moment I felt as though I had to make a choice, like a dope addict or gambler, as to what kind of person I was going to be and what kind of business I was going to run. For me it was an easy decision. I went back to just putting stuff on shelves, wherever I happened to find room for it, and not giving a shit what people decided to buy or not buy. When the landlord raised the rent and I needed to make more money, I was already fully extended. I was moving truckloads of paper towels and cat food, and running a really successful deli business, but that wasn't enough. The only way to make more money was to go into marketing again or to go into a more profitable business. That's when I became a restaurant.

At the restaurant I have certain items on the menu that are very profitable, certain items that are not profitable at all, and certain items that I don't care if I ever sell again no matter how profitable they are, because they're a pain in the ass to make. But I don't design my menu so that people will be drawn to the more profitable items or the easier-to-make items. I just cram it all on the menu somewhere just as I once crammed things on shelves and let people order what they feel like.

That said, I am not independently wealthy, so I do have to make a living. And in any business if you want to succeed—which by my definition just means making enough money so I can keep doing what I do—you have to figure out where the profit center is. Every industry has one, and it's often hidden or unexpected. In the automotive industry it is all in the accessories—stereo, air-conditioning, leather seats, and so on—or at least it used to be that way. In a movie theater you pay $6.00 for a tub of popcorn, and the movie theater probably didn't spend that much on all the corn they popped for the entire week. In the grocery business the way I made money was by doing volume. You put $1.00 into a grocery store, and you make a 10-cent profit. The key is to make a decent number of dimes. And when I started doing more deli business, it didn't take me long to figure out that the profit was in mayonnaise.

Egg salad was my first shot at converting a staple into a profit center, and I learned pretty quickly that I could do extremely well by selling anything with mayonnaise, because I was basically reselling the mayo for whatever the price of the finished product was. Mayo cost about 25 cents a pound, egg salad sold for $2.99 a pound, so I was now getting twelve times my money for the mayo. When I became a restaurant, I discovered that despite everything else I was doing, what I was really making my money on was liquids.

The most profitable item in my restaurant, hands down, is iced tea. I also have a high profit margin on sodas and coffee. But in terms of the bottom line, iced tea is it. In a full-bar type of restaurant, liquor is the biggest profit center, but my guess is that I do even better than they do. My numbers aren't as high, but I also don't have a bartender who drinks up half the profits and pours away the other half trying to get bigger tips from his customers.

I charge $2.00 for a 22-ounce glass of Sweet Southern Iced Tea (page 246) and $3.95 for Frozen Fruit Iced Tea (page 246), which is the Southern tea with frozen fruit instead of ice cubes. Both are really good, and both are a little different from iced teas you'd get at another place down the street. But let's face it: No matter how good the iced tea is or how unusual it is, it's all just water. A person who orders an iced tea could get three refills and then take the glass home with him and I'd *still* make a profit.

The same is true for some nontypical beverages like flavored milks and fountain sodas and egg creams. The milks are $3.00, and what they are is a glass of regular milk with some syrup stirred in. And for $4.00 I sell fountain sodas, which are syrup with soda water. When it comes to liquids, it's all *profit.*

Red Rose tea figurines

Sweet Southern Iced Tea

We make our iced tea in big batches. For many years we had problems with it clouding until I finally arrived at a solution. We now don't make iced tea from brewed tea; we sun-tea it. The truth about sun tea is that you don't really need to put it in the sun; you can just put the tea in water and let it sit wherever you happen to put it. Once we "brew" it, we keep the tea refrigerated, because the one true thing about any iced tea is that it should be really, really cold.

Frozen Fruit Iced Tea

This tea was Minda's idea, and she just loves it. She could have four or five glasses in a day, and it still wouldn't be too much. The fruit that we use as "ice cubes" starts to defrost as it cools the tea, so you basically get a small serving of mushed fruit salad in addition to your beverage. This small, subtle detail makes it special. It's such a simple concept that I wonder why I have never seen it anywhere else. You can use any fruit you want, but the fruit you use will make a difference. Small fruits such as blueberries and raspberries will be just right by the time you have sipped your iced tea down enough to get to it. Bigger fruit such as mangoes and peaches will still be frozen even after you have finished your tea. I recommend that you use small fruit for individual glasses of tea, and larger fruit if you are putting out a big pitcher.

Frozen raspberry ice cubes

To make Frozen Fruit Iced Tea, fill a tall iced tea–type of glass with whatever frozen fruit you like. Fill the glass with cold Sweet Southern Iced Tea (above) or whatever cold iced tea you like. Enjoy.

Egg Cream
Makes 1 tall egg cream

Egg cream is a classic New York Jewish deli item consisting of milk, chocolate syrup, and soda water stirred together into a light, frothy beverage. It is an apocryphal-type thing. If you go on Google and look up "egg cream," not only are you going to get ten thousand entries (or maybe 10 million), but each entry is going to be passionate and insistent that it is the right way to make one. The one fact that all egg-cream enthusiasts agree on is that the chocolate syrup used is Fox's U-bet. The truth is that all recipes for egg creams are basically the same, but people who make egg creams believe that whatever subtle nuances they bring to their method make all the difference. Eve had a special way to do it, which Melinda has since inherited: the addition of a minuscule amount of half-and-half. If you ask Melinda why she makes it this way, she'll say, "Because that's the way Mom did it, that's why."

Ingredients
Cold milk (I use whole milk but I know you will use whatever kind of milk you like.)
Fox's U-bet Chocolate Syrup
½ teaspoon of half-and-half
Seltzer water

Instructions
Fill a clear, tall iced tea–type of glass one-quarter full with milk. Fill it another quarter full with Fox's U-bet Chocolate Syrup. The glass is now half full (or half empty, depending on how you look at it). Add the half-and-half and stir well. Stir continuously as you fill the glass with seltzer water. The egg cream will rise and foam up so that the top third of it is air. That is what makes it an egg cream. Serve immediately.

Chocolate Milk
Makes 1 tall glass of milk

Eve was the one who first started making chocolate milk in the store. It was a product she served with deliberate imperfection. She would stir the chocolate syrup and the milk together by hand using a long iced tea spoon, which would cause some of the syrup to be left on the spoon, and Jackson Pollock–like splatters of the syrup floating in the milk. If you are really anal retentive, you could blend the milk and syrup together in a blender or buy chocolate milk already mixed into a homogenous product. But the layers and flecks of the unmixed chocolate are what strike me as appealing.

Ingredients

3 to 4 tablespoons Fox's U-bet Chocolate
  Syrup (depending on how chocolaty
  you want your milk)
Cold milk (I use whole milk but I know
  you will use whatever kind of milk
  you like.)

Instructions

Start with the chocolate syrup in the bottom of a clear, tall glass. Pour in the milk to fill the glass, then take a long spoon, such as an iced tea spoon, and give the milk a vigorous stir so that it becomes chocolate milk. There will still be a splattered image of nondissolved syrup at the bottom and throughout the milk. This is ideal. Serve the milk with the spoon, which, if you're lucky, also has some of the syrup stuck to it.

I also make a lot of dessert-type soda fountain beverages, which help raise the check average. A milkshake or an "Orange Julius" adds $6.00 to a check, which sometimes doubles the amount a person spends in the restaurant. It's more than I charge for scrambled eggs and toast. What they are doing is having dessert simultaneously with their meal. So I get the money from their having dessert without the restaurant's going through the trouble of providing a separate dessert course where the waiter has to clear the table and put down a fresh napkin and silverware.

"Orange Julius"
Serves 2

When I was a kid, Orange Julius was strictly a California thing. I didn't discover it until late in life, and then I fell completely in love with it and *had* to have it at my restaurant.

It seems as if it would be easy to replicate an Orange Julius because when you go to an Orange Julius store and order one, you can watch them make it right there in front of you. You can see them put in the orange juice, the ice cream, the ice, and a scoop of some white powder. That's where the magic and mystery is in an Orange Julius. If you can figure out what that powder is, you've got it. I don't know how I did it, but I figured out what the powder is: It's egg whites.

The powdered egg whites, coupled with the powdered sugar that is used as the sweetener, produce the foamlike texture that is a big part of the Orange Julius's uniqueness. I am not a food scientist, so I can't tell you for sure why this is, but my theory is that after you have buzzed the shit out of the ice pieces, until they are nearly liquid, on a microscopic level the globules of ice are coated with those powders, giving the Orange Julius its distinctive texture.

Legally speaking, I am probably not allowed to call this an Orange Julius because the name must be copyrighted or some crap like that, which is why I put the name in quotation marks. I could have called it an Orange Julius-ish. Or maybe I can get away with it if I just say that this is *my* idea of what an Orange Julius is. The truth is that mine *is* different from the orig-inal. It's better, because we squeeze the orange juice fresh.

Ingredients
1 cup fresh-squeezed orange juice
1 tablespoon powdered egg whites
½ cup powdered sugar
2 cups crushed ice (or 3 cups ice cubes)

Instructions
Put the orange juice, egg whites, and sugar in a blender and blend quickly to combine the ingredients. Add the ice and blend until the ice is finely crushed and the drink is frothy. Do not overblend, or the ice will begin to melt and the drink will start to flatten.

Milkshakes and Malteds
Makes 1 milkshake or malted (serves 1 or 2)

You know how you go to an ice-cream store and order a scoop of ice cream or a milkshake, and you see those young girls bending over to scoop the ice cream out of the container? The ice cream is *rock hard,* so this is no easy task for these girls. It's good for the customer, because you get a good look up the girls' skirts while they're scooping, but it is a really stupid way to go about scooping ice cream.

We have a clever system for making milkshakes and malteds that bypasses the stupid scooping process. It was my daughter Mara's idea, and it's brilliant. We make our own ice cream—Zack does it every morning. Mara devised a system where we freeze the ice cream in paper cups in 9-ounce portions, which is just the right amount to make one generous milkshake. When a person orders a milkshake, instead of scooping it out like the girls in the ice-cream stores, Zack, who is in charge of milkshake making at Shopsin's, cuts the paper cup to free the ice cream. The ice cream comes out in one big chunk, which he then cuts into cubes. Once the ice cream is cut up, he leaves the pieces alone while he takes the milk and whatever flavoring he's adding to the milkshake and whacks it around in the blender until it's mixed together. Then, with the blender still running, he takes the ice-cream cubes and starts dropping them in—drop, drop, drop. The second the shake gets thick, he stops adding ice cream—or at least that's what is *supposed* to happen.

This is where Zack always screws up. Intellectually, he just doesn't get the basic concept of a milkshake. Zack can understand a lot of complicated things, such as scrambled eggs, which is not an easy thing to understand. But when it comes to the science of making a milkshake, he *just can't get it.* "It has to do with *monitoring,*" I tell him. "When it's thick, asshole, you *stop!*"

I try to explain to him that once a shake gets thick it is never gonna get thicker. I tell him, "You may not use all the ice cream, and you can do anything you want with the extra—eat it, throw it away, throw it at a customer. Just don't put it in the blender once the shake is thick." If you do as Zack does, you have to keep whacking the shake to break up the excess ice cream. Then it's not thick from being frozen and right; it's thick from having too much ice cream in it.

I've explained this to Zack a hundred times, but when he makes a milkshake, he still just whacks the shit out of it. I think he walks away and forgets about it until the shake is milky thin. Then he has to add more ice cream to thicken it, until finally he has added so much that the canister is practically overflowing. Now that I think about it, that's probably why he does it—so he can make enough for himself.

The true secret to our milkshakes, besides Mara's system and the fact that we use homemade ice cream, which is a really big one, is that we put malt powder in them. Even the regular nonmalted milkshakes get malt. We don't tell our customers, we just do it. A lot of people don't even know what malt powder is, but if you asked them if they wanted it, they would say no. Maybe the word *malt* throws them. Maybe it makes them think about beer. I don't know what malt powder is, either, but I do know that it's really good and that it's what makes a milkshake taste special. Without it, a milkshake is just a glass of whacked up half-melted ice cream.

Sometimes when we get busy on weekends, Minda puts a freeze on milkshakes. She won't let anyone order them. Despite the fact that we have our clever system, when there are a thousand other things going on, it still takes a lot of time and attention for one person to stop and make a milkshake—especially when that one person is Zack. People get really upset when they find out they can't get their milkshake, but Minda won't budge. When Minda decides on something, that's it. Don't argue with her. Even *I* don't have any say. Or maybe I should say *especially* I don't have any say. For our milkshakes we use noncustard ice cream, meaning ice cream that doesn't contain egg.

Ingredients
3 ounces whole milk
Flavoring (see Variations on Vanilla, below)
1 tablespoon malted milk powder, or 3 to 4
    tablespoons more if you are making a
    malted
9 ounces noncustard vanilla ice cream

Instructions
Put the milk in a blender with the flavoring, unless you are making a vanilla shake, and blend. While the blender is running, add the malted milk powder and the ice cream, about one ounce at a time, until the shake is thick. You may not need all the ice cream.

Variations on Vanilla
To make all our milkshakes and malteds, we start with vanilla ice cream, and to make flavored milkshakes we add the flavor. The options are almost endless. We have butterscotch sauce, mint syrup, coffee syrup, vanilla syrup, and strawberry, cherry, lime, and caramel syrups. We sometimes add walnuts, pecans, or pistachios. We throw frozen berries and peaches in there. And then we have more creative variations like the Peanut Butter Cup Milkshake that gets peanut butter and chocolate syrup. My favorite is plain vanilla with lots of malt, although I can't remember the last time I had one. Add whatever you want. It's your milkshake.

To make any variations, follow the Milkshake recipe and add the following:

Mocha Nutella Malted
4 big spoonfuls Nutella, 4 big spoonfuls malt powder, and 2 big spoonfuls instant coffee

Raspberry
A handful of frozen raspberries

Chocolate Peanut Butter
¼ cup Fox's U-bet Chocolate Syrup and 2 big spoonfuls peanut butter

Chocolate Chocolate Chip
¼ cup Fox's U-bet Chocolate Syrup and a handful of chocolate chips

Fluffer Nutter
A cup of marshmallow fluff and 3 big spoonfuls peanut butter. At the end, put in 2 tablespoons more fluff and blend quickly so you can see the white swirls in the shake.

Butter Pecan
1 big spoonful butterscotch sauce and a handful of pecans

Pumpkin Pie
2 cups canned pumpkin puree and 1 teaspoon Mara Spice (page 95) or pumpkin pie spice

Coffee
1 very big spoonful instant coffee

Avocado
A whole avocado (peeled and pitted)

Pistachio
A handful of pistachio nuts

Piña Colada
A handful of chopped-up pineapple and a small handful of angel flake coconut

Maple Walnut
¼ cup pure maple syrup and a handful of walnuts

Three-Berry
¼ cup strawberry dessert sauce and a small handful each of frozen blueberries and blackberries

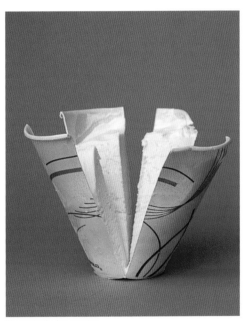

Homemade ice cream

Concretes
Makes 1 concrete (serves 1 or 2)

A concrete is like a milkshake, only it's really, really, *REALLY* thick. It's thick almost like soft-serve ice cream, but it's grainy, like concrete. I stole the name *concrete* from the Shake Shack. But I didn't actually steal it from them. I became aware of concretes in an article in which Danny Meyer, the owner of Shake Shack, talked about the concrete, which he said was from some place in St. Louis. So I really stole it from the place they stole it from. Everything in cooking is like that. There is nothing new.

The major difference between a concrete and a regular milkshake is that a concrete is made with frozen custard ice cream as opposed to regular noncustard ice cream, and it has less liquid. Frozen custard ice cream is made with egg yolks; the egg yolks are cooked with milk until the mixture becomes thick, like custard. After it cools, the custard is put in an ice cream maker and turned into ice cream. The premium ice cream that is so popular these days, the stuff you get in grocery stores in those itty-bitty containers, is technically frozen custard, although for some reason that I assume has to do making more money, nobody calls it that. I use heavy cream instead of milk as the liquid for concretes in keeping with the heavier, richer concept. But the truth is that I don't offer concretes anymore. Zack really couldn't get the hang of those. Finally he refused to try and made me take them off the menu.

Ingredients
2 tablespoons heavy cream
Flavoring (see Variations on Vanilla, page 252)
9 ounces vanilla custard ice cream

Instructions
Put the cream in a blender with the flavoring, unless you are making a vanilla concrete, and blend. While the blender is running, add the ice cream, about one ounce at a time, until the concrete is blended and so thick you have no choice but to eat it with a spoon.

Although I might sound avaricious when I describe the advantages of serving iced tea and milkshakes, where I think I'm different from a lot of restaurant owners is that I don't offer any of it to *try* to make money. In fact, I don't even know if I *do* make money off these things. I don't know what I make money on because I don't cost anything out. I charge $6.00 for a milkshake because that just seems like a fair price for the milkshake I offer. I am not about to waste my time trying to figure out how much the freezers cost me to buy and to run, divided by what's in them, or how much electricity it takes to run the blenders, or how much I'm paying Zack for his time to make ice cream fresh every morning.

What I do know is that it makes me really happy to be able to offer milkshakes, and the milkshakes make my customers really happy. To me that is a winning formula for running a restaurant. I just assume I'm making money. I *must* be, because I'm still in business.

Zack whacking a milkshake

Epilogue: The Art of Staying Small

About the time I finished writing this book, I closed my restaurant on Carmine Street and moved to a small, nine-seat stall in the Essex Street Market on the Lower East Side. The market is an indoor market, mostly Hispanic with some Jewish-type places. There are about thirty stalls including a couple of bodegas, a few produce places selling Hispanic sorts of things like yuccas and plantains, two butchers, and two fish guys. In addition to these, a few upscale businesses have moved in recently that reflect a general gentrification of the neighborhood. One of these is Saxelby Cheesemongers, a small cheese shop that sells only cheese made in the New York area on small farms, where they milk their own cows. The owner, Anne Saxelby, is a really lovely girl, and she is basically the reason I moved to the market, because she is friendly with my daughter Minda. And Minda is the reason I decided to move at all.

As I said in the beginning of this book, as my kids have grown up, I have seen my own philosophies coming back to me through them. One of those philosophies, which could be called "the art of staying small," was the reason behind the move, and this time it came to me through Minda.

The art of staying small more or less sums up my feelings about running a restaurant—and about life. I know it goes against our capitalist system, but I have never been interested in the normal symptoms of success, such as higher profit margins and expansion of income. I never had a goal to make more money so that I could retire or so that I could hire a low-wage employee to do the cooking for me. I have no desire to open a second restaurant, to oversee a restaurant empire with my name on it, or to endorse a line of pots and pans.

Running a restaurant for me is about running a restaurant. It is not a means to get someplace else. I wake up every morning, and I work for a living like a farmer. Running a restaurant is a condition of life for me. And I like everything about this life. I like waking up in the morning knowing I am going to the restaurant to cook, that something unexpected will happen to me in the kitchen, and that no matter what, I will learn something new. I like the actual process of cooking. I like shopping for the food that I cook, and I like my interactions with the people I meet while shopping. I like my customers, and I like working with my kids. It is a simple existence, but for me the beauty is in that simplicity. These are the things that bring me pleasure—and they bring me great pleasure on an extremely regular basis.

Living this way, pursuing your own happiness, is addictive and it's the way I have tried to conduct my life. What this means is doing what it takes to make yourself feel good each day, not to make yourself feel less good today in the hopes that your life will be good in ten years because you're working really hard now or because your property will be worth more money then. The way I figure it, if you make every day of your life as happy as you can, nobody can take that away from you. It's in the bank.

The downside to this way of living is that I haven't planned ahead, and I don't have anything to leave my kids. What's worse, the restaurant we were in cost so much to run every month that if I were to die suddenly or become disabled, I would have been foisting a tremendous liability on them. These aren't things I would have thought about because I just don't think that way. But Minda pointed them out to me—and she also pointed out how hard we were working in order to pay our bills. And it would only get worse, she said. When our lease was up, I would be seventy years old, and the rent would increase to a place where there was no way we could renew. After thirty-five or forty years of hard work and creating what we did at Shopsin's, we would be left with nothing.

Minda also felt that by changing, by downsizing, running the restaurant would be more relaxing for all of us. I would have more fun cooking and interacting with my customers because I wouldn't have to bust my hump just to make rent. If I got sick, it wouldn't be financially devastating to her and her sister and brothers. And after I die, if she chose to, Minda could run the place with the help of Zack and Mara without too much trouble. So she convinced me to move.

Even though I say I don't live in the past, for the purpose of writing this book I was forced to go there, and I was surprised to find that I really enjoyed the experience. It was actually very pleasant to remember all the people I have known and all the stories I didn't even realize were stuffed away in my brain. It was also really special to revisit a time when Alice Trillin was alive and Eve was still here. Of course, it was also sad because all that is done—*gone*. But I enjoyed the visit while it lasted.

Shopsin's logo by
Laurie Rosenwald

One of my redundant theories of life is that one of the reasons to have children is not to *have* the children but that it allows you to go through your life a second time. In that way, writing a book turned out to be a lot like having a baby. I got to see my life a second time. I was able to feel all the pleasure and pain of it, but I saw things differently from the way I saw them the first time, like an educational reenactment. It was a really rewarding thing to do and a great learning experience. There is really so little to life that it seems silly not to chew it a second time—to go over it and over it again until you can distill some kind of meaning from it. It is an experience I would wish for anybody. All that said, I still think the present is the place to be. It is certainly where *I* feel the most comfortable and the only place where I am able to suck the richness out of life.

I just opened the new place, and already I know it is a good move for us. For me it is an affirmation of the future. I wouldn't have made the move had I not had a pretty strong suspicion that I would still be around in six years when the lease expired on the old place. This alone, for a big fat guy at my age, is something. More important, the new place just *feels* right.

I really like being a part of the market. It is like being a member of a church where, even though you live very different lives, you are all in something together because of a common belief system. There is a real cross-section of people in the market, which I like. There are junkies, bourgeois assholes, really rich people, and all the market vendors. I don't like every individual, but I like them as a collective unit. I feel like an orphan who has found his home—or like an alien who has found his home*land*.

I want to say that what I'm doing now is more enjoyable than anything I've done up until now. I don't want to denigrate the other experiences; I had a wonderful time in both of my first two restaurants, and they both brought me a tremendous amount of love and happiness. But somehow I think this is even better. It might have to do with the location and the marketplace. It might have to do with the fact that my children are adults and I am harvesting the rewards of that. Or it might just be that at my age I am better able to feel satisfied and content in any situation. As much as I resisted writing this book, it is very satisfying to be able to end it by saying this: On the simplest, most basic level, I have never been happier than I am today.